ADDICTION
THE HIGH - LOW TRAP

ADDICTION
THE HIGH - LOW TRAP

By Irving A. Cohen, MD, MPH

Health Press
Santa Fe

Published by Health Press
P.O. Box 1388
Santa Fe, NM 87504

Library of Congress Cataloging in Publication Data

Cohen, Irving A.
Addiction: the high-low trap / by Irving A. Cohen
p. cm.
Includes bibliographical references and index
ISBN 0–929173–10–4
1. Substance abuse–Physiological aspects. 2. Substance abuse–Popular works.
3. Stimulants. 4. Central nervous system depressants. 5. Substance abuse–Treatment.
I. Title. [DNLM: 1. Analeptics–pharmacology. 2. Hypnotics and Sedatives–pharmacology. 3. Substance Dependence–psychology. 4. Substance Dependence–rehabilitation. WM 270 C6775a]
RC564.C624 1995
616.86—dc20
DNLM/DLC91–35374 CIP

Edited by Susan Victor
Design by Jim Mafchir

TABLE OF CONTENTS

■■

PART I

■■

PART II

▪▪

PART III

▪▪

FOREWORD

Alcohol and drug problems have been a priority concern in the United States since 1975. Alcohol is implicated in nearly half of all deaths caused by motor vehicle crashes, suicides and homicides. With greater public awareness of their dangers the general use of alcohol and other drugs for recreation has generally declined in the United States since 1985. However alcohol is still the foremost abused substance in the United States leading to dependence and many alcohol illnesses. In addition, approximately 20 million Americans use marijuana at least once in a year and nearly as many Americans have experimented at least once with crack cocaine, placing themselves at risk for developing drug dependence and other problems.

Public health professionals are actively engaged in reaching out to inform the public about the extent of the national problem and the effectiveness of treatment for alcohol and drug dependence. The development of effective treatments for alcohol and drug dependence has encouraged more individuals to acknowledge alcohol and other drug problems. Even while general use of alcohol and drugs is decreasing, the number of individuals addicted to alcohol and psychoactive medications has remained about the same or even increased in the population. National recognition of the gravity of alcohol and other drug problems has changed the social climate so that more people are willing to consider the possibility that they, too, may have a problem.

Dr. Cohen's specialty training in preventive medicine and addiction medicine work together to produce a writing style which puts the reader in the office of an experienced, concerned, and caring doctor explaining the things any concerned person or family need to know.

Many individuals are concerned that they may have inadvertently become the addicted victims of alcohol or other drugs. Such individuals will find the clear clinical descriptions of personal experiences provided in this book very helpful. People who cannot understand the rapidly changing emotions they feel and those who feel their life is becoming unmanageable will find in this book an easily understood scientific explanation of the role alcohol, tranquilizers, and other psychoactive medications may play in producing their strange condition.

Dr. Cohen's book goes beyond previous writing in this area by describing the process of simultaneous addiction to more than one substance. He carefully depicts how drugs may interact to produce a roller coaster experience of emotional highs and lows. Dr. Cohen captures the experience of addicted persons and at the same time offers solid scientific explanations of their experiences. His warm, friendly, personal style enables him to share his considerable experience in treating addicted people with readers, family, and friends who need to understand addiction in order to help. Readers will be informed about the process of recovery from addiction and the important contributions physicians, treatment programs, Alcoholics Anonymous (AA), and Narcotics Anonymous (NA) can make. Hopefully all will take courage from Dr. Cohen's message.

Wallace Mandell, Ph.D., M.P.H.
Chairman, Department of Mental Hygiene
School of Hygiene and Public Health
Johns Hopkins University

Preface
"No Pussycat Drugs"

"There are no pussycat drugs" thundered the Professor. I was in medical school, listening intently as the professor lectured in this important class in Pharmacology and Therapeutics. He was referring to legal, prescription medications and his point was that any physician prescribing a drug must fully understand and weigh the adverse risks to the patient against the potential benefits. The only drugs that were ever totally safe, he explained, were the fake or placebo drugs, used in an earlier era of medicine when it was acceptable to offer someone hope by pretending to treat them when no therapy was available. The very nature of drug therapy for any disease, he went on, meant that any drug powerful enough to be of some beneficial use must carry with it the potential for adverse consequences. He admonished us, that as we became physicians, our desire to aggressively fight disease must be tempered with caution. Primum non nocere. First, do no harm.

I had entered medical school as an older student, giving up a stable and financially rewarding career in the computer field to contribute to what I considered the greatest health crisis that has ever faced the United States, the epidemic of addiction.

I thought I knew about the power of addictive drugs but that professor's lecture taught me that there have been virtually no effective drugs ever introduced that have not later proved to have some adverse consequences. As I listened I thought, if even under a doctor's control all drugs have the potential to be dangerous, what chance does a young person have, doing self-experimentation with "feel good" drugs.

Unfortunately, for the last several decades, national policy has been either lacking entirely or totally ineffective following from that simple truth. There remains a pervasive myth, a myth that states that there is such a thing as safe use of feel good drugs. How can this be? If all drugs can be dangerous, then addictive drugs that are taken at the discretion of the user are bound to be the most dangerous. The daily death toll from addiction is proof enough of this. Whether the death is an overdose from illicit fentynal, a murder of a family member by someone undergoing crack paranoia, a family killed because a train operator was a pothead or a young boy watching his mother die of alcoholic liver failure, it is all the same. There are no pussycat drugs.

In our desire to feel good, each "breakthrough" heralded by the press seems like a promised miracle of science. This is not new, for the designer drugs of today are simply another chapter in history. When distillers were first able to increase the strength of alcoholic beverages, this was looked at as a miracle and whiskey was named "Water of the Gods." When German chemists were able to purify an extract of the coca leaf to a form of injectable cocaine, Sigmund Freud thought it would be a cure for depression as well as alcoholism and morphine dependence. Even heroin and amphetamines were first introduced with the idea that they would be "non-addictive" substitutes for the drugs they replaced.

Why do people turn to drugs? There is a perception that the addict is a bad person. In truth, addicts come from every background and are of every nature. No one wants to live next door to an addict, but no addict was born that way. A few may have been people we would characterize as "bad" before becoming addicted but many times more were people just like you, the reader and your neighbors. Good, decent people just trying to get on in life. Addiction trapped them all.

Understanding the societal problem of addiction is not possible unless we look at individual cases and see the people involved as the quite ordinary human beings that they are. This book attempts to do just that. Only when we understand this face of addiction can we step back and look further, look for solutions that will benefit society, solutions that will prevent human suffering.

Today, as a nation we lack this societal plan. Politicians have succumbed to business interests. Ineffective prevention and phony treatment programs grow and multiply as they drain our tax dollars. Look at the ballyhooed "drug czar" of the recent Federal administrations and look at the increase in the number of young men and women who die each year as a result of AIDS and explain the effectiveness of our national drug policy.

The purpose of this book is to help you, the reader, understand what is going on around you regarding addiction. As you read it, you will begin to understand that what we need is not to spend more money or resources, but to be able to use our resources wisely. As you see this, join with others around you to demand effective addiction prevention, detection and treatment policy for our nation. This can only happen when it comes from you, the ordinary citizen.

Today, there are only a handful of physicians in the world who have credentials in both Preventive Medicine and Addiction Medicine, although the greatest gains in improving the health of the public will come only when we can effectively join those two important bodies of knowledge.

In the past, good-intentioned people, who lacked the knowledge to understand how little they knew of the question, led the fight against addiction. Many of them were misled, perhaps by people of less than good intent, so that our government policy on many occasions was responsible for additional men and women dying as a consequence of addiction.

The words of British Prime Minister Benjamin Disraeli, over a century ago explain why we must expect more than this sorry performance in the United States today: "The health of the people is really the foundation upon which all their happiness and all the powers as a state depend."

As a first step, learn something of addiction yourself from the pages of this book. As a second step, think of what you can do. Understand the enemy of addiction and understand that indeed, there are no pussycat drugs. Keeping in mind the principle "first do no harm," demand more of yourself, your neighbors, your community and your nation.

Demand competence on the part of your elected leaders and demand first priority to this problem. No economic plan can survive if the American working man and woman is not fit to carry out a days work. No plan to deal with health care cost can work if we do nothing to greatly improve the health of Americans. No grand educational scheme will work if the educated boys and girls of today become the crack-heads of tomorrow.

ⅠⅠ

Tolerate your neighbor, as a person, for he or she may be no better or worse a person then yourself. Be intolerant of your neighbors actions. Do not accept addiction all around you, for your intolerance will make a difference. There is no magic pill that can protect your son or daughter from addiction if swimming in a sea of drugs. Clean up your home, your neighborhood and your city. Ask your neighbor for help and respond in kind when she asks you. Ask God for help. It is too big a job for us alone.

Irving A. Cohen, M.D., M.P.H.
Topeka, Kansas

Introduction
THE HIGH-LOW TRAP

═══════

Millions of Americans have been trapped by a vicious, biologic phenomena called addiction. No sane person ever started out intending to become an addict, yet millions of our neighbors are either addicted to chemicals today or may have spent years trying to free themselves from this vicious trap.

This book is dedicated to those who have been trapped on the roller coaster ride of chemical dependency. I wrote it because I have found that both patients and the general public rarely understand the real nature of the disease of addiction. Disease is neither "good" nor "bad". Addictions have a biologic as well as a behavioral basis. The peculiar, irrational behavior of anyone who is addicted is no accident. It is the result of the highs and lows, a result of the trap.

Addiction is a complex disease that involves both behavior and biology. The High-Low Trap describes a condition that ensnares most people who have had a problem with cocaine, pills or alcohol. This trap is the relationship between stimulation and sedation. Stimulants (cocaine, crack and amphetamines) and sedatives (alcohol, tranquilizers, barbiturates) trap people on a biological roller coaster before they even recognize that they are addicted.

A ride on an amusement park roller coaster is a good analogy for understanding the experience of the High-Low Trap. Your bravado, which got you on the ride in the first place will vanish as you go through a succession of terrifying falls, twists and turns and you may wish to change your mind. However, once the roller coaster ride has begun, you cannot reverse course or leave the car.

The High-Low Trap is not a character flaw or personality disorder, it is what I call the syndrome of swinging between sedation and stimulation–the chemical roller coaster ride our nervous system takes as a result of addiction. This roller coaster is biochemical, a result of physiologic processes in the body and brain and carries our emotions and perceptions of the world along with it on a confusing and terrifying ride. It is a direct result of the original addiction, a result that complicates the process of recovery.

This book is dedicated to those who have been trapped on that roller coaster ride of chemical dependency. I wrote it because I have found in my work as a therapist, that there are many people who can not get better until they really understand the nature of the disease of addiction. The experience of having an illness, any illness, is always a bad experience. That does not make the person who suffers from the disease either a good or a bad person. Addictions affect both good people and bad people, just as heart disease and cancer affect both good and bad people.

Addiction is rarely looked at as rationally as heart disease or cancer. The irrational way addiction is treated by society interferes with adequate prevention and treatment. All who live in the United States are aware of many of the consequences of our current addiction epidemic. The terror of AIDS effecting both high and low risk people, the senseless shootings in the cities, the loss of innocent lives on the highways are reported daily in our news media. The continuing emotional pain of a family member who has suffered verbal, physical and even sexual abuse from an addicted spouse or parent is more private but no less devastating. Even the current economic recession, which some would blame solely on exploitation of our nation by predatory foreign competitors, has been worsened by the increase in health care costs and the drain on the work force excellence resulting from the addiction epidemic.

BEHAVIOR VS. BIOLOGY

Some would have you believe that addiction is purely the result of bad behavior. If you ascribe to such a theory, you might surmise that addiction is simply the consequence of willful wrong behavior and can be reversed through the application of right behavior. This simple approach, although it may be useful in limited circumstances, has never truly succeeded by itself. When it is found that this behavioral approach has not worked, you may have concluded that the sufferer was simply a bad person or beyond help.

Others want you to believe that addiction is purely a biologic event and that the complex behavior of addicted people can be understood solely within the chemistry or genetic laboratory. If you held to such theories, addiction cannot be caused by wrong behavior and any use of a drug is predestined by biology. Therefore, any societal or religious norms concerning behavior are in conflict with biologically predestined needs. If the disease of addiction could be described simply by understanding the complex chemistry of brain cells, then the underlying chemical imbalance could then be prevented or corrected by the addition of some missing substance.

Depending upon whom you hear describe such a theory, the missing substance may be a drug synthesized by man or a natural nutrient. You might be lured by news coverage describing some new and important drug research into believing that such a cure or panacea is just around the corner. Or if you have come to mistrust conventional medicine and supposedly sound science, you may be seduced by another breed of profiteer–those who claim to have discovered alternative forms of medicine. They may use this same biologic theory enhanced by their own jumbled version of current research to support their case. They will often claim the rediscovery of an important nutritional or herbal remedy known to the ancients but forgotten by modern civilization.

If you had been willing to believe these purely biologic cures–whether the magic talisman was a new drug or an ancient substance–failure of the remedy could be explained in the same way. Proponents of such wonder-drugs would explain that it was not the fault of the remedy but rather was the fault of the person. Perhaps some inherent genetic or biochemical abnormality placed the affected person outside the realm of correction. Despite the totally different approach, once again the person who can not be cured by a biologic method is hopeless or bad. This time, however, please don't blame the victim. Blame his or her ancestors because it is genetic or blame society because of our unbalanced environment.

If you had at one time believed that there was a chemical panacea for addiction, you were in good company. A century ago, Sigmund Freud convinced many people that a new drug, cocaine, was the panacea for addiction to alcohol and opium. Since cocaine is a chemically refined form of an ancient herbal substance, it was the perfect solution. Only after Freud saw the resulting epidemic of cocaine addiction sweep Europe and effect him personally did he reject his quest for a talisman and turn to psychotherapy for answers to human behavior.

Looking solely at either biology or behavior as a cause is insufficient if you wish to understand addiction. Either of these theories alone can be taken to ridiculous extremes. Addiction is both biologic and behavioral. The irrational behavior of addicts is no accident. The behavior is the result of brain chemistry and the brain chemistry is the result of behavior. Consider a roller coaster with an entrance station but no exit. This High-Low Trap is my way of describing the tremendous power of the worst addictions afflicting people.

RESEARCH AND CLINICAL EXPERIENCE

For you to understand addiction I must discuss some recent neurochemistry breakthroughs. Research into the natural chemistry of the brain has revealed that addictive drugs override several powerful and complex natural systems. Behavior and brain chemistry can no longer be considered unrelated sciences. These discoveries show that they are components of an extraordinary control system. The complexity of this control system, whether you believe it was created by nature or God, greatly exceeds the sophistication of any control system or computer ever devised by scientists and engineers.

This book may help you understand these recent discoveries and give you some idea of where this new knowledge may be integrated with existing clinical treatments.

The rift between biology and behavior is not the only division that has interfered with the prevention and treatment of addictions. Recent observations by experienced and honest doctors and counselors did not fit older theories about the brain and behavior. Clinical observations about what did and did not work in treating addictions were frequently rejected in academic circles.

Respected academic scholars who conducted costly experiments to test scientific hypotheses often provided little useful information that could increase the effectiveness of addiction treatment. As a result, the search for a workable solution has been caught in a rivalry between those practicing the healing arts and those providing a sound scientific foundation for that practice. Those that have suffered the most–the addicts themselves–have not really benefitted from the vast sums of money and national resources already expended for prevention and treatment. Look around and you will find that they are found in our streets and our homes.

The need to solve the problem of addiction cannot be ignored. The first step in doing this is to make people aware that both sides can be right. With more recent scientific and clinical information, there should no longer be a chasm. In this book, the reader will be shown a path through the maze of conflicting ideas and theories. Following this path can lead to both treatment and prevention that really works.

WHAT THIS BOOK IS ABOUT

There are three parts to this book. The first part deals with addiction itself, in its many forms. The second part is all about recovery, what it is and how to begin. Finally, the last and most important part of this book is about prevention.

This introduction–The High-Low Trap–is an overview, to set the issues and the problems in perspective. The chapters that follow are about people. They are not all pleasant individuals but they are real people and except for changing names and other information that could identify them, their stories are all true. Each personal story was selected to illustrate a specific point about addiction, whether about biology, behavior or both. Most of the people described have recovered. Through their own stories they not only tell us about the despair of addiction, they also teach us about the joy and the process of recovery.

The six chapters of Part One look at different aspects of addiction, including an understandable view of the relationship between events in the brain and behavior.

In Chapter One we meet Alice and Jim. They both were addicts, however neither of them became addicted because they were trying to get high. Instead, they were people who had turned to others for care and inadvertently become addicted. The chapter title, "Innocent Addicts," describes their plight. Once addicted, one remained innocent while the other contributed to a worsening of the addiction process. Yet they were both victims. Only by looking at who these two individuals were before they became addicts can we respect them as people. These are familiar stories, but represent a very small percentage of addictions, yet they are useful in understanding the powerful trap that ensnares good people who have no intention to do wrong.

Subsequent chapters will introduce men and women who are more typical, people who by their own actions participated in their entry onto the road to addiction. Introducing the innocent addicts first will help you to understand the power of addiction before rushing to judge other addicts. Whatever the chain of events that led to addiction, once that point is reached, original intent matters little.

Chapter Two, "Alcohol: The Addictive Sedative," relates the first part of Bill's story. Bill was not a skid row bum. He is a very typical alcoholic, an educated upper-middle class businessman who appears to be successful until his long-standing alcoholism destroys his life. This chapter explains why alcohol is so widely used. Alcohol is a sedative that fools a natural relaxation mechanism in the brain. Knowledge about this mechanism is new and has forced us to discard earlier theories of how alcohol worked in the brain. In Bill's case, you will learn through his experience how this powerful drug disrupted the balance we call mental health. As you read about Bill, you may understand why the psychiatrist and counselors who treated him believed he was suffering from panic attacks and an anxiety disorder. You will learn why Bill became sicker when he received the wrong form of treatment.

In Chapter Three, "The Pill Person," Bill's story is continued as he progresses from a functioning alcoholic to an unemployed and disabled mental patient. Bill's unfortunate experience with alcoholism went further downhill as he became severely addicted to tranquilizers. The medication that was given him in an effort to restore his mental health instead worsened his disease. Bill's case is used to show why tranquilizers are almost always the wrong drug to treat alcoholism and why alcoholics compound their addiction when they receive this popular form of prescription medication.

Chapter Three is also a hopeful chapter because you will see that Bill was able to recover from his personal hell. The path that he followed took him from his private nightmare through a process called recovery. Bill did not just stop his sedatives. He also used the program he found at meetings of Narcotics Anonymous (NA) and Alcoholics Anonymous (AA) to rebuild his life and find a peace of mind he never knew while on either alcohol or medication.

Cocaine addiction is discussed in Chapter Four. Cocaine is a central nervous system stimulant, a drug that increases the activity of the brain. Stimulants have been used for centuries, but the recent destructive epidemic created by cocaine has done more damage than many other curses of the past.

Stimulants produce very different experiences then sedatives and downers. They are used to increase alertness and to brighten mood. This sounded very attractive to Lisa, who you meet in this chapter—an intelligent woman who was on her way up professionally. It took very little time for her cocaine use to destroy the business and reputation that she had developed over the years.

The attractive nature of stimulants is the reason for their popularity throughout history, that is, until their true danger is realized. You will learn why even Sigmund Freud was lured into this trap a century ago, why hardened criminals and street drug users fear cocaine addicts, and how the most severe forms of mental illness—the psychoses—are mimicked in cocaine users.

Chapter Five "Dual Addictions," describes the worst aspects of the High-Low Trap. Don, an executive in the entertainment business, recognized his cocaine dependence and fought it, only to fall victim to alcoholism. He was a victim of a syndrome of sedation and stimulation, a trap that many cocaine users succumb to.

Recovery from the High-Low Trap can be achieved and is being done every day. However, it is so serious that chances of recovery are low unless every available tool is used and used properly.

Chapter Six, "Other Addictions," discusses a number of other drugs which are addictive. The issue of certain activities popularized as addictive behavior is also explored. This book focuses on the relationship between addiction to the stimulants, such as cocaine and the sedatives, such as alcohol. Since victims of addiction don't always follow such neat plans, it is impossible to talk about a few addictions, even if they are the most common and most important, without relating that discussion to other addictions.

Chapter Seven, "Recovery and Thinking," and Chapter Eight, "Recovery and The Body," offer hope to the battered victim of this disease called addiction. We follow Mark and Phyllis through their early recovery and see them both become younger in their appearance as their thinking clears. We will learn of dangerous traps during early recovery and hear of an unfortunate death that could have been prevented. The reader who has not witnessed recovery from severe addiction will discover that it is more than just the absence of drugs, it is a new beginning, a rebirth on a path to enhanced mental health.

Chapter Nine, "Recovery and Sex," breaks the puritanical taboo often surrounding recovery and discusses common problems about sex, relationships and sometimes, unfortunately, abuse. Many recovering people discover that their addiction had hidden difficulties which are painful to face during recovery. Fear, shame and confusion caused by these problems can equally sabotage the recovery of both men and women. Fear aroused by sexual issues should not prevent anyone from progressing in their recovery. Family and friends need to know that patience, honesty and understanding will go a long way in helping but further help from a professional sources may be needed. We will see how Jim relapsed from an otherwise good recovery program because he had nowhere to discuss a common male fear.

Chapter Ten, "Finding Recovery," is the instruction manual for anyone wishing to find recovery or help a loved one. It discusses the choices available regarding widely respected self-help groups, such as Alcoholics Anonymous and Narcotics Anonymous, professional treatment centers, detoxification, inpatient and outpatient rehabilitation programs and factors that may limit your choices. It takes an honest look at the enormous value of voluntary effort in this field, and why for some, the least costly path to recovery may be the best. This chapter tells the reader what to expect in a rehabilitation center and at self-help meetings. It discusses the ways that family and friends may help a reluctant person take the first steps upon this new road.

Chapter Eleven explains how to utilize twelve step programs. Those who choose a path of recovery using the program of either Alcoholics Anonymous, Cocaine Anonymous or Narcotics Anonymous will all find that their recovery is based upon following a simple twelve step program. This chapter, entitled "Following the Twelve-Step Path," is an explanatory guide to doing so. It shows the importance of using all twelve of these steps in their given order. When used as intended, it shows how such a program is neither folklore or religion, but is a sound therapeutic plan that may equal other therapies for maintaining a sane and balanced life.

Chapter Twelve discloses "Other Paths to Recovery." There are many people who free themselves from the yoke of addiction in many ways and this has been true throughout the ages. There are also special programs that may be excellent for a few and wrong for many. Religious cures, oriental medicine and high-tech cures seem to have worked for some. No one has the right to deny the success of another. If any cure has actually helped even one person, then it has merit, if only for that one individual.

The danger of these other paths is many fail the people who try them. The true danger is that many of these paths to recovery are used as alternates to well accepted paths to recovery. Instead, if used to strengthen current approaches, these could conceivably increase the chance of a successful recovery.

The natural history of addiction is quite varied. Relapse is always a danger. Even untreated, some people will see their addiction wax and wane over the years. True recovery is not transitory. Recovery is not complete unless it breaks this cycle and prevents relapse. Chapter Thirteen is dedicated to "Avoiding Relapse." Permanent recovery requires a constant investment of time and work. The work of avoiding relapse is the most pleasant work one could imagine. The "task" of learning to keep life in a pleasant and useful order is it's own reward.

In the last part of this book, the emphasis changes from helping those who have already been scarred by this epidemic to preventing the further spread. Chapter Fourteen is titled "Prevention is Possible." Americans have been cheated. They have been led to believe that prevention is not possible or that it is simple. Few sensible people believed that there could be any hope to prevent addiction by mouthing slogans and printing posters, but most of us would have been very pleased if this had been enough. It was not enough, of course. It discouraged those who felt that we were doing the best we could do. Yet the government spends fortunes on programs that are called prevention. The final chapter explains why current efforts are likely to fail again. Prevention can work but requires knowledge, planning and leadership. If the United States utilizes the tremendous power and resources that it already has, the addiction epidemic will be brought under control. Until that occurs, we will need a never-ending supply of good addiction treatment programs, because without prevention, we will have a never ending supply of addicts.

Four appendices are included at the end of the book. These contain detailed information to help you find help. Separate appen-

xxii ıı   ADDICTION: The High-Low Trap

dices deal with "What Your Doctor Should Know," "How to Recognize A Specialist," "Knowing Who Needs Treatment" and "Locating Help." Addresses and phone numbers are included for your use.

This book was written for you.

I hope you enjoy it, learn from it and use it.

This book is intended to help you understand the disease of addiction. It may help you seek out the care you need for yourself or a loved one. It is not intended to offer individual medical care. If you require such care, please consult your own personal physician for individual attention.

ADDICTION
THE HIGH - LOW TRAP

1

INNOCENT ADDICTS

Addiction makes people think about guilt. We often prejudge addicts. Even if addiction is a disease, didn't the addict start it all himself or herself? No, some did not! This group, that I call "the innocent addicts," demonstrate that the tremendous strength of addiction can trap people who are not trying to get "high" from drugs. This powerful biological/psychological phenomenon is "The High-Low Trap." Cocaine and crack users, people who are not "innocent" by any definition, provide some striking examples of what this is and why it occurs, but cocaine addicts are not its only victims. Anyone who uses sedative drugs, tranquilizers or alcohol may find themselves affected by this. People who are recovering from alcoholism may face considerable stress and even relapse because of this problem. Whether a person has been an alcoholic or a cocaine addict, a "pill-head" or a junkie, the High-Low Trap will complicate their disease and may rock the foundations of their recovery. In this chapter, I will tell you about some innocent addicts. Understanding how powerful the trap is for them helps in appreciating the even greater problems of people who deliberately sought a chemical high.

ALICES'S STORY

Alice belongs to one of the most common group of drug addicts in the United States. She is not suffering from AIDS. She is not a criminal. She has never used a needle and syringe to inject herself with drugs. She is a middle-class widow in her late sixties–a grandmotherly woman–who slowly realized that she was "hooked" and was asking for help. Legitimately, she could be called an "innocent addict."

As I listened to Alice talk, my frustration mounted. I was angry because I knew the difficulty that she would soon face. She thought that she was suffering from an addiction. And, she was right. Yet, none of the drug addiction treatment programs that were available locally were appropriate for her. She sought my help because she had heard that I was experienced in treating addictions.

Alice seemed grateful that I was paying close attention to what she was saying. She answered my questions hesitatingly but honestly. Alice had lived in the same neighborhood most of her adult life. She watched her children move away and her friends die. Her husband passed away, and she lived on his pension and social security benefits. Her family physician had known her for years. He had treated her high blood pressure and arthritis, listened to her complaints and dealt with her other problems as they occurred.

When this kind and compassionate man died, she was left without a physician. She located another doctor who had recently-moved to the neighborhood. This doctor, a specialist, seemed to have less time to listen to her. She felt that he was annoyed with her questions and complaints. "...He always ordered tests but never told me what they were for..." she recalled. "Then, he started me on tranquilizers. I had read a little about them and wondered why I needed them. But, he told me it would help my blood pressure." She looked at me in a way that let me understand she was a person who would not deliberately ignore her doctor's orders.

Using detailed questions, I asked her how and when she used alcohol. Heavy alcohol users, past or present, or those who are drinking while taking tranquilizers, represent a different problem from that of an innocent addict. If Alice had a classic alcohol or drug addiction problem, I could help her on the road to recovery more easily than I could aid an innocent addict. I continued to listen carefully and asked more pointed questions. An important psychological defense mechanism called "denial" makes many people who are addicted unwittingly minimize their problem. These extra questions often uncover a much more devastating addiction then the person seeking help first admits. Alice did not seem to be alcoholic nor did she seem to have ever deliberately sought drugs. She claimed to have taken one or two drinks at social occasions a few times a year when her husband was alive.

She began to drink more frequently after he died. A few months later, still without any heavy pattern of use, she realized the futility of this and simply stopped drinking. She had not used an alcoholic beverage since. When I asked about her taking drugs, particularly "street" or illegal drugs, she appeared shocked and puzzled. Again, I believed her.

Now, I started to ask her more about the addiction she felt she had. Occasionally, a patient comes to me, unnecessarily worried, looking for a problem because of a book or magazine article warning of the evils of a particular medication. Unfortunately for her, Alice was correct in her suspicions.

She had exhibited mild symptoms of clinical depression for several years. Those symptoms started shortly after her doctor changed her blood pressure medicine. This timing made sense because one of the two medicines she was on for high blood pressure (hypertension), worked in her body by blocking "beta-adrenergic receptors" in her autonomic nervous system. This means that it helped keep her body from over-reacting to normal signals of stress by increasing her blood pressure and heart rate. The "beta-blocker" Alice was taking is a very common medicine with the generic name *Propranolol*. It is used very widely and, for its purpose, it is an excellent medicine. This is a nonaddictive drug, but it may produce depression and a feeling of a loss of energy in some people.

Sometimes, patients continue to have problems from medication because they do not let their physician know about them. Many good drugs exist for controlling blood pressure. A patient who has a side effect from one drug usually is switched to another. Alice had let her doctor know about her depression, but he did not change her medication.

Instead he put her on a tranquilizer. His reasons for doing this may have been wrong, but he is not alone. Many physicians prescribe tranquilizers for patients with vague complaints that the physicians do not understand.

In Alice's case, it could not have been a worse move. Tranquilizers are "sedative-hypnotic" drugs. They make you calmer (sedate you) while they make you sleepy (hypnotize you).

Alice continued to answer my questions openly. She had felt calmer as soon as she started taking the drug. But, she certainly did not feel better. She was lethargic, and lacked energy and spirit. Her memory did not seem as good, and she became confused more easily. These symptoms came as no surprise to me. She was not on a large dose of tranquilizer, but she was taking it three times a day. The effect of such a dose on a young healthy person is roughly equal to drinking three strong shots of whiskey a day. That would not cause a profound problem under other conditions. But, Alice was *not* a young healthy woman.

For six substantial reasons her tranquilizer could produce such a profound effect:

1. First, her age limited the ability of her nervous system to tolerate change. As many older people, her nervous system had an adequate ability to handle normal functions without showing any deterioration. However, under the stress of disease or drugs, it could not function as well.

2. She was already depressed as a side effect of Propranolol, her blood pressure medicine. Since a tranquilizer may increase this type of depression, the combination was especially bad for her. When two drugs may both increase one effect, the word "synergy" describes what often happens. The combination of these effects may be even greater than the simple addition of the two effects.

3. She was taking another blood pressure medicine as well. This medicine, a diuretic (often called a "water pill") increases the body's elimination of fluids. It makes people urinate more. Most diuretics cause the loss of other body chemicals (called electrolytes) along with extra urine. This fluid loss may cause a shift of fluid levels among different parts of the body.

Diuretics do not have any direct behavioral effects, but they can change the way other drugs are distributed in the body. Sometimes this change in fluid distribution can increase or decrease the impact of other medications. Older people may also react more to shifts in body fluid by feeling dizzy or lightheaded when they stand up quickly. Understandably, these changes are confusing and alarming to some people.

4. Her body might break down a tranquilizer at a slower rate than a younger person. All medicine has a limited life in our body. As a first step in eliminating many tranquilizers from our body, our liver chemically takes the tranquilizer apart, breaking it down into new chemical compounds. Immediately after any drug enters our body, our system starts to either break it apart or simply eliminate it. Years of research help drug manufacturers determine the "life", the specific length of time that a partic-

ular drug will remain in the body. Physicians use this information to determine the best dose of medicine for an individual
patient, as well as to decide how often that medicine should be
taken.

As people age, the ability of their body to break down many
medicines slows down. If the doctor accounts for this possibility of a slower rate and the levels of the drug or its effects are
carefully monitored, the medicine does its job and no problems
should occur. If a medicine is given to an older person without
considering the possibility of a slower rate of elimination, it will
build to a higher level than is necessary in the body. This is why,
over time a level of a drug that would be right for a younger person can have effects that are more powerful than intended in an
older person. That is why the tranquilizer dose that may have
been considered mild for a younger person was actually a high
dose for Alice!

5. Alice's brain adjusted to the presence of the drug. This
attempt to be "normal" on the part of her brain resulted from the
prolonged use of this medication. Because "benzodiazepine"
tranquilizers mimic natural chemicals in the brain, after her long
use of these tranquilizers, a new balance of natural brain chemistry was achieved.

When the amount of medicine circulating in her blood fell, that
new balance would have been disturbed. That disturbance is
known as "withdrawal." There are many types of drug withdrawals. In the case of a benzodiazepine tranquilizer, such as
the one Alice was taking, the mildest symptom of withdrawal is
anxiety. Anyone who suddenly stops taking a tranquilizer after
years on the medication should go through a period of increased
anxiety. That temporary rebound of anxiety is to be expected
from the withdrawal.

Since this temporary anxiety (which is an important part of the
High-Low Trap) is expected, it should not make sense for a doctor or a patient to assume that this signals a return to her (or his)
underlying symptom of anxiety. Alice had learned that she
could not easily stop taking her tranquilizer. Others have tried
to stop suddenly on their own, only to find they were unable to
tolerate the withdrawal, and returned to using the benzodiazepine tranquilizer. Some have been unfortunate enough to
have their doctor change their prescription to an even stronger
tranquilizer, as a result of their attempt to break the bond of
their addiction.

6. Alice was "labeled". Once a person in our society is diagnosed as having a psychiatric disorder, rightly or wrongly, this

"label" follows them. For years, organizations that care about the mentally ill have been fighting this stigma, but as a society we like to categorize people. Several years ago, a well qualified and competent politician was forced to withdraw as a candidate for Vice President because it was disclosed that he had once sought psychiatric help. The debate that raged over his candidacy was not based on this man's qualifications; the powerful image of a "former mental patient" was enough to exclude him from serious consideration.

Public ignorance cannot be blamed for this powerful prejudice; professionals with extensive training often are guilty of the very same behavior. Research demonstrates that once a patient is "labeled," even qualified mental health workers continue to assume that the original diagnosis was correct, even if all behavior they see is normal. This phenomena occurs even when the first diagnosis was not arrived at in an appropriate way. Just as in Alice's case, her doctor had little qualification to label her as having an anxiety disorder. But, once he did, he and other doctors and mental health workers continued to believe it.

Alice trusted doctors and was slow to question their judgment even when she did not agree. Eventually, as she experienced the negative effects of the tranquilizer, she began to believe that perhaps she was "a little crazy." Once she accepted this label, even partially, she began to interpret everyday events as "caused by my sickness." Along with accepting this label, she also accepted her physicians erroneous belief that hers was a chronic state. She no longer was sure she could feel "normal" *ever again.*

Alice was really an addict. Biologically, she became hooked on a legitimate medication. Society would not label her as a "drug addict," because she really was an innocent addict. She did not intend to get hooked. Few people reading this account will accuse her of seeking a thrill or wanting to get high. Still, biologically, Alice was *very* addicted.

Both the innocent addict and those whose behavior actively contributes to their own addiction are considered "addicts," when using a scientific definition of addiction. Most of the people described later in this book suffer from a more conventional form of addiction. Some addicts (including alcoholics) would even say that Alice was not a "real" addict. Yet, the suffering that Alice endured was real. The addiction that she had was quite tangible. The emotional pain she felt and the lost years of a meaningful life were very real, as well.

Understanding the biological side of addiction helps to counteract the various explanations of all addictions as being based purely upon behavior. Many years ago, the founders of Alcoholics Anonymous (AA) described the disease of alcoholism in lay terms as "physical, mental and spiritual." These differing aspects mean that the addict must be seen as a whole person to comprehend the sometimes baffling nature of this disease. The physical or biological aspect of addiction does not fully explain addiction. On the other hand, denying the biological basis of addiction is the same as saying that addiction is caused by a character defect or some form of wrong behavior. Understanding the innocent addict, the purely biologic addict, helps us to come to grips with all addictions. Our understanding may enable us to view addiction as a disease, and then, see recovery as a very complex process.

Innocent addicts may be treated as effectively as other addicts. However, there are few programs geared toward them. Their disease does not get much attention. Drug treatment programs are available in most cities, but the programs were really not available to patients such as Alice. Alice was not a threat to society; programs established to deal with patients viewed as a "threat to the fabric of our society" did not know what to do with her.

What Alice, and others like her, need is detoxification to bring them off their tranquilizer without agony; this may need to be done in conjunction with counseling to help them rebuild self-esteem. Alice's family physician (despite his earlier shortcomings) needed to be involved, since he was her primary care provider. She needed consistency in her continuing care.

If any of the local long-term drug treatment programs had taken Alice, they would have assumed that her behavior had contributed strongly to her addiction. Clearly, she would not have fit in. The local detoxification program would not accept her because her withdrawal was not life threatening. Local detoxification programs are overcrowded and have to deal with the most urgent cases first.

Alice would have fit in well in several excellent private psychiatric programs if she had not already been labeled. The danger to Alice in a psychiatric program was that she was already believed to have a mental illness. The likelihood was that her insurance carrier would rush her through the system, to prevent a long hospital stay. If her withdrawal was too rapid, she could be expected to develop symptoms of anxiety. Since she had been labeled, this would be dealt with as "... another manifestation of her pre-existing anxiety disorder." The result would have been a prescription for yet another tranquilizer and the downward spiral would have continued.

Instead, Alice was treated through the cooperation of several professionals. She had sought help only after acknowledging that something was very wrong. There were many agencies and professionals available, but she had been bounced around before finding people who would listen and not stereotype her. This lack of appropriate treatment options is not always the case. The city and state you live in can and will influence the nature of treatment available. The willingness of government and insurance agencies to deal with a full range of addictions problems can be the crucial factor when a patient does not fit a stereotype. The difficult question of finding the correct care is important and will be discussed in depth in later chapters. For now, it is enough to realize that Alice was one of the lucky ones. She did get the care she needed.

JIM'S STORY

Jim was not nearly as lucky. Anyone dealing with Jim now would question why his story is here, in a discussion of "innocent" addicts. Jim has broken the law. He has lied and cheated to get drugs. He is not a sweet, white grandmotherly woman. Jim is a black man in his thirties. He is street-wise and aggressive. A veteran who served his country honorably, he now is fighting with the system. Many other veterans would prefer to put the past behind them. Some even resent the attention paid to a veteran like Jim, one with so many difficulties. Jim fits a stereotype, that of the troubled veteran that Hollywood and the entertainment media are all too willing to portray. Each reader may judge whether Jim is an innocent addict.

As a young man, Jim was asked to serve his country. Like many who served during the turbulent years of the war in Vietnam, he faced serious personal conflicts. Doing his job, staying alive, not letting his buddies down were simple, short-term goals. This was a time when long-term goals were not appropriate. Counting the days left on a tour of duty became a ritual that served as a link to home. Jim used drugs, but he did not develop an addiction while he was overseas. He did use alcohol heavily, but he seemed to be like many of the young men with whom he was stationed.

War is often filled with irony. In Jim's case, the irony was he survived Vietnam unscathed only to be seriously injured in an automobile accident while on duty in the United States. His injury meant the end of his Army career and the beginning of the long road of physical rehabilitation at a Veteran's Administration facility. Unfortunately, Jim was left with a physical condition that would cause pain for the rest of his life. He received good treatment, by very capable doctors at several specialized centers. Despite thorough evaluations and several attempts to remedy his problem, nothing has been sufficient.

During Jim's treatment, a pattern clearly developed. Pain killers, or "analgesics" were used since Jim was first injured. Sometimes these contained narcotics (or "opiates") in combination with other ingredients; sometimes, they were non-narcotic, and when pain was extreme, they were pure narcotic. At the beginning, Jim's doctors took a "wait-and-see" attitude. They conveyed this attitude to him. They gave Jim the medication he needed, and followed his case closely. Since the doctors expected improvement, they gave Jim these drugs with the understanding that they were needed. As with anyone who takes narcotics on a regular and frequent schedule, Jim's body adapted, and he became biologically addicted. This did not mean that Jim acted like a drug addict. He was being given a medication for a very real and legitimate purpose.

Once the staff at the hospital felt that there was going to be little future improvement, the situation changed. Jim was still seen by a physical therapist on a regular and frequent basis, but his doctors had less time for him. Since pain medications had helped him, they were continued but with less supervision. Jim seemed like a good person to the staff; he certainly deserved, as much as anyone, to have his pain relieved. His specialists were needed on other cases that seemed more important; so, when he did see a doctor, it was at one of the hospital clinics. Often, his physician was someone who had not seen him before.

Slowly and gradually, Jim increased his use of narcotics. He became despondent. He now realized that he would have a chronic pain problem. In his despondency, he seemed less able to tolerate his pain so he began to take more. Jim was honest with his doctors. He explained that he had run out of medication early because he had been in pain and had taken extra doses, based on his own judgment. Obligingly, his prescription was increased.

Once in a while, a doctor balked. Some expressed concern and tried to limit his narcotic dose. This seemed unfair to Jim; but, he had been around the system enough to know how to work it. He could get the medication he wanted by changing his clinic visits to another day of the week, by showing up as an emergency patient at night, by claiming he had lost his medication, or simply by being belligerent.

Jim was a legitimate patient. He was a veteran who had served his country in wartime. His injury, although not combat related, still had resulted from his military service. Jim knew that he was supposed to be given the highest priority within the V.A. system. If he was denied pain medication, he would threaten to contact his congressman. It often worked, but his ploy was at the expense of changing his relationship with the hospital. Now his complaints were brushed off, and he was given what he appeared to need with no attention to the serious addiction problem that had developed.

The V.A. Medical Center staff reacted to Jim's anger by labeling him. Although he never received any type of psychiatric evaluation, as with Alice, his complaints brought a psychiatric diagnosis (of an "anxiety disorder") from his doctor and a prescription for tranquilizers.

Jim always drank alcohol, but he appeared not to be having a problem until now. He was never told not to drink while taking tranquilizers, although the relationship of alcohol and tranquilizers is very clear and synergistic. That synergy caused the effect of alcohol to be multiplied when he took his tranquilizer. As he got worse, Jim began to question whether drugs affected his life, but he continued his scams to get more and more. If he had an ample supply of one type of medication but wanted something else, he knew the street value of his medications and easily traded one for another. This illegal dealing was not for the profit, but just to obtain what he wanted–when he wanted it.

His combined use of narcotics, alcohol and benzodiazepine tranquilizers created a profound and obvious effect. The changes in Jim were as obvious to his wife as they were to the medical center staff. Now he was so intoxicated from this combination that he could barely function.

Once again, Jim became a victim of the system. Although he had still not been seen by a psychiatrist, another psychiatric diagnosis was made. This time, the diagnosis was "depression." That diagnosis, of course, was added to his earlier diagnosis of "generalized anxiety disorder." Now, Jim had two labels!

Very effective medications, called "tricyclic anti-depressants" are now commonly used to treat genuine cases of depression. These medicines take several weeks to begin to work. On the other hand, powerful stimulants, such as amphetamines, can quickly and temporarily reverse some symptoms of depression but are not a safe or effective treatment. Stimulants are a common ingredient in powerful pain relief "cocktails" used in other countries for dying patients. Carefully used, they may increase alertness in a dying patient who is heavily drugged with pain killers.

Jim was not given an anti-depressant for his "depression." He was instead started on amphetamine, a powerful stimulant. Amphetamine, a stimulant with many characteristics similar to cocaine, is highly regulated because prescriptions are subject to extraordinary misuse. By this time, Jim had developed a pattern of misusing any medication he was given. It was inevitable that he would quickly try to increase his use of this drug, too. When he did, he found out first-hand that amphetamine use can lead to psychosis. Psychosis is a severe form of mental disorder characterized by a loss of contact with reality. In other words, because of the medicines his doctors prescribed–the amphetamines, narcotics and tranquilizers, he "flipped out."

Jim endured a living hell, but this low point became the turning point in his life. His frightened wife had called the police to control him. The police followed normal procedures and brought him to the nearest hospital emergency room that had a psychiatrist on call. He received strong medications to quiet him and was about to be transferred to a state mental hospital with a locked ward for his own protection. If he had gone to the state hospital, the doctors would have difficulty obtaining a full explanation of the medications he had received. Without the availability of his Veteran's Hospital records, he might have received yet another label, based upon the severe psychotic state he was now in.

However, his wife followed the police to the emergency room. She informed them that he was under the care of the Veterans Administration Medical Center. The emergency room staff quickly changed their plans and transferred him to the V.A. hospital. Now, twelve years after his initial injury, he would finally receive a complete psychiatric evaluation.

Recovery from his addiction has not been easy for Jim. He still has chronic pain from his injury. Thanks to a psychiatrist at the

Veteran's Hospital who took the time to review his record, the problems of simultaneous addiction to several different types of drugs became clear. The drug-induced psychosis and the problems of detoxification from multiple drugs (including alcohol) meant a complicated and long hospital stay. Only after that was done could she send him to the hospital alcoholism and drug addiction rehabilitation program.

Jim now uses an electronic pain killer, called a transcutaneous electronic nerve stimulator (or "TENS") when his pain is severe. He learned behavioral techniques from a counselor in a special pain treatment program so that he does not need drugs for pain. He has accepted the fact that he is addicted and regularly attends meetings of Narcotics Anonymous (NA). As a recovering addict, he has developed a new approach to life by living and practicing the NA recovery program.

Jim is now on the road to recovery, and he is grateful. He clearly participated in his multiple addiction, as he is now participating in his recovery. Would Jim have become an alcoholic or a drug addict if his life had gone differently? Many people would emphatically answer "Yes, he would!" There is no way to tell what would have happened to Jim had he not been injured. Certainly, his behavior contributed to his downward spiral.

However, before condemning Jim, realize that this pattern of addiction is not unique to Vietnam-era veterans. Over a century ago, there was an equally terrible epidemic of drug addiction in wounded veterans of the American Civil War. Were these men, separated by a century in time, and by very different circumstances, all "predestined" to become addicts? It is more likely that, in both cases, some combination of world events, chance and biology acting together made them unlucky victims.

▪▪

Jim and Alice seem to be two very different people; yet there are two important similarities in their stories. First, in both cases, their doctor's involvement played a crucial role in the development of their addictions. Sickness that results from medical treatment is called "iatrogenic illness". These were both cases of iatrogenic illness. If either Jim or Alice were not being treated for other illnesses, these events could not have occurred.

Iatrogenic illness does not necessarily mean any medical malpractice was involved. It may mean that something unfortunate happened as a result of treatment, even though that treatment was the best that could be given. Both of these people are grateful to be getting better now; they are not looking for legal remedies to their problems.

The important questions are: what is the "accepted medical practice" in the local community; are these isolated cases and should their doctors have known better?

।।

Recently, the New York State Health Department imposed tough regulations that allow the state to monitor benzodiazepine tranquilizer prescriptions as stringently as narcotic prescriptions. This resulted in a marked decrease in careless prescribing by physicians. As a result, illegal "street sale" of tranquilizers decreased in that state.

When Otis M. Bowen, M.D., was the United States Secretary of Health and Human Services, he endorsed a policy statement developed by the Committee on Scientific Affairs of the American Medical Association outlining what doctors should know about addictions. He had the Federal Government mail a copy of that statement (which can be found at the back of this book in appendix A) to physicians across the country. If the doctors who treated Alice and Jim were as aware of addictions as this policy recommends, neither of these stories could now be told.

।।

The second similarity between Alice and Jim may surprise many readers. Both were "high risk" candidates to develop addictions. Why were they at high risk? Because both Jim and Alice had an undiagnosed case of "addiction in remission" before they were given medication. They each had a problem with an addicting drug before, but had "controlled it."

Understanding why they were at such high risk requires dispelling one of the widely believed myths about addiction. Professionals, as well as recovering alcoholics and addicts, are repeatedly told that, left untreated, no case of alcoholism or drug addiction ever gets better. There is supposed to always be a progressive, downward spiral that leads to insanity or death.

When addiction is looked at in the long term, over a person's lifetime, there is truth in this for many people. When viewed in the short-term, over a period of a few years, this idea is rubbish. It is an idea that developed from interviewing older men who had already progressed far down the spiral. The misunderstanding that results from this concept prevents many cases of addiction from being recognized in their early stages. Incredibly, men and women are forced to suffer more before getting help.

Addictions are chronic, progressive diseases. But, the downward progression is not the same for all people. For years, cases labeled as "spontaneous remissions" have confused those trying to make some sense of this painful and costly disease. Alcoholics can never drink safely again. Drug addicts can never safely return to using psychoactive drugs (including alcohol) no matter how long they have been clean and sober. The disease of addiction, when not active, should always be thought of as "in remission." There is a temptation to say, as we do with cancer, once it has been in remission many years, it is "cured."

Addiction is never really cured. These cases of "spontaneous remission" are part of the natural history of addiction. There is no accurate estimate of the number of undiagnosed alcoholics or addicts temporarily in remission; however, the facts are straightforward. The number of alcoholics and other addicts is usually conservatively estimated (by government agencies and authorities in the field) at between seven and ten percent of our adult population. In contradiction to this, studies of high school and college age groups sometimes report as many as twenty to thirty percent of that group as "heavy users" of alcohol or other drugs. What happens as these young people grow older? This phenomenon has been observed for years. When adults are questioned extensively about earlier problems associated with alcohol or drugs, the percentage who admit they had problems at some time in their life is always much greater than those who appear to have current problems. In longitudinal studies, when the same people are questioned repeatedly over several decades, many seem to drift between having problems and appearing normal. Clearly, the lifetime course of addiction is far more complicated and tortuous than commonly portrayed.

This supports the stories that older recovering alcoholics tell. Many alcoholics try to control their disease. In doing so, they may go through temporary periods of abstinence. Years ago, such people were said to be "on the water wagon" or today, "on the wagon." Recovering alcoholics call this "white-knuckled sobriety" because of the extraordinary stress that many have felt during those periods. People who are practicing abstinence under these conditions may admit that they have a problem but feel it is under control. At other times, they may deny a problem by closely attempting to limit or control the amount or type of alcohol or drugs they use. Alice's earlier alcohol problem had been mild, but she had clearly found it necessary to control it, by abstaining from alcohol.

Whenever a person describes such attempts at *control*, I always question them more closely. Periods of time when a person has felt the need to control alcohol or drugs are another clue to high risk or hidden addiction. People who have never had problems do not know what to say when I ask, "How do you control your alcohol or drug use?" People with ready descriptions of control techniques always can describe a period of time during which they were worried about alcohol or drug use. This is true even when they feel that this period of control "proves" that they really did not have a problem after all.

Jim, when he returned from Vietnam, was trying to practice controlled drinking. He had a problem before he got hurt. At a young age, and in the Army, he had been drinking heavily and had used drugs. This behavior did not stand out in his environment.When he returned to the United States, he had abandoned his drug use and controlled his drinking. Many other veterans and current members of the armed services can tell similar stories.

Jim's behavior did not label him, but it certainly could have identified him as a person at high risk. Alice too, could have been identified as a person at risk of addiction. Unfortunately, the picture of Alice and Jim, as people at risk, becomes clearer only after they have suffered.

Since neither Jim nor Alice had been identified as being at high risk of addiction, neither of them had been warned. They had both originally obtained medical help for legitimate and innocent reasons. They might have refused the medications they were given had they known of the risk. Jim and Alice paid a high price, a price of suffering, to learn about addiction. That suffering could have been avoided.

2
THE ADDICTIVE SEDATIVE

■■■ There are thousands of drugs that are only slightly different chemically, drugs are classified into groups that have similar effects. The drugs to be discussed in this chapter all fall into the group called "sedative/hypnotic." A "sedative" is a drug that produces a soothing or calming effect. A "hypnotic" drug is one that causes sleep or drowsiness. Most drugs in this category have both soothing and sleep inducing properties. Some are better at causing one or the other result.

ALCOHOL

The most popular drug in the United States is the one that society sometimes forgets to call a drug. It is alcohol. It has been used for medicinal purposes as far back as we can trace the practice of medicine. The medicinal uses of alcohol have relied on its properties as a sedative and as a solvent. (It is commonly used to thin certain types of spray paints and lacquers.) This solvent property has been known to chemists and apothecaries for centuries. Old medicinal preparations used alcohol to dissolve and extract the active ingredients from plants and herbs. Many an old elixir's supposed "active ingredient" had little value as a medicine, but those elixirs would still have a powerful sedative effect because of their high alcohol content. Today, most of those old medicines are no longer on the market, but the tradition of using alcohol in medicine continues.

The United States government still allows virtually any form of liquid medicine to contain a strong dose of alcohol, as an "inert ingredient," although the "active ingredients" are closely regulated.

Many popular liquid medicines, such as cough and cold remedies and vitamin mixtures, contain mostly alcohol. Drug manufacturers have shown that this hidden alcohol is not needed by developing and selling identical liquid products that are "alcohol-free." However, the tradition of using alcohol in medicine dies slowly.

Most alcohol used today is not deliberately taken as a medicinal drug, but rather is consumed as an intoxicating beverage. Although it is still just as much a sedative, no matter why it is taken, the typical person drinking alcohol today does not think this is the same as using a drug.

SLEEPING PILLS AND TRANQUILIZERS

Barbiturates and benzodiazepines are two other types of sedatives commonly used today. These drugs are generally known as sleeping pills and tranquilizers. In the United States, drugs of this type are available only with a doctor's prescription and can be taken orally or by injection. However, sedatives are almost never injected except in a hospital. Sedatives taken orally–usually in pill form–are one of the most popular prescription medications in use today. About eighty million individual prescriptions are filled annually in the U.S. for the benzodiazepine type of sedative alone.

Millions of Americans now use or have used tranquilizers without becoming addicted, just as most of the tens of millions who routinely use alcohol have no problems. Because of the huge numbers of Americans who drink alcoholic beverages or use tranquilizers, the relatively small percentage of people experiencing problems numbers in the millions.

Knowledge of the danger of addiction is not new. Many books have been written over the years, by authors who have accurately observed and described the problem. Doctor Benjamin Rush, a famous physician, who was also a signer of the Declaration of Independence, wrote such a book over two hundred years ago.

Although alcoholic beverages have been consumed for thousands of years, the science of understanding how alcohol works in the body is new and fundamental discoveries are still being made. Scientific theory begins as an educated guess. Accepted theories are often proven wrong as science progresses. Once in a great while, true breakthroughs occur and what was once theory can be called fact, however, there are still many things that physicians cannot explain.

Bill's Story

A few years ago I worked in the evenings as the medical director of an outpatient alcoholism clinic. This program was part of a community mental health center, that included separate programs and staff for various forms of mental illness. One evening one of my counselors approached me hesitantly. He asked if I would agree to see a client from the "other" program. This was a rare occurrence since there was a strong sense of territory within both groups. A mental health counselor wanted to refer Bill to us but hoped to clear the way first because of resistance from other mental health staff. Bill had already been treated for two years in the mental health program. I readily agreed and a few days later I met him.

Bill was an unemployed college graduate in his early thirties. He was dressed in good quality clothing but looked very untidy. He had previously held an executive position at a major industrial firm. As we talked, it was clear that he was concerned about his drinking. Bill had been treated for two years for "agoraphobia" and "panic attacks." Agoraphobia means an unusual fear of open spaces (literally "fear of the marketplace"). It is usually applied to people who are afraid to leave the privacy of their home for the crowded conditions of stores, streets and shopping centers. Panic attacks are sudden episodes of unreasonable anxiety and fright without a discernable cause. Panic attacks are often accompanied by a number of changes in body functions that cannot be controlled, such as a rapid heart beat. These types of involuntary bodily functions are controlled by a very basic part of the nervous system called the autonomic nervous system. The reaction of Bill's body to panic was a result of activity within a portion of his autonomic nervous system called the sympathetic system. The response of the sympathetic nervous system to panic has been known since early in this century, thanks to the work of Doctor Hans Selye. This sympathetic response is called the "fight or flight" response. It is the body's way of preparing for extreme physical activity and is a very logical response to imminent and extreme danger. People suffering from this problem may find both their mind and body responding inappropriately when there is no danger. They go through an internal living hell.

Bill came from a white, middle class background. He was brought up in a suburb of a large city, in a neighborhood where most of his acquaintances were, like himself, Protestant and of

English, Scottish or German descent. Both his parents had attended college. He had graduated from an ivy-league school and gone
on to receive a Masters in Business Administration from another
excellent university. He had been a perfect model of the young,
urban professional. His first job was in management and he rose to
an executive level quickly.

   When Bill first began having problems at work, his company
suspected that alcoholism was the cause. They arranged an evaluation by a psychologist. As Bill describes it, the psychologist
seemed to suspect alcoholism but did not confront Bill with a diagnosis. She did send a report to his company and they recommended that he go on extended sick-leave while getting care. They also
told him that the same psychologist would be willing to see him
for therapy, but that he had his choice of practitioners. They were
willing to keep him on sick-leave indefinitely as long as a doctor
kept in touch with their insurance company. Both Bill and his
employer felt there was good reason to expect an early return to
work since he had never been seriously ill before and had no previous history of psychiatric problems.

   Bill now believes that if he had gone back to see the original
psychologist, she would have told him that he was having a problem with his drinking. At the time he did not think he was an
alcoholic. He had never thought that his drinking was the cause of
his inability to work. He had realized, however, that during his last
year at work, his drinking pattern had changed. He assumed that
he was drinking because of his problems, and he was able to
admit that it worried him.

   On long-term sick leave, Bill was actually covered by a disability insurance policy his company had paid for. Since he received
less than his usual take-home pay, he had become very nervous
about the psychologist's fee. His insurance would have covered
part of her charges but left him with a substantial bill to pay. As Bill
explained it to me, his reasons for not returning to her were purely financial. He felt comfortable with her and more importantly, he
trusted her. He felt that he would have been willing to continue
going to her, even if she had told him he had a drinking problem.
In fact, he claimed, he would have been relieved, since he had no
satisfactory explanation for the increased drinking. Worried about
the cost of his care, he discovered that if he used this community
clinic, his portion of the bill would be substantially less. He decided he would come to the clinic for treatment of his illness, which,

at that time had yet to be diagnosed. Bill certainly was secure financially, even on his reduced income. Nevertheless, I believed him. Patients as troubled as he was can take an issue, such as financial security, and become obsessed with it. As I heard him describe these events I accepted the reasons he offered for not returning to her care. If he had, he may have begun to get well earlier, instead of entering the living hell of the past two years of his life.

As I listened to Bill, I began to reconstruct what had occurred. Often, the toughest part of practicing medicine is obtaining a complete history of the course of a patient's illness. I had his chart in front of me. I could see exactly what care he had been given since coming to our clinic. At the moment, it was more important that I do exactly what I was doing. I needed to concentrate on what I could learn directly from Bill. Once I did that, I could see him as a new patient, and not prejudge him by a diagnosis he had been given or care he had received.

Bill was an alcoholic. That much was clear to me, but alcoholics can have other illnesses, and if he was an alcoholic who was also mentally ill, he deserved treatment for the mental illness just as much as anyone else. A question that I could not answer that day was what the relationship was between the two illnesses that Bill appeared to have. Whether his problem was an independent illness, or the symptoms had resulted from his alcoholism was an important question to answer, but not that day.

That day, there was one priority. Bill was an alcoholic who needed help. Because he had been diagnosed as mentally ill he had not been treated for his alcoholism.

Didn't he still deserve treatment for his other illness? If Bill had broken his leg, he would have been taken care of. Our society would not have stood still if a mental health worker had prevented Bill from having his leg evaluated and treated. If an orthopedic surgeon in our local emergency room had refused to treat him because of mental illness, there would have been a furor. The doctor's colleagues would have taken action against him, the local news would give it full coverage and advocacy groups for the mentally ill would take up the issue. He would have been much better off if he had broken his leg. He would not have had to wait two years for treatment.

Bill was my last patient for that evening. I chose to take more time with him than was scheduled and did not have to keep other patients waiting. I explained to him that he was an alcoholic. I carefully went over what he had told me. I noted details he had given me of when and how he drank. I repeated back to him the concern he had expressed about his drinking. I pointed out to him the changes in his drinking pattern as he had described them to me. I carefully explained to him that any one of these details, by itself, should be enough to make any doctor suspect alcoholism. I could see the change, the relief in Bill as I went on to discuss the multiple reasons for my diagnosis. There was little room for doubt that he suffered from alcoholism. I explained to him that I preferred to wait before considering his other diagnoses. Later, I would explain to him why. That evening, it was sufficient to discuss his disease of alcoholism. In doing that, I offered him hope that his life could improve dramatically. That hope slowly materialized as reality as my diagnosis and prediction was proven correct.

Why had Bill become an alcoholic? His early behavior will seem familiar to many people. He started to drink alcohol for what seemed like good reasons. Curiosity, availability and peer pressure all play a part in why someone takes their first drink. At some point during the very early drinking experience, the drug effect of alcohol took over. Alcohol is our oldest tranquilizer. I have never met an alcoholic who did not say that at the beginning alcohol made them feel good. Most alcoholics envy the social drinker who can continue to get the same effect that they experienced at the beginning. As Bill and I discussed it, he acknowledged that he was no different.

As the emotional pain of alcoholism sets in, the pleasant aspects do not always disappear. At some point, however, the pain overwhelms the pleasure. Below a certain threshold, the pleasure can be maintained in balance with the consequences. That is why most social drinkers, unlike alcoholics, can continue to enjoy alcoholic beverages throughout their lives. It is also the principal behind many strategies to deal with alcohol problems. Talking about responsible drinking, temperance or knowing your limits is for social drinkers. These strategies will not work for most alcoholics, but some will never stop trying. The lure of regaining the pleasure, only "this time" without the pain is a powerful and deadly trap for most alcoholics.

The alcoholic quickly begins to develop tachyphylaxis or tolerance to the intended effect. Tolerance increases with some drugs when people take them frequently. Bill found that when he was in college, he enjoyed the pleasant effect of alcohol. By the time he was in graduate school, he was an experienced drinker. He recalled that he had noticed then that he had to drink considerably more than when he was younger to achieve the same results.

ALCOHOL AND THE BRAIN

A dramatic discovery was made a few years ago. Scientists testing an experimental drug, Ro15-4513, found that it appeared to reverse drunkenness. This is not a new wonder drug, but it was a research breakthrough. Ro15-4513 showed scientists that alcohol has a profound effect at certain very specific points in the brain. This discovery helped scientists and the public understand how the brain works and how it is altered by alcohol.

Earlier, in the 1970s, another startling discovery dealt with a very different but equally dangerous group of drugs. It was found that narcotics, such as morphine, opium and heroin work because of "natural receptors" that exist in the brain. These drugs, called opiates, are all related to opium. Apart from the terrible addiction problem of opiates, they are wonderful pain relievers. Scientists are able to alter their chemical structure just slightly and observe the effects, but they had never understood how the opiates influenced the brain.

The breakthrough came when scientists recognized naturally occurring brain chemicals that resembled opiates. That led to the discovery of a wonderful, natural system for dealing with pain. Today we know that the brain produces these chemicals as it needs them. They have been called "endorphins," from endogenous (meaning developing from within) morphine. Natural points inside the brain are "receptor sites." The body produces endorphins in tiny amounts, yet these natural opiates are very potent. Endorphins are designed to fit the pain relief receptors. It takes a very small amount of endorphin to produce the same pain relief as a larger dose of morphine or heroin.

Any time the brain produces an effect by generating or releasing a chemical, that chemical is a neurotransmitter. Some neurotransmitters only work within the part of the brain that produces them, like a signal on a private telephone circuit. Other neurotransmitters work like signals from a radio or television broadcasting station. A broadcasting station sends out a signal that goes

to every location within its range. If there is a receiver turned on
and tuned to receive that signal, it gets through. If several thousand receivers are set to receive that signal, they all will pick it up.
If a severe snowstorm forces an elementary school to close, concerned parents can learn the news rapidly by listening to the radio.
Those same parents would tie up all the telephone circuits at the
school and overwhelm the school secretary if they each called individually to check if the school is closed. Broadcasting is a very efficient way to transmit this information. Some chemicals in the brain
are like powerful transmitters, reaching different parts of the brain
at once with the same message. The discoveries of the endorphins
and their receptor sites revealed much about the way certain powerful signals travel across the brain.

   The discovery of endorphins created much speculation about
how other drugs that affect the brain might work. Two conflicting
theories to explain how alcohol works have been especially popular. Remember, theory is just an educated guess until science
demonstrates it is right. One theory was that endorphins explain
how alcohol effects the brain. According to this theory, as alcohol
is broken down by the body, compounds called isoquinolines are
formed through a series of chemical reactions. These compounds
then act like endorphins, setting off the opiate receptor sites.
Although it was widely publicized, there are a number of problems with this theory. One problem is that a number of the intermediate chemical reactions needed to make this work have never
been found in humans, although there has been considerable
searching for evidence that they exist. Another obvious problem is
that alcohol does not produce the same changes in the brain as
narcotics. Although many people suffer from "polysubstance
addiction," alcohol and opiates are clearly not similar. A third problem is that certain drugs used to treat narcotics addictions are of no
value in treating an alcoholic. There are powerful drugs available
that block opiate receptor sites in the brain, drugs such as naloxone
hydrochloride. Inject this drug into opiate users in a coma from a
narcotic overdose and they will quickly awaken (if no other damage exists) because the naloxone takes over the receptor sites and
"jams the signals" by blocking the opiates. In addition to saving
his life, you will have put the person into sudden and extremely
uncomfortable withdrawal. Now, if naloxone is given to someone
who has passed out because they are drunk from alcohol and has
not taken any other drug, there will be no effect, no change. If alco-

hol worked chiefly through opiate receptors that person should have awakened. Chemical reactions between alcohol and opiates may exist, but, if they do, they play a small role in the chemistry of alcohol in the human brain.

The second theory is that the brain has other powerful ways of transmitting or modulating signals, through endogenous chemicals other than the endorphins. Alcohol somehow influences how these other endogenous chemicals work on different receptor sites. The location of these other receptor sites differs from the endorphin or opiate receptors because they influence the brain in different ways. These other chemicals play a part in a powerful internal system within the brain. Research based upon this theory has produced some startling results. The most dramatic result has been the discovery of the relationship between alcohol and Ro15-4513.

Research has now provided strong evidence that at least one of these other endogenous systems does exist. Simply for the sake of discussion in this book, I would like to introduce my own term, "endoseren" for endogenous serenity. When more is discovered about this system, perhaps a better name can be found. Endorphin allows the brain to modulate or control pain. Endoseren may be the way the brain modulates or controls anxiety.

The pharmaceutical companies that manufacture benzodiazepines have spent years attempting to learn exactly why and how these tranquilizers work. The National Institute of Mental Health has spent tens of millions in research in order to gain a better understanding of anxiety. This research is paying off, as scientists have demonstrated specific receptor sites in the brain that benzodiazepines attach to, sites that are related to another chemical within the brain called gamma-aminobutyric acid (GABA). GABA itself seems to be part of the body's natural tranquilizer system, with the effectiveness of GABA modulated, or changed, by the endoseren system. These endoseren receptor sites are like a lock looking for a key. Since there is a beautiful plan to our bodies, when we discover a natural lock, a natural key usually exists to match it. Scientists are now trying to discover whether the key to the endoseren system is a naturally occurring chemical called octadecaneuropeptide.

Scientists have produced further findings that show that an endoseren system exists. Knowing the chemistry of tranquilizers that bind to receptors, pharmaceutical company scientists have developed drugs that block these receptor sites. Tranquilizers, are said to be "anxiolytic," that is, they break up or "lyse" anxiety. Benzodiazepine blocking drugs have just the opposite effect. One such experimental drug, FG 7142, has been shown to be "anxiogenic." That is, it generates anxiety. This drug causes anxiety by blocking tranquilizer receptor sites even when no tranquilizers have been given, so it appears to be blocking a natural or endogenous system. FG 7142 is stopping a natural brain chemical from providing a serene state of mind.

Even more recent research confirms this second theory, that there is a distinct system in the brain overpowered by alcohol. Scientists have now discovered that the modulation of GABA by alcohol takes place at a specific point, called the gamma-2-long-form sub-receptor. Why is this important? Because it provides more scientific evidence that each of us has a normal system jimmied by the sedative alcohol. It shows that alcohol tampers with a circuit that was left in our brain for a specific reason. It shows that what happened to Bill could happen to anyone of us.

ıı

Bill probably was normal before he started to drink. There was no family history of alcoholism or mental illness. Research to determine more about the nature of endoserens will give us a better understanding in the next few years. Right now, there is speculation that if Bill's parents had been alcoholic, his brain might have had a low level of a naturally occurring chemical called serotonin before he took his first drink. Since Bill had no increased genetic tendency for addiction and no behavioral problems prior to that first drink, none of several theories about "high risk" individuals apply to him. That means that before Bill took his first drink, his brain was able to cope with anxiety in a normal manner.

I explained all this to Bill, because it was important that he understand that he was neither bad nor crazy. Once he had taken his first drink, subtle internal changes began. In his case, he was not an instant alcoholic. Alcohol gradually shifted his brain chemistry as well as his patterns of behavior. He became another victim of the High-Low Trap. The research on Ro15-4513–the pill that blocks alcohol in the brain–has given us the evidence to understand how.

TRANQUILIZERS AND ALCOHOL

We have known for years that there is an interaction between tranquilizers and alcohol. Tranquilizers can prevent alcohol withdrawal problems and are used to prevent dangerous medical complications during detoxification. Alcoholics who have never before used a tranquilizer have a high tolerance to them. This means that if an alcoholic must be given a tranquilizer, such as before surgery, he or she must be given more of the drug than is required in an average person before it begins to take effect.

Since Ro15-4513, a drug that blocked a natural tranquilizer site, could also block the effect of alcohol explains much about how alcohol works in the brain. When alcohol first entered Bill's brain, it exerted some of its pleasant effect by broadcasting a signal picked up by circuits tuned to the endoseren network. Tuned to receive the special signal from a small natural transmitter, they instead responded to a very strong signal that was quite different. Imagine for a moment what happens when you are listening to your car radio and you pass the broadcasting tower of a large station that is not the one to which you are tuned. Your radio suddenly starts bringing in this strange signal. Even though it is tuned to a different frequency, the stronger signal is powerful enough to trick your receiver until your car moves away from the station.

In a similar way, alcohol tricks the brain's receptor sites. The endoseren network is only one of several points that alcohol affects in the body. This is because alcohol is a solvent. That solvent quality allows alcohol to enter the protective membrane of many of our body's cells.

When tranquilizer receptors were first discovered, it was not apparent how alcohol could influence them. Alcohol is so chemically different that it seemed as if it must bypass that system and go straight into the cells. Since alcohol gets into many cells, that did not explain why it was so powerful in affecting certain brain systems or interacting with tranquilizers. Blocking alcohol from brain cells by locking up receptor sites has given us the answer. Even though alcohol cannot match the key needed to fit the lock at receptor sites, that was where it worked.

Alcohol works just like the car thief equipped with a jimmy. The thief may not have the key to your car door, but he has learned how to slip a piece of metal in through your window frame and catch the door mechanism at the back of the lock. Alcohol works like the jimmy. Bill's endoseren system did not match the chemical structure of alcohol but alcohol could get in and operate his receptor sites by slipping into the "lipid-soluble membrane" and jimmying the lock at the gamma-2-long site. His body never knew whether it was getting a signal from alcohol or a natural system.

When Bill first began to use alcohol, his brain reacted like any social drinker. At moderate levels, his brain reacted as if natural levels of relaxation were turned up. He was away at college, and new situations could produce both excitement and anxiety. Alcohol was always present at college social occasions and with good reason. Learning about adult social behavior is exciting but can also be terrifying for young men and women. Having "a beer or two to loosen up" was one way of dealing with the stress. This made the occasion enjoyable, and the first change was underway. This first change was not chemical; it was behavioral. The association between alcohol and social interaction was learned. The rewards were positive. Bill was no longer terrified of talking to a young woman he found interesting. He enjoyed the conversation and was able to feel good about himself. This is a normal part of emotional growth, but Bill attributed his "courage" to the alcoholic beverage. Many of his college friends had the same experience and will associate alcohol use with the enjoyment of social occasions for the rest of their lives. Unlike Bill, their pattern of social drinking remained moderate and pleasant.

During his first years of college, Bill limited his alcohol use because he limited his social time. He was a serious student so he restricted his social activity when it would interfere with study and school assignments. The stress of this began to get to him. When he did have free time, he was more isolated than his less studious roommates. Although he dated several women, he didn't date on a regular basis. There were weekends when he just wanted to relax, but had no social setting to drink with others. This might have been the first hint of events that would occur later. He began to drink on weekends, when he did not have classwork to do. He still enjoyed drinking with friends but he became comfortable drinking alone as well. If he did not have a date or a party, he could slip down to the rathskeller located in the basement of his dormitory. Here, he could start out to have "a few" and just relax. Often, the few would turn into many, and he would get very drunk. This never caused him serious problems since he didn't have to drive to get home. His body reacted to some of these occasions but he was not the only student in his dormitory that experienced that. The vomiting and the hangovers were looked at as "rites of passage," not only by his friends but by his parents and the school administration.

Remember the hysteria about widespread drug use on campus a few years ago? Bill's parents never have fully appreciated the problems he was beginning to have. Many parents, at that time, were relieved to hear about the drinking episodes of their sons and daughters. More than once, I have heard of a young adult who was told "Thank God–you are not using drugs." Bill, however, was using a legal and socially acceptable drug–alcohol. As he began to increase his use of alcohol, biologic changes began to take place.

The human body is wonderful. It has a design that exceeds our ability to duplicate in a machine. There are complex systems to regulate many functions. If we were designing a robot to mimic a person, the most difficult part would be including all the control circuits and feedback loops. Our bodies are loaded with feedback loops to control our functions. We call the normal setting homeostasis. When we are not sick and everything is functioning right, our bodies maintain homeostasis. If something goes beyond a normal setting, the sensor of a feedback circuit sends a signal to correct the condition.

Compare the human body to a very simple feedback loop, the thermostat in your home. If it is too cold, the thermostat signals the furnace, and the house is heated. Once the house is warm enough, the thermostat senses it and the furnace stops. You may also have an air-conditioning system that the same thermostat controls, and it will send a signal to cool the house if it is too warm.

If you live or work in a larger building, you know about the problems that can occur when such a simple system is not used correctly. Suppose all the people in one office were very unhappy about the cold. Let us imagine that they chipped in and bought several portable heaters for their office. You may have seen what happens next. The office they share becomes warm and cozy. Unfortunately, the engineer that designed the heating system had expected that corner of the building to be the coldest and located the only thermostat in that office. Now, the building heating system receives a signal that the building is warm enough and the furnace turns itself off. The people in the rest of the building begin to shiver. Even worse, perhaps the air conditioning in this building turns on automatically, even in the winter. The corner office has become so warm and cozy that the workers don't notice the cool breeze as the air conditioning takes over, but the people working in the rest of the building can't understand what is happening.

This discussion about furnaces illustrates some principles regulating the body. Whenever a system that is closely regulated is overridden, the feedback loop is defeated. Whether it is the human body or the heating system of an office building, confusing the feedback loop can have disastrous consequences. In the hypothetical case of the office building, it meant that the small amount of heat from the portable heaters confused the system and the remainder of the building was cooled when it should have been heated. We could call it a Hot-Cold Trap. In the human body, similar but often more complex changes can occur. This is the basis for homeostasis.

■■

Now, back to Bill. As he began to drink more and more, and on a regular basis, his need for alcohol began to change from just a behavioral need to a biological need. Remember the social situations in his freshman year? He used alcohol to augment his natural system for dealing with anxiety. As long as this was infrequent and moderate, there was little change in his body chemistry. By his junior year, he had gotten into the habit of using alcohol fairly often and in larger amounts. Since the alcohol jimmied the lock and turned on his relaxation circuits without the help of endoseren, the feedback loop was satisfied. Natural production was reduced. As long as this happened infrequently, the system was only out of service when he was actually using alcohol.

His original problem was behavioral. He had never learned to cope with certain social situations without a chemical aid to relaxation. This stymied his emotional growth. Now, there is a biological problem. His system had learned and adapted to the frequent presence of alcohol. It had attempted to compensate for having it's endoseren system jimmied. Now the High-Low Trap was sprung. Bill now was having difficulty during the week and felt greater tension and less satisfaction from his normal activities. Although he still was an honor student on the coveted Dean's List, his actual school performance suffered. His grade point average dropped slightly during his junior year but not enough to hurt his chance of getting into a good graduate school.

His senior year grades dropped more. Many of his classmates would have been thrilled to get the marks he got but they were well below what he could do. This did not hurt him, since his application to graduate school was based upon his performance through the previous year. If during his junior year he was uncomfortable, his senior year was misery. Since his body believed it did not need to turn on his endoseren system often, when he was not drinking he was always tense.

Bill had entered college with little experience drinking alcohol. He explained that he "matriculated in drinking like an adult and graduated a full-fledged binge drinker." He was rarely at ease during his class week and he looked forward to the weekend to "relax." Relaxation, as Bill explained to me, always included alcohol. He still enjoyed being with others, but he was becoming more isolated. Since he seemed so different during the class week, people he knew in his daily environment were not on the best of terms with him. He seemed to separate these people from his friends, those people with whom he could relax. In truth, he was losing friends. As he described his relationships, it was evident to me that the people he had called friends were actually only drinking companions. Even worse, more and more of his weekend drinking was becoming solitary.

Sometimes, during the week, he would decide to relax and spend an entire evening drinking. This did not happen every evening. Even back then, Bill had sensed something wrong with daily use. He used the calendar to control his drinking. By imbibing heavily on certain days and abstaining on others, Bill was following a classic pattern of binge drinking. Binge drinking is sometimes mistaken for a behavioral problem. It is assumed that if people can control their drinking during the week and binge only on weekends, they are not alcoholic. Instead, they are often labeled "problem drinkers" or "alcohol abusers."

All this had happened many years before, but it was enough to discuss that evening. At our next visit, Bill and I could review the more recent events in his life. It was time to begin to involve him in his treatment plan.

Since Bill welcomed help, he was willing to cooperate in the treatment plan I outlined for him. I explained that the first step for him was to stop drinking any form of alcohol. He agreed to do that. I was not concerned about the serious medical consequences of withdrawal. His drinking pattern, his medical history and the fact that he had certain other medications in his system all indicated that he should be able to stop with little risk. He agreed to join an alcoholism group counseling session that met weekly at our clinic. I arranged this and assigned one of our certified alcoholism counselors to his case. He was not as happy about my recommendation that he also attend Alcoholics Anonymous (AA). He felt that despite his problem, he was not as bad as the people he pictured attending AA. I suggested to him that he try going to three AA meetings in the next week and jot down his feelings after each meeting. He agreed to that, because it gave him more control over the situation. We scheduled an appointment in a week. He left the clinic looking as if he were overwhelmed and relieved at the same time. This was a far different person than the man who had shuffled into my office less than two hours earlier.

3

THE PILL PERSON

━━
━━

A week later Bill walked into my office on schedule. He looked very different than he had the previous week. He was neater, and even though he still looked a bit nervous, he carried himself as if he felt good about himself. He had a "glow." He was anxious to talk and I could anticipate why. I had already checked with his new counselor, who had seen him once at the group session and once individually. I also overheard him talking easily to the receptionist. In terms of change, that week had been like a year.

The first part of the treatment plan was working well. He had accepted the fact that he had a problem and had identified with others he had met at the group session who were getting better. The change in his bearing and his eagerness to talk told me as much as the words he actually spoke.

We reviewed our previous discussion and he recalled several incidents that more strongly confirmed the diagnosis. He found the alcoholism group different from the mental health group he had been assigned to before. The process seemed the same, even the room was the same, but the focus was very different. He was scared of the new group but he identified almost immediately. Following my suggestion, before he had attended his first group meeting, he had gone to AA. I had asked him to attend at least three AA meetings before this visit, and he had been to eight! Obviously, he wanted more of what he had found there.

At this second meeting he had been referring to himself as an *alcoholic* throughout our conversation. This was positive, because many people have difficulty in identifying themselves that way. The psychological defense mechanism of denial is a barrier that can keep someone from admitting the obvious. Such denial can harm or kill those who refuse to seek treatment during the early stages of cancer or heart disease. A woman who dies of breast cancer because she was scared to find out the truth about a small lump in her breast is an example. She may have died unnecessarily because her denial kept her from treatment when she had a good chance of recovery.

In addiction, denial can be just as deadly. The addict may continue to deny his or her problem right to the grave. For those individuals attempts at treatment will be futile until they recognize that they have a problem. Bill got past his denial stage because he identified so strongly with some of the stories he heard at Alcoholics Anonymous.

One thing surprised me. I sent him to an AA group in his upper-class neighborhood, thinking he would find much in common with the doctors, lawyers and corporate executives he would meet there. But he preferred to attend most of his AA meetings near our clinic in a neighborhood that seemed out of character for my "yuppie" patient. It was a good place but an older factory area with a blue-collar population. Bill explained that because he felt he was down-and-out, and had "hit bottom" he could relate to the "gut-level honesty" he sensed at these working class AA meetings.

All AA groups have the same dynamics. However, on the surface there may be extreme differences. Addiction is not limited by race, social class, religion or education. Similarly, participation in AA is not limited by these parameters. This may come as a surprise to a person trying to recover. Many newcomers feel most comfortable attending meetings in their own neighborhood, because they see other people who look and sound like themselves. Later, they may recognize that they can learn as much from the recovery of a person who lacks a high school diploma as they can from someone with a doctoral degree. Once that occurs, they may find themselves attending many different AA meetings and interacting with people with a wide variety of experience.

For Bill, the opposite was true. Perhaps guilt and shame over his own addiction played a part in his recovery. He may have needed to associate with people he would not ordinarily have come into contact with when he was drinking, as a way of recognizing his own humanity. Many months later, he began to attend meetings in his own neighborhood. It took him that long to get over his stereotype and understand that the bankers and lawyers in his neighborhood had experienced the same problems as the mill workers he now met.

Bill had taken an important first step. He had remained abstinent from alcohol for the past week. This went smoothly because he was already getting much of his addictive need satisfied by the tranquilizer he was taking. Stopping his tranquilizer was going to be an important part of his recovery from alcoholism.

This second step seemed to be a contradiction. Tranquilizers are excellent drugs for certain purposes. One of these purposes is to protect patients from the sometimes lethal effects of withdrawal from alcohol. Benzodiazepines are a perfect drug for this because they mimic the effect of alcohol at endoseren receptors without the deadly effect of alcohol on some lower portions of the brain. A physician can detoxify a very addicted patient from alcohol by substituting a tranquilizer then smoothly tapering the patient off the tranquilizer dose. This is usually done in a hospital setting; it takes three or four days for most people. This is a first step in recovery and is recommended when a patient might develop serious medical problems by stopping alcohol too quickly.

Unfortunately, tranquilizers are too much like alcohol. Although they are the best drug for alcohol detoxification, they cause continued problems when given to alcoholics for any other purpose. This is not because they are bad drugs, any more than alcohol is a bad beverage. However, they can continue an alcohol dependence in an alcoholic who is not drinking. I had read Bill's record and knew what had happened to him during the past two years he was treated at the clinic. Now, I went over this with him so that he could understand the other side of his addiction.

Bill had been treated for two years for agoraphobia and panic attacks. He had not been treated for alcoholism until one week ago. The treatment that had been used for his panic attacks had worsened his alcoholism and was going to make his treatment much more difficult. If Bill were not an alcoholic, there would have been several ways to treat his panic attacks, including psychotherapy, biofeedback or medications, either alone or used in combination. Since no two people are the same, there is no single accepted therapy. A combination of several methods is often used.

When medications are utilized, doctors and patients should be aware that there are different types of medications available to break the cycle of the anxiety which causes a physiologic response (or panic) which, in turn, creates greater or excessive anxiety. Some medications such as the anti-depressant drugs and the new non-benzodiazepine anti-anxiety drugs (such as the non-addictive drug *buspirone*), work in indirect ways. This means that the person experiencing the attack does not sense rapid relief from the drug, even though the condition will eventually be helped. On the other hand, benzodiazepine tranquilizers are sometimes used. These can bring rapid relief or they may prevent an attack taken immediately before a stressful situation. They are very popular medications, because initially they seem to relieve the problem.

When Bill first came to the clinic, he probably was not suffering from agoraphobia or panic attacks. He had been seen by a good clinical psychologist and his drinking problem was being explored. When he came to the clinic, he was seen by an equally good psychiatrist. There were no hints of agoraphobia, except one. His alcoholism was isolating him, and his desire to remain at home and drink was mistaken for agoraphobia. He described times and situations, both at work and when visiting his parents, when he would become very anxious.

These episodes of anxiety were mistaken for panic attacks because their relationship to alcohol was not explored. Bill was a daily drinker, but not a continuous drinker. He could not appear intoxicated at work, certainly not before lunchtime. Every working day he had been subjecting his brain to the alcohol withdrawal syndrome. Vacations and weekends were the only times that he felt comfortable having a morning drink. The rest of the time, he experienced alcohol withdrawal–the High-Low Trap. His irritability, anxiety and bodily reactions were not panic attacks. They were a clear indication of his growing dependence on alcohol.

Bill's psychiatrist had taken a gamble that he was not alcoholic. He may have been reluctant to make this diagnosis in a bright young executive. Alcoholism often kills because others (including physicians, psychologists and loved ones) are unwilling to hurt someone with this terrible label. Imagine professionals who were disinclined to label people who had treatable forms of cancer. Many would die unnecessarily out of a deadly form of politeness. Alcoholic men and women do die because of this. Studies have repeatedly shown that many professionals are reluctant to diagnose alcoholism in their patients and clients, even when the diagnosis is clear.

In Bill's case I don't know why his psychiatrist did not recognize his addiction. His psychiatrist lived in the same upscale neighborhood as Bill. Perhaps he thought Bill did not fit the stereotype of an alcoholic. Bill claimed he had asked the doctor about his drinking. He said to me that he had been told it was not related to his problem, and he could continue to drink, as long as he "kept it under control."

Then, Bill came under the care of a treatment team at the clinic. He was seen by a mental health counselor who would discuss his case monthly with the psychiatrist. He would also be seen by a physician for about ten minutes every two months for a "medication visit." Prescriptions were renewed or changed based principally on what the psychiatrist had learned from the counselor, rather than from his own observations. From the beginning, his care included tranquilizers. Since the tranquilizers replaced the falling alcohol level during the parts of the day he was not drinking, they seemed to help slightly. Alcohol and tranquilizers should never be mixed, but somehow Bill did not get that message from his treatment team. For two years this treatment continued, with the tranquilizers worsening the effect of the alcohol through their synergistic relationship.

Eventually, his panic attacks began to look more like the real thing. This reassured his treatment team that they had made a correct diagnosis. So, they continued his therapy and completely forgot the original question: was he alcoholic? Bill had continued to deteriorate. His treatment team did not see the alcohol connection because Bill reported he was drinking less. He even reported being able to stop for a few days at a time, which he did occasionally in that two year period. The synergism at the receptor sites in his brain allowed him to do this. He was like other alcoholics who switch from whiskey to beer. Since the effect at his receptors was virtually the same, his condition could not improve.

Why did his panic attacks appear to worsen? His brain was now on a roller coaster. Tranquilizers have a withdrawal syndrome, too. It is characterized by increased anxiety and increased autonomic nervous system activity. The autonomic nervous system controls many involuntary actions, such as the rate at which our hearts beat.

Now, whether his tranquilizer level or his alcohol level was falling, he would become anxious and feel his heart racing. This would be relieved by his taking more tranquilizers.

Although he appeared to get better at first, subsequently he got worse, and so the search for a better tranquilizer began. His prescription was changed several times, each time to a newer benzodiazepine. Since benzodiazepines were introduced, drug companies have come out with newer, "cleaner" versions. These newer tranquilizers require a smaller dose and are effective more quickly. They also leave the body more quickly. This means that they also produce faster changes. Whenever the addictiveness of a drug is measured, the speed of the changes are important. The faster the onset of action, the more powerful the psychological reinforcement that is given to the behavior of taking the drug. The faster the drug leaves the body, the more noticeable the withdrawal that results from the falling blood levels of the drug. This meant that the newer benzodiazepines trapped Bill in a cycle of rapidly rising and falling drug levels.

Bill then began to experience real panic attacks. The constant rising and falling levels of benzodiazepines were part of his problem. The other part was that his brain forgot how to regulate anxiety on its own. The benzodiazepines he was taking flooded the feedback controls that regulate his natural responses to anxiety. Without that, every provocation resulted in unchecked anxiety. Every episode of anxiety produced temporary physical changes, such as an increased heart rate. This in turn caused Bill to be more aware of his body and more fearful. The anxiety caused fear and the fear caused anxiety. His therapist had taught him some good techniques to recognize and break the cycle, but, with his natural tranquilizer system turned down, his response was not adequate. The only short-term solution was to take another tranquilizer. The short-term solution became the root of the long-term problem.

Bill is not unique in terms of what happened to him. His problem was still alcoholism. He continued to drink heavily, so the diagnosis was made a little easier. I have seen men and women who had never been diagnosed as alcoholic tell similar stories. Many times, they had experienced several years of drinking in a clearly alcoholic manner. Some event or insight had caused them to question their own drinking and they had quit. They had clear cases of undiagnosed alcoholism in remission and, as discussed earlier, were practicing white-knuckled sobriety. Rather than return to drinking, they had sought help for their anxiety and been given a tranquilizer. Eventually, usually several years later, they fell into the same pattern but without any recent use of alcohol.

Bill seemed intelligent enough to understand all this, although he did not need all the intricacies of this information to get better. My plan was to work together with Bill to help him deal with his tranquilizer addiction. If his tranquilizer problem was ignored, his alcoholism would never truly be treated.

Fortunately, Bill had always suspected that his tranquilizers were part of his current problem. He was ready to hear me but he was fearful. This fear, that his pills were actually contributing to his problem, had been a conflict since he had started taking benzodiazepine tranquilizers. He had seen new problems develop and old problems appear worse, creating a strong suspicion that his pills were to blame. As much as he mistrusted his pills, he also had become quickly attached to them.

The pills were his friends. As his psychiatrist had prescribed faster acting tranquilizers, the effect was even more noticeable. The rapid relief of anxiety provided reinforcement of the behavior of taking a tranquilizer. He not only took tranquilizers when he was already anxious, but he began to anticipate when he might become anxious and would take a tranquilizer in advance. He clearly had become addicted to tranquilizers both psychologically and physically. Attempting to separate these two powerful components was not possible. However, he had to understand that his addiction was both psychological and physical.

Bill both feared his pills, and feared giving them up. He clearly was identifying himself as an alcoholic, and wanted all the help he could get. His willingness to admit his alcoholism was cathartic. It enabled him to acknowledge that he also had a pill problem. He was scared, and it began to show. In his two years of therapy this conflict had never been discussed.

Bill had developed a trust in our alcoholism program in the short time he had been under our care. Now that I had identified tranquilizer addiction as a second problem, he hoped for a quick, easy solution. I warned him that it was not going to be quick or easy, especially as an outpatient. Tranquilizer withdrawal took much longer than alcohol withdrawal. As an outpatient, he would face normal, stressful everyday situations during the very time that he would be getting physical cues from the withdrawal. He would have ordinarily taken a pill when he felt that way. Now he would have to deal with or accept the stressful situation. This is too much for many people to handle.

As a patient at an inpatient treatment unit, he might do better because of the supportive environment. But, he turned down that option. He said that he trusted us because of the progress he had made in such a short time. Although glad that Bill felt so positively about us, I told him what to expect. My recommendation was the inpatient unit. He would fit in very well and his dual addiction would be understood and treated. It would take a month, then he could return to our clinic. He did not want that. Perhaps he felt he was not "sick" enough to need it. I explained to him that as an outpatient, tranquilizer withdrawal often takes much longer. I chose to slowly and gradually wean him from his pills. Quicker withdrawal would have been easier, but it would not have worked in Bill's case. A quick withdrawal is more severe, and the unsupervised patient will often use extra pills if they are available. The patient may then give up, believing that he or she is not capable of living drug-free. Unfortunately, the time involved is the chief disadvantage of a prolonged withdrawal. Impatience in reaching a goal of abstinence can be reason for dropping out of treatment and returning to addiction. Success is possible with many types of detoxification, but, because of the innumerable problems of outpatient withdrawal, professionals often favor inpatient care, so that this phase of treatment is rapid and clean cut.

Bill needed a great deal of reassurance over the next two months, which is what this phase of his treatment took. Withdrawal in a controlled setting takes far less time, but this was done in small increments because Bill was an outpatient. If, as often happens, he had dropped out of treatment or obtained additional pills elsewhere, this approach would not have worked. To prevent this, extra time was allowed at each step. The level of tranquilizer in his blood stabilized at a new, lower level with each decrease, and only then was his body able to adjust and take over more of its own control.

Whenever the treatment went too fast, he cheated. Addicts, even respectable middle class ones, can lie. At these times, Bill took extra pills but did not mention them. Deliberately I gave him very small prescriptions without automatic refills. Thus, I could gauge whenever he was taking any extra pills and discuss the situation with him. He was trying hard and very much wanted to be drug free. He wanted approval and so, at first, tried to hide when he had taken an extra pill. At these times, I explained to him that he was not to take medication on an as needed basis. The only way this would work is if he let me know when he felt anxious, and we agreed on any change in his detoxification schedule.

Bill did complete his detoxification successfully. That set the foundation for his early recovery. Now, as an active member in both Alcoholics Anonymous and Narcotics Anonymous, he celebrates the day he took his last tranquilizer as his birthday. For Bill, alcohol and benzodiazepines were one and the same. His was clearly a case where addiction to one meant addiction to both.

Bill was like the majority of men and women who become dually addicted to alcohol and tranquilizers. He had several psychiatric symptoms but since he had no other disorder, these symptoms disappeared as he progressed in his recovery from addiction. There are people who have psychiatric problems in addition to an addiction. For those unfortunate people, true recovery may not begin until both problems are recognized.

The vast majority of alcoholics and other addicts do best by conservative treatment. Psychiatric symptoms that do not indicate a condition which is dangerous to the patient or those around him do not always require prompt treatment. Conservative treatment, in this case, means not over-treating the patient. Bill continued to attend group and individual counseling for about a year. I was able to watch him, to see if any other problem developed after he was free from alcohol and medications. If he had been one of those few with other problems, he might have needed further help. Such help may include using certain carefully selected, non-addictive drugs. There are many people who receive medications that do not aggravate addictions.

Since Bill did get better, it was a pleasure to watch him change. Contrary to fiction, people with addictions do get better. He regained his self-confidence as he discovered he was no longer isolated. He acted and looked like a different person. Within three months he was working for his old employer. He was grateful for this, having been considered disabled for two years. If he had not been treated for his addiction, he would have been considered "permanently disabled" because of the erroneous psychiatric diagnosis. Instead, as a recovering alcoholic and tranquilizer addict, Bill has returned to a productive and full life.

Years of alcoholism and addiction are not cured in a day. Those first few months for Bill were his "early recovery." Both biologically and behaviorally, he had undergone subtle changes over the years. As he progressed in his recovery, newer and healthier ways of dealing with life were needed to replace his old patterns, or he would have been at risk of having a relapse. He learned these new patterns at Alcoholics Anonymous, often without realizing that he was changing his behavior. By following the examples of sober people he encountered and trying to follow the suggested steps for living that AA provided, he was "working a program of recovery."

In our treatment program, Bill gained better understanding and insight as to why and how that worked for him. The synergism of working a program and understanding how it worked for him speeded his recovery. It was important for Bill that this understanding focused on his recovery. Later chapters may help you understand and choose the program that is right for you or someone close to you. As Bill put it "I got worse during my earlier two years of therapy, but I learned some fascinating things about myself. If my addiction had not been treated I would have been very insightful, but I probably would have died!"

4

COCAINE ADDICTION

━━━━

■■ This chapter is about cocaine and other stimulants. It will help you understand why cocaine, speed, crack and ice are the most addictive drugs that exist today. It will help you understand why cocaine traps smart people, people who feel they are too bright, too powerful, too much in control to become addicted. It will help you understand why so many cocaine addicts relapse again and again. Finally, it will discuss newer and possibly better treatment becoming available for the crack addict.

Cocaine has trapped so many people because it is a powerful central nervous system stimulant. Crack is a newer form of cocaine. Speed or amphetamine and its newer forms (such as "CAT" and "ice") are equally dangerous stimulants. A stimulant is a drug that temporarily increases the activity of different parts of the body. Central nervous system stimulants, such as cocaine, are drugs that increase the activity of the brain. These are the opposite of alcohol and tranquilizers, sedative drugs that calm the brain. Many stimulants have been known and widely used for centuries. These ancient forms of stimulants, which include tea, coffee and the notorious coca leaf, all can be addictive, but have been used in a much milder form than the drugs purified by chemists in the past century.

Stimulants are used to increase alertness and to brighten mood. If you are reading this book while relaxed in a chair, reach for that coffee or cola drink you placed nearby. You may already understand that our society condones the social use of a mild stimulant (caffeine) but recognizes the danger of abuse and addiction of more powerful stimulants. Stimulants do not produce the exact opposite effect of sedatives but there is a relationship. Increased alertness and brightened mood sound very positive. The introduction of new stimulants, throughout history, has traditionally been welcomed as a very positive step until their true danger was realized. Stimulants make people feel better. If you are a coffee drinker, imagine Monday mornings without that cup. Caffeine-containing beverages, such as coffee, have long provided mild stimulation. Occasionally an alarm is sounded about negative consequences, such as centuries ago, when coffee houses were eyed with suspicion. Most people use caffeine very sparingly and have little desire to increase its use. In addition to the caffeine found naturally in coffee and added to soft drinks such as cola, tea also contains a stimulant called theophylline and hot chocolate contains another stimulant called theobromine. All of these beverages are similar in how they are used and these three drugs all belong to the same category called methylxanthine.

The similarity between the mild stimulants and the more dangerous ones is worth understanding but should not be carried too far. The coffee drinker reading this book may understand the increased alertness and brightened mood at a moderate, pleasant level, just as the social drinker understands the pleasant effects of alcohol. This gives no clue, however, to understanding the enormous craving experienced by the late stage crack addict any more then the social drinker can understand the late stage alcoholic. Cases of abuse of milder stimulants have been known for centuries, yet it never has proven to be a major problem for most users.

Stimulant problems did not begin until about a century ago, when German organic chemists were able to extract and purify the drug Cocaine Hydrochloride from the leaves of the South American coca plant, scientifically known as *Erythroxylon Coca*. The coca leaf was well known to native cultures for thousands of years and to Europe for hundreds of years. European and American chemists had included it in various widely available tonics. Chewing the coca leaf was as much a part of the working ritual in some places as the morning coffee break is in our culture. Purifying cocaine changed all that. Using this new, purer form of cocaine, it became possible to inject it with the recently available hypodermic syringe. This meant that the alertness and brightened mood could be brought about quickly and at a higher level.

The more quickly a drug exerts its effect, the more powerful the psychological reward. The cocaine purified by the chemists was the same drug already present in the natural coca leaves.

Delivering it to the brain quickly, it had far more deadly potential. This point is crucial to our understanding of the newest stimulant epidemics, "crack" cocaine and "ice."

Today, we are dealing with several types of stimulants. Cocaine, available and used in different forms, and amphetamines, including "ice" and "crack," are the most dangerous stimulants. Many of us heard the myth a few years ago that stimulants were not addictive drugs. This has never been true. The addiction is based upon a powerful combination of biological activity and psychological conditioning. That is a very real addiction, one so powerful that it equally affects bright, powerful people, average people, as well as disenfranchised people.

Animals, used in laboratory tests, quickly become addicted to stimulants. Researchers often use animals to evaluate the actions of drugs without subjecting human test subjects to high risks. Animal addiction to stimulants is a remarkable finding. Most animals are too smart to become addicted to other types of drugs. It is difficult to study many aspects of addictions in animals, such as the laboratory rat. If scientists can make a disease behave the same way in an animal as it does in a person, valuable knowledge can be gathered quickly and human suffering reduced. This has never worked well with most addictions, because animals do not like to take many of the drugs we like. Special breeds of rats have been bred, just to get them to drink alcohol without forcing it into their system. Animals do not overdose on drugs, except one. That one drug is cocaine.

Lab animals are often taught to perform small simple tasks. As an example, a rat may be taught to press a bar in its cage to get a certain reward, such as a food pellet. This forms the basis of many experiments in behavioral psychology. The pellet of food is a reward. The experimental apparatus can be modified so the rat receives an intravenous dose of cocaine through a tube or catheter implanted in the animal. When this is done, it has to be limited. If it is not, the rat will kill itself. It will continue to press the bar to get more cocaine until it dies of an overdose. The rat will not do this for any other type of drug, not alcohol nor even heroin.

LISA'S STORY

Lisa provides a story describing another point of entry into the High-Low Trap. She related her story over a period of several months during her early recovery. "I am here for my `coke' (cocaine) addiction. I never believed I could end up addicted to anything. I always had it my way. Addicts were weak people, people who could not handle things. I could always handle things. I ran my own business, had everything going for me. Well, here I am, thirty-three years old, sitting in a group therapy session for all kinds of people with addictions. You have told me here and my NA friends have told me, too. I should know by now that the first step in recovery is to admit that I am powerless over my addiction. I just was not used to being powerless over anything. If I was, how could I have built up my own business? But I know it's true. Cocaine won, and I didn't even realize until near the end that I had a problem. I had only been using cocaine for three years, and the first two I was kidding myself. The business was good, and I could afford it. The last year was bizarre. I guess my use increased because I started to use my savings. I knew this was not right but I thought if I could increase my business, my income would improve enough to stop using savings. This was ridiculous because as a consultant, my business was mostly me. I was already doing as much as I could but I became somewhat grandiose with all that coke.

"That last year, I started to dip into savings. Before the year was out, it was gone. Seventy thousand dollars were sucked up my nose. Can you believe that, seventy thousand? I am still in business, but I was so erratic that last year, I have ruined my reputation with most of my clients. There were a few people I got to know over the years that I socialized with. I found out that some of them liked to do a line of coke and that was great. In that last year, I even helped them out. Since I traveled, it was easier for me than my friends to get drugs in some cities. So, I helped them out. Not dealing, really, just friends. When I could save them some trouble, getting drugs, it enabled me to get more myself.

"I really was dealing drugs. I still shake when I think about it. I could go to jail for that, but I did not see that at the time. It was just a way for me to get cocaine for myself. I mean, that's not really dealing. I never made money from it, and these people were all my friends. Some friends, but that's what I thought at the time.

"Finally, I realized I was dealing. I couldn't kid myself. I am disgusted with myself now to think about it, but it happened. I was using so much cocaine now that I was real erratic, real paranoid. I couldn't look good, have it all together to deal with my clients. I still saw the clients I was supplying, but was really getting less consulting work from them. Only some follow-up on some old jobs. Just an excuse for my dealing. I began to believe that one was a narc and I was about to be caught. Like I said, that last year was bizarre.

"I can't believe this happened in just three years. I mean, I liked drugs, but never got addicted or anything. We used to party in high school when we could get away with it, but the good times started in college. It was ok to get bombed on alcohol or smoke some dope. Everybody I knew did, and you could see the ones who were developing problems. My boyfriend at the time, he's my ex-husband now, used like I did. Never a problem. We didn't have cocaine then, but there was speed (amphetamine). Hell, that was for studying. None of our friends shot up. Amphetamine helped us cram. Especially my ex. He wanted to get to medical school and things were tough. Lots of competition, so he needed to get perfect grades. Pills helped. He would have those all-nighters, right before exams. Afterwards, when he couldn't do anything for a while, he crashed. But, finals were over and as soon as he could we were off to party. Me, I tried amphetamines and I liked them, but I didn't need the grades, so I skipped the all-nighters. Still, they helped me keep the weight off. It was easy then, one old doc near the college didn't mind helping you out if you had a weight problem. I guess I liked amphetamines but not the way I liked cocaine when I started that years later."

STIMULANTS AND THE BRAIN

Lisa made some powerful statements about her stimulant addiction. While there was no earlier pattern of addiction before trying cocaine, there was a clear pattern of abuse of many drugs. She was not afraid to try new things. She saw other people develop problems but did not believe it could happen to her. Perhaps her amphetamine use in college days was more of a problem than she admits. If she had never used cocaine, she still may have ended up with a drug dependence, though it is likely that it would have taken a few more years to surface.

Cocaine and amphetamines work in similar ways. The brain uses a number of well-known neurotransmitters: norepinephrine increases alertness; dopamine is associated with instinctive cravings and reward-seeking behaviors; serotonin, also known as

5-hydroxytryptamine, is important in regulating sleep cycles. Interestingly, serotonin and norepinephrine work in opposite ways. Both cocaine and amphetamines temporarily increase the amount of these three important brain chemicals that are in use and actively stimulating the brain. In effect, these chemicals temporarily force the brain to put more of its own neurotransmitters to work.

All this happens quickly. The more quickly the change occurs, the stronger the reward and the more the potential for addiction. Two interesting things happen when any stimulant is taken at high levels for a period of time. First, the brain runs out of neurotransmitters. Lisa described her ex-husband using amphetamines as a study aid, allowing him to go without sleep for several days during exams. Truck drivers have often used amphetamines to allow them to drive continuously without sleep (resulting in one of the street names for illegally traded amphetamines, "road dope"). This practice often depletes the neurotransmitters in the brain, rather like a car running out of gas. This is called a "crash." Since there are no more neurotransmitters to push out, taking more stimulants has no effect. The result is sleep, whether the person wants it or not. Lisa described this phenomenon in her ex-husband. He was lucky. He made it to exams. Some hapless students have misjudged and crashed just before examination time. Truck drivers, of course, are in an even more dangerous situation. A crash can mean just that.

The second phenomenon that may occur has to do with the brain's automatic regulation of its own neurotransmitters. The temporary increase confuses the control mechanisms. As the brain level of cocaine or amphetamine drops, neurotransmitter levels rapidly return to normal or below normal. Another dose of drugs is needed to feel normal again. This results in a reinforcement of the addictive cycle. This cycle is a form of withdrawal known as "jonesing." It is not dramatic or life-threatening like sedative withdrawal, but it can be quite powerful.

Again, the same principles apply. The quicker the fall in drug level in the brain, the more severe the withdrawal. The quicker the rise in drug level and action in the brain when the drug is taken, the more powerful the reward. The more powerful the reward, the more it reinforces the behavior. The down-side can mimic the disease of depression, and for good reason. In depression, the brain's levels of serotonin and norepinephrine are decreased.

Remember the previously described problem with a simple heating system—one system, with one set of controls. Now, we are looking at three neurotransmitters, each doing something different. Like a separate heating and air-conditioning system, serotonin and norepinephrine sometimes appear to work in opposite ways. Imagine that someone is tampering with separate thermostats on the office heating and cooling systems. One system may be trying to heat up the office while the other is trying to cool it down. Any balance that existed is gone. Now, substitute "brain" for "office" in this discussion. Cocaine turns the activity level up, then down. More cocaine is needed to turn it up, and so on. Like the rat pressing the bar, the situation can get out of control quickly.

‖

Lisa described her bizarre belief that a friend might be a federal narcotic agent. Paranoia such as this can be a result of schizophrenia. Acute paranoid schizophrenia is a psychosis, a major mental disorder, characterized by delusions and irrational suspicion. The underlying biological cause for schizophrenia is overactivity of the dopamine pathways. Dopamine is one of the three neurotransmitters that cocaine and amphetamines increase. Lisa was paranoid but she was not schizophrenic. She was acting irrationally because her high brain levels of cocaine eventually mimicked the very serious disease of schizophrenia.

Lisa described her situation further. "My sister flew up from Dallas. My family was afraid I was going crazy or about to kill myself. Thank God they got me into inpatient treatment. My business is a mess and my savings are gone, but I am recovering. I feel like I never knew my family before. Since I got into recovery, I've been able to talk to them about things we never talked about as kids. My sister dropped everything, stuck her husband with taking care of the kids. I've always acted like I didn't need help before, probably because I was afraid I wouldn't get any and would be let down again. When my sister came to help, everything broke down. I would never have expected her to do that. We were not that close. I am older and was always the strong one. Now, it's OK to not be strong. Admitting I was powerless over my addiction (the first of the Narcotics Anonymous Twelve Steps of Recovery) was like opening a floodgate for me. I now can see that I don't have to be perfect at everything.

"Treatment opened my eyes. The first few days all I needed was rest and support. I had a tremendous craving but felt I was doing the right thing. The warmth and encouragement helped me through. As I got better physically, my thinking started to straighten out and I began to participate and learn about my own disease. It was a beginning for me. Recovery started to feel good. I don't remember feeling good about life without any drugs or booze. Even though I don't think I had a problem before I started using cocaine, I always associated feeling good with alcohol or drugs. This is as far back as I remember.

"Even sex...I liked sex, but I always associated it with getting high. I'm being careful now. I've been like a nun since I left treatment. That will change, eventually, but right now I am too scared. If I get involved with someone, it will be a whole new experience. I've never done it clean and sober. Right now, I'm feeling very good about myself, and I'll let it go at that. When I am not so threatened about it affecting my sobriety, maybe I'll be ready.

"Anyway, about my treatment. I really felt good. I learned about the disease of chemical dependency. I thought I would get off the cocaine and would be able to use alcohol and other drugs the way I did before I got hooked. They told me I was like a pickle. A cucumber is a cucumber until you age it in brine, then it becomes a pickle. That was me. Remove me from the brine and wash me off and I was still a pickle. It was funny but I understood it. Me, the self-assured management consultant. I pictured being a cucumber in my mind and chuckled, but the concept stuck. The pickle was never going back to being a cucumber. I was never going to go back to being who I was before I first used.

"Treatment was four weeks, period. When I signed in that didn't bother me one way or another. Then, it started to feel good to be there and I was glad I had that time. Later, as I got near the end, I was uncertain. The old me popped up and said I could handle this. I felt I understood the program and had it under control.

"Thank God I had learned to ask for help. The new me admitted I was scared. The treatment center was too far from home to commute for aftercare. I seriously considered moving nearby, just to feel the security of still being linked with them. I shared this with my counselor and he encouraged me to move, even to consider this half-way house they ran just for women. That wasn't for me. I recognized that I needed to get back home and back to work. I felt that eventually I would end up back with family, friends and business acquaintances. I needed to deal with being clean and sober in a normal world. Once I made that decision, they supported me. The staff and the group all made me feel like that was the right thing for me, even though I was beginning to get scared.

"Since they were not tied in to any outpatient programs here, they gave me information about NA and AA meetings in my area. I was told to start going to meetings as soon as I got back. I thought NA was the place for me, but they don't have enough meetings around here. The staff had told me that I qualified for both groups so I could go to either one.

"The staff at the treatment center was right. The day I got home I started to go to AA meetings but I felt I needed to talk more about drugs. Some people who were alcoholics but hadn't been into drugs asked me if I really belonged. Luckily, most of the people I met seemed to understand my suffering, whether they had used only booze or had tried everything. In treatment I had learned that I couldn't drink again. The AA people I met said that was enough, I could belong to AA as long as I had a desire to stop drinking. They did tell me I probably would benefit from NA, but it was OK to belong to both fellowships (as they often refer to themselves). The treatment center staff had warned me to quickly find a member of NA to be my sponsor. They told me a sponsor is a member of the self-help group who sets a good example that I can follow, someone to turn to for comfort and guidance. Three days out of treatment, I heard this woman at an AA meeting and could identify with what she said. I asked her to be my sponsor on the spot, and she agreed. Jane became my sponsor both in NA and AA, and she took over my life for the next few months. Since I was a consultant, I had flexibility and Jane let me know that for the next few months I was going to be putting my recovery program ahead of my business. I did as I was told and threw myself into recovery the way I have thrown myself into everything important in my life.

"I had felt so good about myself in treatment that I thought my life was under control. I thought that this was all there was to recovery. The last few days I had been anxious and had thoughts that frightened me. It was a fear, an obsessive fear of my using again. When I shared this with my counselor, he attributed it to my thinking about going home and asked me to reconsider going to the halfway house. This fear got worse when I was home and I thought I was going out of my mind. These thoughts were no longer so innocent. I really wanted to use again, despite knowing what I knew. I tried to work my recovery program even harder and to live life 'one day at a time,' but I began to feel desperate. I didn't

know how I could still have these feelings. I assumed that my program was failing. I saw others who had gotten better and assumed
they had some inner quality that I lacked.

"Jane, my sponsor, saved my life. I broke down and told her
how I felt. I was ready to stop going to NA meetings. A few weeks
out of treatment and I was suicidal. My mother and my sister had
both started telling me how well I was doing. My sister even went
to a few Naranon meetings (for the family and interested friends
of addicts) back in Dallas. Everyone acted as if I was cured and I
felt that secretly I had failed. I don't know to this day if I would
have taken my own life but I had never felt so bad or so desperate.
Jane told me that she had those same desires about a month after
she last used and had thought she was going to return to using.
Jane had a far rougher life then I had, so I believed her when she
told me that if she went back to using she would be dead in a
month. Fear kept her clean and activity kept her going. She made
sure she kept in daily touch with me and made sure I stayed busy.
The important part was that the craving for cocaine she described
had left her. Just knowing that what I was going through was not
unique was enough. The fear that it was going to continue this
way subsided and I could continue to not use and work my program. After a few weeks, it got better for me just as it had for Jane.
I am grateful for what happened to me in treatment, but angry that
I was not prepared for this. I don't know why they didn't warn me
that this happened to a lot of us. Perhaps they didn't know or they
were scared of frightening me. If it were not for my NA sponsor, I
am sure I would not have made it."

RESURGENCE OF CRAVING

Lisa is lucky to be alive. What she has described so far hints at
the frightening problems that stimulant addicts have in early
stages of recovery. Stimulant addicts may die from using a toxic
dose of their drugs, but they do not die from their withdrawal.
Knowing this, hospitals and insurance companies may refuse permission to treat a cocaine addict in withdrawal, stating it is "not
medically necessary!"

If they are withdrawing or crashing, the stimulant addict des-
perately needs a supportive environment. A very real, biologically
based craving exists. Medical care is needed, untreated and unsupervised, the addict may use again or, in despair over the situation,

may take his or her own life. Unfortunately, they may look well enough so that they are unable to convince busy or inexperienced emergency room staff that they need attention.

After the first few days the addict is often feeling better. This is what Lisa described. For a few weeks, she assumed that she was free of the effects of cocaine and therefore back to normal. Far from being back to normal, the addicts's brain is in disarray. The systems that produce and regulate neurotransmitters are just starting to get back in gear. As the brain produces more of it's own neurotransmitters, the receptors and the regulators have to readjust. Several weeks after their last use, many cocaine addicts exhibit a resurgence of craving that can continue for a month or two.

This resurgence of craving could not come at a worse time, because most treatment programs are sending people home just when this delayed craving is starting. Unfortunately, high costs to insurance companies limit the treatment stay at inpatient programs. We know more about this craving now, and need to be better prepared for it. This is one time in the treatment of addiction that medication may help. This craving is not the result of bad thoughts or a poor attitude in working a recovery program. Craving is a genuine medical problem and so severe that some users will take desperate steps. Whether or not they are treated with medication, both the early and the delayed stages of craving are very real. The recovering addict needs assurance and support.

Some currently available medications appear to be effective in reducing cocaine craving. Research is underway in an attempt to better understand when and how medicine helps to prevent relapse. Fortunately, none of these medicines are addictive, an important consideration. Physicians who treat addiction prefer only to use a medication when it is clearly needed. The use of any medication can never be a substitute for a complete recovery program. The high relapse rate in the first few months of recovery from stimulant use has created an urgent situation which physicians and researchers are trying to respond to with any tools that are available.

Right now, at least five groups of chemicals are being tried. The most widely used is the tricyclic antidepressants group. These drugs were intended to treat the disease of depression. Many drugs in this group, including the widely used drug Desipramine have an effect on regulating the levels of the neurotransmitters norepinephrine and serotonin. When Desipramine is used to treat depression, it takes weeks before any improvement is noticed. In sharp contrast to this, when a cocaine user who is abstinent for a few weeks begins to have powerful cravings and drug nightmares, Desipramine may bring relief within a day or two.

Because Desipramine is an anti-depressant, it sometimes does double duty and is continued for an extended period when there is also depression present. However, when used solely to deal with cravings, it is typically prescribed at low levels for only a few months.

Another group of medications used successfully to deal with cocaine craving are two powerful medicines that influence the brain's regulation of the neurotransmitter dopamine. One, amantadine hydrochloride, is normally used to treat viral infections and Parkinson's disease. The other, bromocryptine mesylate, is used to treat rare endocrine disease as well as certain types of tumors. They are both useful in both early and delayed cocaine craving. They are sometimes preferred by physicians who wish to avoid using an anti-depressant. However, both of these medications have powerful side effects. They must be used cautiously and patients should be seen frequently. Because of this limitation they are often limited to use very early in recovery.

Another group of chemicals sometimes used in an attempt to control cravings are nutritional supplements. There is no question that good nutritional habits are a useful aid in recovery from any addiction. There is a theory that if a person consumes nutritional supplements containing massive amounts of amino acids their brain will replenish it's supply of neurotransmitters burnt up by cocaine use. If this is true, it might be useful shortly after quitting when neurotransmitters may be low. If such a shortage existed, once it passed, craving is more likely a result of imbalance and poor regulation than a lack of neurotransmitters. The danger in taking these supplements is how they have been promoted and sold. Substances normally found in food should be considered drugs when extracted, concentrated and sold as drugs. Unfortunately, due to a weakness in U.S. drug laws, many products are called "nutritional supplements" but actually promoted and sold as remedies for disease. Since the people peddling these products are not qualified to either diagnose or treat disease, they should not be giving advice or making claims about their use. Since most true nutritional supplements are not patented and many are inexpensive, some of the peddlers of these products claim to have invented proprietary mixtures with special unique properties. These arguments are used to justify exorbitant prices for ingredients worth only pennies.

This profiteering and huckstering has clouded the issue as to whether there may be some benefit to using such supplements with proper controls. At least two amino acids, tyrosine and tryptophan, seem to have a drug-like effect when taken in this manner. Some physicians were using supplements cautiously before disaster struck. Since supplements were available without a doctors prescription, they were sometimes innocently recommended by counselors who would never dream of prescribing a drug. At other times, they were pushed by store clerks giving advice in health food stores. Many people were taking such chemicals without any medical monitoring.

In 1989, physicians noticed a new and devastating disease, which was named the eosinophilia-myalgia syndrome. Investigators were baffled by this disease until it was realized that everyone who was suffering from it had been using the supplement tryptophan. Once the connection was made, the U.S. Food and Drug Administration acted to remove tryptophan from the market. The culprit was not tryptophan, but a contaminant. A major Japanese drug company had devised a new way to increase production of tryptophan less expensively and was supplying this to American "health food" importers. The new process was flawed and contained a contaminant that has left many Americans weakened and crippled. If this had been a prescription drug, safety testing might have prevented this disaster. Unfortunately, it seems as if nutritional supplements can be marketed with as much concern for the public as street drugs.

In the future, some use of nutritional supplements may prove to be an important addition to treatment. At the present time, the public should be wary of health claims made by suppliers of nutritional supplements or those who have a financial interest in their use. The best advice is to use nutritional supplements only when an individual recommendation is made by a physician, experienced in the treatment of addiction and actively involved in the treatment.

Physicians are closely watching the research being done in the use of antidepressants other than the tricyclic antidepressants described earlier. A number of these have been explored and were helpful in small numbers of patients.

Lastly, an anticonvulsant drug, tegretol, which normally is used to control epileptic seizures, has seemed to help a small number of patients.

As physicians are cautiously increasing the use of medicine to deal with cocaine craving, they sometimes meet resistance from counselors who prefer to deal with patients only when they are taking no medicines. Fortunately, these non-addictive medicines are gaining wider acceptance.

Lisa did get through her early and delayed craving, which was fortunate. The early craving occurred while she was in treatment. The delayed craving was just starting as she left treatment. The despair she described is too common. Cocaine addicts often consider and sometimes do commit suicide during this period. Her treatment program had failed to prepare her for a very real biological event that was likely to happen. Since the treatment center had no contacts in her city, they failed to see that her treatment was continued on an outpatient basis when she went home. Recovery from cocaine addiction still has a high relapse rate. The conflict from the biological process of delayed craving can occur even though the recovering addict is "working" an excellent recovery program. As physicians and other professionals are better able to understand and deal with that craving, the chances of success for a recovering cocaine addict should improve.

BEHAVIORAL CRAVING

A third type of craving also exists. This type is purely behavioral, but it occurs because of the biology of cocaine. Lisa describes her experience. "I got through those rough times because of Jane and a lot of other recovering people who helped me. I have been working the suggested steps of recovery and was beginning to really feel good about my whole life. As I started to spend more time rebuilding my business, I had some terrifying experiences. I was going out of town and went to use the bank machine to withdraw cash. As I stood in front of the cash machine and found my card in my purse, I started to think about doing a line (of cocaine). I felt excited about it, and it terrified me. I drove to a NA meeting and spent several hours afterward talking with people there. Some of them told me about the exact same experience. I was too scared of what was happening to me, despite working a good program. I made excuses and postponed my business trip. Some of the people at the meeting suggested an outpatient chemical dependency treatment program might give me some extra help, so I came here. Now that I am here, I wish I had followed my inpatient treatment program with something like this right away. Anyway, I'm glad I made it here now."

Cocaine, more than any other drug, helps us understand the power of conditioning. Lisa was experiencing euphoric recall as a result of classical conditioning. Psychologists have talked about conditioning ever since Pavlov conducted his experiments on dogs nearly a century ago. Pavlov was not a psychologist. He was a physiologist, a scientist exploring basic biological mechanisms. In his famous experiment, a bell rang every time a dog was fed. After this was done many times, the dog would salivate whenever the bell was rung because the dog's body reacted as if it were being fed. The animal's nervous system was showing a conditioned response, anticipating the act of eating, because the bell had become a conditioned stimulus. For many years, some psychologists attempted to use this principle as the basis for explaining much of human behavior. Human behavior is far more complex than simple animal behavior such as this, so although many of these theories are correct, they do not completely explain human behavior.

Cocaine is an exception. Many recovering cocaine addicts can no longer handle certain innocent everyday items, such as bank cards or mirrors. This is a result of classical conditioning. The mirror is a good example. Many cocaine users take cocaine by inhaling it through their nose. Before snorting it up through a straw (or, for "the rich and famous" through a rolled up hundred dollar bill), the powder is divided into thin white lines on a hard surface. A small women's make-up mirror does the job nicely. The bank card is associated with a cash withdrawal to buy cocaine. So strong is the reward from cocaine that these everyday implements have taken on the same meaning as Pavlov's bell. If they were frequently associated with using cocaine, the ex-user may have an anticipatory response far more troubling than Pavlov's dog salivating.

CRACK

Once again, consider the addictive strength of drugs that get to the brain rapidly. One of the reasons cocaine is so effective in producing a conditioned response is that it is so powerful a reward. When Peruvian Indians chew the raw coca plant, they feel some of the same good feeling that cocaine users feel. What they do not get is the rapid onset of those feelings that modern chemistry has unfortunately provided. Chewing the coca leaf allows some very weak coca to be absorbed directly through the lining of the cheek and some more to be swallowed and come through the digestive system. Snorting cocaine hydrochloride packs very pure cocaine against the rich blood supply of the nasal mucosa. It gets into the blood rapidly, and a peak level is reached in the brain in minutes.

Many people are afraid of using a needle to take drugs. The use of a hypodermic syringe for intravenous injection of cocaine is an invisible line that many users were unwilling to cross. For those who did, they found that the same amount of cocaine taken by injection had an even stronger euphoric effect. Cocaine no longer had to be absorbed. It went through the return circulation of the veins and once past the heart, directly to the brain in well under a minute. The same level was reached, but the feeling was different. Consider going from zero to sixty miles per hour in a truck, then doing the same thing in a standard passenger car. The top speed is the same, but the change is much faster. It is the acceleration that impresses you. The reward is stronger when taking cocaine by a faster method.

Next consider what has happened in the past few years. Cocaine "freebasing" was found by users to be an even quicker way to get the drug to the brain. Freebasing refers to a chemical change that converts cocaine to it's alkaloid form or a "base." In that form, it can be smoked without destroying the drug. Inhaling cocaine into the lungs, it is rapidly taken up by the bloodstream. The difference is that it gets into the blood the heart is processing to send out to the brain. By bypassing the return circulation, precious seconds are saved. Freebase cocaine now shaves more time off the already rapid rise in brain level that intravenous use gives the user. Still, this difference is measured in seconds. Can that be so important? It certainly can. Consider the comparison in acceleration we just discussed. A family passenger car going from zero to sixty in thirty seconds certainly is faster than a truck that takes two minutes to get to the same speed. Now compare the passenger car to a fast sports car that is able to accelerate to sixty in ten seconds. The difference in time is less, but the rapidness of the acceleration is exhilarating.

Experienced cocaine users whose addiction fooled them into thinking that they had cocaine under control have been overwhelmed by freebasing. Like the rat pressing the bar, freebase users rapidly allow their addiction to take over their lives. The powerful psychological reward of freebasing was limited for several years by its complexity and danger. A cocaine user who wanted to experience freebasing had to use complicated paraphernalia and handle an explosive mixture. The percentage of users who tried freebasing was small and accidents scared off many. Human ingenuity once again has presented us with an unwanted extension of knowledge. In the past few years, cocaine has become available in the United States and Europe in the form of "rock" cocaine or "crack." This form of cocaine looks like small dirty brown particles or rocks and it makes a popping noise or crack when it is smoked. The drug dealers have learned enough chemistry to preprocess cocaine hydrochloride into crack so that it may be smoked as freebase without the danger of explosion. The chemistry of this conversion is so simple that some teenagers have become home processors, using kitchen equipment. The real danger of crack is the rapid rise time. The small crack crystals are being sold for a few dollars. Even young children can afford this. The cocaine really doesn't go further with crack. The rapid rise in brain level provides euphoria quickly and cheaply with less cocaine. This means that it wears off rapidly and has to be repeated more often. So, it turns out not to be cheaper, and the necessary repetition means more rapid addiction.

■

Lisa had never used a needle or freebased. She had quite literally snorted seventy thousand dollars straight up her nose. The powerful effects of cocaine were enough to make her anticipate the euphoric feeling of cocaine just from taking out her bank card. Understanding what was happening in her life made it possible for us to work with her to extinguish this response. That part of her treatment was only a small element in the total picture of her recovery, but it helped her deal with circumstances that threatened to cause a relapse. If she had been using crack, she may have had a much stronger experience from this phenomena.

Lisa is doing well now in her recovery. The high of stimulant use and the low of neurotransmitter depletion are behind her now. Stimulant addiction is another path to the High-Low Trap. Addictions have different natural histories and each individual takes his or her own path. Some, like alcoholism and other sedative addictions, are slow and insidious. Others, like crack cocaine addiction can be so rapid they are overwhelming. Each has its own cost, both to the individual and to society. The greatest number of number of addiction problems are caused by alcohol, but the rapid deterioration from cocaine addiction brings cocaine problems to our attention faster. In a typical chemical dependency program, we usually see alcoholics and heroin users coming to treatment only after many years of suffering. Cocaine addicts, like Lisa, usually ask for help after several years of suffering. Some crack addicts are now showing up asking for help after only a few months use.

The addictive power of cocaine should never be underestimated. News headlines tell stories of bankers and ballplayers, teachers and mayors, all whose lives were shattered by cocaine. These were all strong people, capable people, educated people. They were seduced by cocaine, seduced into believing they were in control when, in fact cocaine was in control of them. Another famous person, a brilliant physician once started experimenting with cocaine while still in training. Whether he was addicted is not known. What is known is that it made this scholarly man seem like a coarse raving fiend in his personal writings. It made him become the leading scientific advocate of cocaine use in Europe. That happened over a century ago, and that brilliant physician was Sigmund Freud. Once this liberal attitude had helped to encourage a European cocaine epidemic he recognized the danger and reversed his position. Perhaps the recognition of that early mistake helped shape his career as one of the founders of modern psychiatry. Cocaine addiction can trap anyone. Intelligence and education are no barriers.

In this chapter we have seen how stimulants work. The short-lived up of cocaine has always been a powerful trap. Modern chemistry has intensified this and made the trap far more powerful. Heavy use of cocaine or other stimulants can temporarily cause changes resembling major psychiatric disorders. Many cocaine and speed addicts wish to stop, but the rebound in their brain chemistry triggers powerful cravings when they attempt to quit. Even those who go through good treatment programs and put first priority on their recovery experience these cravings. Knowing what they are and how they can be dealt with can help get past this craving period. Medicines may help, perhaps nutrition may help, but physicians and researchers still have a lot to learn.

⦙⦙

Anyone can be trapped by cocaine, there are no barriers to addiction. Never using cocaine is far safer than using it and trying to stop.

5

DUAL ADDICTION

▀▀▀▀

▀▀**T**he epidemic of cocaine use is doing more than ruining lives directly through stimulant addiction. Often, people recognize their cocaine problem and fight it, only to fall victim to alcoholism. These people are victims of a sedation-stimulation syndrome, or High-Low Trap. Cocaine addict's histories provide examples of what this is and why it occurs, but they are not its only victims. Anyone addicted to sedative drugs–tranquilizers or alcohol–may also find themselves affected by this, and may experience considerable stress during recovery and even relapse because of the High-Low Trap. Whether people are alcoholics or cocaine addicts, the High-Low Trap complicates their disease and rocks the foundations of their recovery.

DON'S STORY

Don was not my patient, and I first heard his story after he was well on the road to (what I hope proves to be) a permanent recovery. Don is a bright, creative man who used his talents to found a successful business in the entertainment industry. He is a third-generation Italian-American–a group that many people falsely believe is immune from addiction.

"I am an alcoholic," Don began. "My alcoholism was very hard for me to accept. In my family, it was a terrible shame to be an alcoholic. It was unthinkable. Accepting what has happened to me has taught me humility. The entertainment business is not for the humble. It is full of bright, aggressive people who have to act like winners. I think that many of us secretly believe that we are just ordinary people and someday someone will find out. When I realized I was addicted to cocaine it did not have the same shame for me. Thinking about myself as a drug addict was made easier because the drug was cocaine. I never shot up, but I had gotten pretty bad with freebasing. Cocaine addiction had a different connotation, because cocaine was so "in." I would spend months at a time on the (west) coast and it was part of the business scene. At many of the parties I went to I was greeted with a handshake as the host handed me some cocaine. This was always considered a cost of doing business, and everyone I knew accepted the situation nicely. When I had to go spend a month in treatment for my cocaine addiction, I didn't buy into any of the chemical dependency stuff I heard. I accepted the fact that I was a cocaine addict and I was willing to deal with that, but only that. I had used other drugs and alcohol without experiencing problems, so I couldn't see how I had any drug problem, aside from cocaine. Cocaine addiction had more prestige than other addictions. I needed that. Two weeks in a hospital intensive care unit changed my mind. Less than a year after completing one of the best cocaine treatment programs on the west coast, I nearly died, even though I never had used cocaine again. I ended up hospitalized as a consequence of alcoholism. Maybe I was an alcoholic all along and didn't know it, but I don't think so. I started drinking and using tranquilizers as soon as I got out of treatment. After all, I had seen shrinks for years and been on and off tranquilizers without problems. I always drank but alcohol had not been that important a part of my life. I was too scared to ever use cocaine again, but I continued to drink. Tranquilizers were ok, too. My shrink still prescribed them for me for a while, which made me feel they had to be safe.

"When he stopped, it was easy enough to get more on the street, but I also increased my drinking. In that year, I crossed the line and became an alcoholic. I still don't know how it could happen so quickly. By the time I was hospitalized, the doctors told me I was in the physical shape of someone who had been drinking heavily for years.

"I was discharged from the hospital straight to another treatment program. Some friends of mine helped to arrange it. The program was not very different than the first one I was in, but this time it was different for me. I identified more with everyone. I had lost that elite superiority that I thought I had as a cocaine user. I still don't think I was a real alcoholic until those last few months, but I can look more at how I used alcohol differently once cocaine became a regular thing with me.

"Alcohol helped me get down after using cocaine. If not alcohol, then tranquilizers. As long as it was a downer. Some of us had to work in the morning–that meant really early. The industry is not the glamorous place to work that many believe. Often you have to be on the set when other people are still asleep. There was always someone passing out something to help. Up or down, life had become part of one big chemical cycle. When I stopped using cocaine, I didn't realize what a tolerance for alcohol and tranquilizers I had developed. Without the cocaine in my life, I continued and increased my alcohol use.

"I have always been excitable and it is part of this business. When I stopped doing cocaine, any time that I was on the set and something was not going right, I felt like I needed a drink. Whether or not I was an alcoholic before I used cocaine, I definitely had become one by the time it was over."

Don's case is a clear example of the High-Low Trap. There are some very definite clues. He had used tranquilizers and alcohol before becoming addicted to cocaine. He may even have been in the early stages of alcoholism before going downhill on cocaine, but there is no evidence of that. What is clear, however, is that his addiction to the stimulant cocaine worsened his addiction to the sedative alcohol. We do not have a complete understanding of all the brain chemistry involved in this phenomena but there are certain points that Don has in common with millions of others who have been caught in this trap.

THE YO-YO EFFECT

Don was already drinking heavily during the time he was using cocaine. Alcohol is a sedative–a downer. Cocaine is a stimulant–an upper. In the chapter about Innocent Addicts, Jim had deliberately been given amphetamine, an upper, to counteract the effect of the painkillers and sedatives he was on. This principle is well understood by people using cocaine. Don had to use a sedative–either alcohol or a tranquilizer–to be able to function. Chemicals brought him up, chemicals brought him down.

Unfortunately, people trying this eventually discover that they do not control the process. They alternate chemicals in order to feel at the right level, like pushing a button and having the elevator stop at precisely the right floor. Instead, they find they are controlling their feelings like a yo-yo–going up and down at will–but unable to stop at a desired level. The fact that Don had reached a point where he was drinking at an alcoholic rate would have been evident if he were not using cocaine. It was not until he stopped the cocaine that the full effect of his alcohol use became apparent.

THE CRASH

Don's drug use confused his brain's regulation of its own neurotransmitters. We know that serotonin is one of the three neurotransmitters that cocaine increases in the body for a short time. Serotonin is temporarily made to work harder by having more of it pushed into active use in the synapses (the junction points of electrochemical communication in the brain). When high levels of stimulants are taken the serotonin is used too quickly to be replaced; the brain cannot produce it fast enough. When stimulants are used continuously the user experiences a crash, from neurotransmitter depletion. The brain is running too fast, not stopping to fill up, and runs out of fuel. More often, users don't push themselves quite that far. Instead of running out, they run low and have to use more stimulant to get back up that hill on a dwindling supply of neurotransmitters.

Some alcoholics also appear to have an altered level of serotonin. Researchers are trying to determine if this is something with which they are born–a genetic trait–or whether it is a result of their drinking. Another recent breakthrough was the discovery of an altered gene for dopamine levels in some alcoholics. Dopamine is another important neurotransmitter whose level is altered by drug use.

If neurotransmitter level differences prove to be a risk factor for developing alcoholism, *any stimulant that alters the regulation of that neurotransmitter would biochemically increase the risk of alcoholism in anyone, whether in a high or low risk group.*

ANXIETY

Stimulant use generates anxiety, that is, it is anxiogenic. Sedatives are anxiolytic–they break up the anxiety. The pattern of using alcohol or tranquilizers to deal with anxiety might not exist before cocaine is first used. Don repeatedly said that he did not think he was an alcoholic until after he started to use cocaine. The repeated anxiogenic challenge for the brain may have been too much. Many people first get into trouble with alcohol or tranquilizers because of stressful events. Some are able to stop their heavy use when the stressful event is past, but others are hooked. For the cocaine user, the stressful event is really internal, although the user may believe it is external. Don felt the pressure of the job; working on the set was overwhelming. Before he started using cocaine, he thrived on that excitement. *Once he started using cocaine, anxiety became overwhelming without a downer.* Once the cocaine stopped, the pattern of using a downer to deal with anxiety stayed with him. The job had not changed, Don had.

ALTERATIONS IN THE BRAIN

Don may have suffered permanent change to some receptors in his brain. This is a very speculative theory, but some physicians believe that all heavy users of alcohol or drugs have had their brains permanently altered. The reasons they believe this are based upon experience with two types of patients. During the 1960s when hallucinogenic drugs first became popular, users having a "bad trip" were often difficult to differentiate from people suffering from a major psychotic illness. The difference usually became apparent after a few days, because the person who had used psychedelic drugs would return to normal in a few days. Some, however, would not get better and appeared to be schizophrenic. This sudden onset of the illness in people who previously had no hint of a mental disorder was puzzling. Since schizophrenia usually first appears in the early adult years, one plausible explanation was that these people would have developed schizophrenia anyway, but the episode of using hallucinogenic drugs brought it to the surface earlier.

Another explanation was that these drugs somehow altered receptors for the neurotransmitter dopamine and by doing so, mimicked schizophrenia. In the sixties, however, there was no convincing evidence for the theory that drug use could alter such brain receptors. A tragic event in the 1980s provided further information.

Some illegal drug chemists started to turn out a drug called MPTP (1-methyl-4-phenyl-4-propionxypiperdine) which was sold on the street as a synthetic substitute for heroin. These illegal synthetic drugs are known as "designer drugs." Since they are being produced in illegal labs and are never tested, the users become the ultimate guinea pigs. In the process of creating a batch of MPTP, some of it was inadvertently converted to another chemical, MPPP. When users tried this deadly designer drug, the MPPP was converted in the brain to MPP+, which selectively killed certain brain cells that utilized dopamine.

The result was a devastating epidemic of Parkinson's disease in young people. Parkinson's disease is normally only found in older adults. It is a progressive disease that affects the brain circuits that control movement. It seems to occur because of a breakdown in certain brain cells that use the neurotransmitter dopamine. Seeing this condition suddenly occur in young people, without hope of reversal, puzzled physicians until it was traced back to the deadly designer drug. This one example has convinced many doubters that, under certain circumstances, abused drugs can cause permanent changes in neurotransmitter functions.

Despite this MPPP evidence and other convincing research of permanent alterations in brain function, no clear evidence exists that most drugs can produce permanent changes. Those who do believe that all drugs can cause such changes describe a post-drug impairment syndrome and believe that all recovering alcoholics and users may permanently suffer from it.

In the last chapter, Lisa described her belief that she would never be able to return to her previous condition. She compared herself to a pickle, who could never again be a cucumber. Lisa, like most people after a successful recovery from addiction, returned to a functional and physically healthy life. The return to normal mental health was gradual but steady. The realization by Lisa that someone who is addicted may never safely use drugs or drink alcohol again is not evidence of a permanent brain dysfunction. Instead, it is a healthy reflection of her understanding the seriousness of her addiction and her need for total commitment to her recovery. Much more needs to be learned before we can answer the questions about addiction and permanent changes in the brain.

॥

Don's drinking and drug use threw the regulation of his natural tranquilizer system out of control. The natural control system, called the endoseren system in this book, was responsible for the regulation of Don's anxiety. Cocaine constantly altered the controls. The artificial alteration of neurotransmitter levels, up and down, would have a profound effect on the ability of the brain to produce its own tranquilizing chemicals. The use of alcohol and benzodiazepine tranquilizers would worsen that effect. The high-low effect, like a yo-yo reaching the end of its string and reversing direction, completely confuses the normal regulators in the brain.

Finally, Don and millions of others like him establish a pattern of behavior in response to feelings of a biochemical origin. Ordinary events that should have no biochemical importance can produce feelings that trigger old learned responses. (In the last chapter, Lisa described how a bank card made her think about using.) Patterns of response can differ, and the anxiety about using may be handled by the active user in two ways. He or she could use a stimulant or could respond to the anxiety by using a sedative. The triggering event and its response can be purely behavioral but just as strong as a biochemical connection.

All of the reasons for altered responses to events and feeling the need to drink or use overlap. Currently, some scientists and physicians have pet theories but most of us are not sure of the relative importance of these different components. There is a solid connection in practice, that the increased use of uppers, such as cocaine, clearly changes the pattern of abuse and addiction to downers, such as alcohol. It may be that several of the reasons discussed, acting together, form the basis for the link between sedation and stimulation. Whichever explanation is correct, this relationship, this High-Low Trap, is real and powerful. Some, such as Lisa, accepted this from the beginning. She had a tough recovery but because she accepted the idea that she had a disease, she never had a relapse. Don could not see this at first. Don's belief that his cocaine addiction was an elite disease had serious consequences. His relapse to alcoholism and sedative addiction was actually a relapse to his cocaine addiction. He finally came to understand the trap of the linkage between upper and downer addiction. It was a lesson he learned by almost losing his life.

6

OTHER ADDICTIONS

The complex problems of addiction to sedatives and stimulants have been emphasized since these are the two types of addictions that cause the greatest harm today. Of the cases discussed only a few were simple addictions; other drugs were included in many discussions. In the real world, there can be no practical or simple separation and classification of people based on the chemistry of the last drug they used. The reader of this book may have a special interest in one type of drug, but addicts can not be separated into neat little compartments. Heroin addiction is, once again, becoming a major problem in the United States. Marijuana addiction has faded, but has never really disappeared. Treatment programs at some institutions and government organizations attempt to deal with a single addiction, yet their patients may have may been using many drugs. I have yet to meet the addicted patient who read an institutional organization chart before deciding which drugs to get hooked on.

Growing concern over so-called physical and mental enhancers will be discussed in this chapter. The questions about physical performance enhancers, such as steroids, and a relationship to other drug use later in life will be explored and the fad of using "smart drugs" in an attempt to increase mental performance will be reviewed. This will be compared to earlier similar movements which eventually resulted in many addictions. Also, the trap of addiction to the deadly drug nicotine will be examined. I will also explore the reason that cigarette smokers continue to smoke, as well as the hope offered by new aids to quitting.

Equally confusing is the recent trend to label many forms of behavior as addictive. In many cases these patterns of behavior, whether related to inappropriate patterns of eating, sex or gambling follow a pattern that is extremely similar to drug addiction. Some believe this is going too far. Is everything addictive? Looking at the High-Low Trap will help in understanding this difficult issue.

First, consider the trap of other drugs. Many of the people who were used as examples in this work were addicted to or had used opiates, such as the narcotic heroin. Narcotics work in a special way in the brain. There is an opiate receptor network in the brain, first discovered only about twenty years ago, that is quite separate from sedative receptors. The chemicals that the brain uses in this network are called endorphins, a name derived from "endogenous morphine." This network is a sophisticated system and several types of endorphin receptors have now been discovered. One function of this network is the natural modulation of pain signals, but other important functions of endorphins are not yet understood. Every time a heroin addict floods his brain to get high, systems we do not yet fully understand are overwhelmed and cannot function correctly. Every time that addict tries to kick methadone or heroin, her nervous system goes into withdrawal. There is a powerful backlash in those systems.

Narcotic withdrawal is not lethal. When it is compared to alcohol withdrawal, it seems relatively safe, for it rarely causes death. Yet, it can be the worst withdrawal that exists. "Uncomfortable" is far too mild a word to describe the symptoms. After experiencing heroin withdrawal, many addicts will do almost anything to avoid it. Without medical help, many addicts will remain addicted to heroin or methadone for years. Fortunately, there are ways that an opiate addict can be helped through a rapid and successful withdrawal. Although addictions to sedatives and opiates are different addictions, some features of withdrawal share common pathways. Both withdrawals activate portions of the autonomic nervous system, the system that regulates involuntary functions of the body. In the case of narcotics, this allows detoxification to be controlled with the assistance of a relatively safe blood pressure medication that works in the alpha-adrenergic portion of the nervous system.

This common feature, however, is often a reason for relapse. This similarity, a withdrawal signal caused by use of an unfamiliar drug, may be interpreted by an addict as a craving for a more familiar drug. There was a time that heroin treatment programs allowed their addicts to continue to use alcohol. This disastrous mix created a situation where the "cured" patient kept jumping between the frying pan and the fire until turning to complete abstinence or dying.

MARIJUANA ADDICTION

Another common drug is marijuana or "pot." The powerful addictive nature of THC (the drug in marijuana) has been recognized in the Middle East for years. Religious and social condemnation of alcohol made marijuana or hashish (a powerful marijuana extract) a more acceptable drug. The result was an addiction problem of epidemic proportions, recognized over a century ago.

In the United States, where only a weak form of marijuana was common until the 1960's, a false belief that marijuana was not harmful led many people to try it. Many people who continue to smoke pot regularly today became addicted during this "innocent" experimentation. Today people are more fearful of this drug and the casual use of marijuana has dropped.

Pot is clearly addictive. When it is smoked, it breaks down into several drugs in the brain, all variations of THC (tetrahydrocannabinol). Researchers have now identified a withdrawal syndrome that marijuana smokers experience, making the behavior of these regular pot smokers more understandable. Many who have smoked marijuana from childhood tell of anxiety that preceded their first use. Some of these addicts can be assisted in their abstinence by a non-addictive anti-anxiety medication, such as Buspirone.

Several types of marijuana receptors have been identified in the brain. One natural use for marijuana seems to be the alleviation of nausea and the stimulation of appetite. This has led to the development of legal, prescription THC pills for patients nauseated by cancer chemotherapy.

Other features of the natural systems that marijuana overrides are not yet understood. However, a common finding in heavy pot smokers today (which was also described in Middle Eastern hashish smokers a century ago) is the amotivational syndrome. The ability of THC to make the user not have to deal with the conflicts of everyday life was attractive to some young people twenty years ago. Today, tragically, many of these same addicts are just getting by–middle aged men and women holding the same type of irregular minimum wage positions they did in their teens. By flooding their brains with THC so that conflict was minimized, they have not been motivated to progress in life.

Marijuana is the longest lived of common drugs taken today. Anyone who smokes several joints each day will continue to have detectable levels of marijuana in their body for several weeks. Most regular pot smokers will say that their thinking has cleared remarkably after only a few days away from the drug. It is only after they have been away from pot for several months that these ex-addicts can fully recognize how muddled their marijuana-soaked thinking actually was.

It must seem obvious to most readers that anyone attempting to recover from alcohol or cocaine addiction cannot safely use pot. Unfortunately, it has not been obvious to many alcoholics and addicts. Many have tried to stay away from alcohol and cocaine without giving up pot, with disastrous results.

HALLUCINOGENS

Other drugs, including hallucinogens such as PCP or LSD, inhalants such as glue, solvents, and nitrous oxide have their own peculiar idiosyncrasies. The exact place that each of these work in the brain is still being determined, but one fact is understood. Although each works in a somewhat different way, they each are addictive and distort the user's perception of reality. They must all be treated equally by chemical dependency treatment programs and all have the potential for doing great harm, whether used occasionally or regularly. Anyone attempting to remain clean from other drugs has no business using them. Anyone fearful of trying one drug should not be fooled by false claims made for another drug. There are no pussycat drugs.

STEROID DANGERS

There is growing concern over the use of so-called physical and mental enhancers. The use of physical performance enhancers, especially the steroids, has drawn attention to this problem. Although it has been outlawed by international athletic organizations, some trainers and coaches secretly encouraged use. Young athletes, both male and female, are given a mixed message regarding such drug use. Unfortunately, as with other drug problems, there is often a short-term benefit and a long-term loss. Lyle Alzado, a former National Football League star, recently died of brain cancer–which he and his physician attributed to his years of steroid use. Before he died, he described how the need to be bigger, better, and more competitive fueled his continued use of steroids and growth hormone. He also describes how steroids clouded his judgement and behavior, leading to violent mood swings and rage. These steroid rages have been commonly described by other athletes. They are as terrifying to the athletes as they are to those around them.

Mr. Alzado did not use other drugs, but with widespread steroid use in sports, is it surprising that many athletes have gone on to develop cocaine and alcohol problems? If the steroids themselves were not bad enough, the changes in mood that they cause can easily lead to alcohol and cocaine problem use as a way of attempting to deal with the mood swing. The problem of steroid use in both professional and amateur sports is not exactly the same as the problem of other drug addiction. However, a society can not tacitly allow one and totally condone the other. Lyle Alzado killed himself as certainly through his steroid addiction as he could have through cocaine addiction.

"SMART" DRUGS

Can an equally terrifying problem occur from the fad of using "smart drugs" in an attempt to increase mental performance? This seemingly well-intentioned movement is not new. The quest for a natural substance to make oneself smart is described in a rather old book–*Genesis*. When Eve first ate the fruit of the tree of knowledge, was she any different from those who today seek an easy chemical or nutritional path to knowledge? Men and women have always sought substances that would enhance their mental properties. So far, as in the biblical tale of Adam and Eve, there has always been a high price to pay for their successes. This newest fad is far from innocent, and those pushing it should be trusted as much as the serpent who encouraged Eve to ignore God's warning.

Today's serpents rely upon incomplete research into powerful drugs being tested to treat specific diseases of the brain, advocating that these experimental drugs be given freely to the public. Some of these drugs may turn out to have value for people who are suffering from diseases which reduce their mental capacity. Advocating that healthy people take these same drugs, particularly before their dangers are known, is advice comparable to that which Eve received. Even seemingly harmless nutritional substances can turn out to do great harm when used as drugs. Remembering what recently happened to users of tryptophan should make most people cautious. Remember that Dr. Sigmund Freud (when he was an early advocate of the widespread use of cocaine) and drug guru Dr. Timothy Leary (who was the 1960's leading advocate of LSD) both described their respective drug as mind-enhancing. The families of those who had to be institutionalized as a result of such advice may have come to a different conclusion. Frighteningly, a leading work on the use of "smart drugs"published in 1990 and sold in some health food stores, contains a testimony to the value of that book by none other than the same Dr. Leary. Drug enforcement investigators have warned that "smart drug" parties on the west coast, where teens and young adults pay a price to supposedly drink nutritional substances to enhance brain power, are actually a cover for the widespread sale of LSD. If we cannot learn from the ancient wisdom of the Bible, can't we at least learn from the horrors of the drug cults of the 60's?

TOBACCO ADDICTION

No book on drugs should ignore addiction to the deadly drug nicotine. Cigarette smokers each start to smoke for a variety of reasons. Research has clearly shown that a large proportion of adult smokers in the United States would like to stop but have not been able to do so. The reason that they have not been successful is that nicotine creates a powerful physical addiction. The only difference between cigarette smoking and other drug addictions is that the consequences are primarily physical, not mental. This is terrifying and testimony to the power of tobacco. The alcoholic and the crack addict have had their judgement clouded by their drug. Their inability to stop is worsened by their inability to fully recognize the extent and consequences of their addiction. The nicotine addict, whether he is using cigarettes, snuff, cigars or chew has no such excuse. Today, virtually everyone knows and understands that this is harmful. The power of this addiction is such that the use continues despite this clear-headed understanding of the problem.

The recent development of methods to slowly withdraw from nicotine, using special nicotine patches in place of cigarettes, offers hope to those unable to quit without this aid. Still, this is only an aid, and, like detoxification from other drugs, it should not be used alone. Nicotine patches work best when they are used in conjunction with support groups, usually run by local affiliates of cancer, heart or lung groups.

NICOTINE LINKED TO OTHER DRUGS

Often ignored is the deadly link between alcoholism and cigarette smoking. In the United States today most alcoholics and addicts continue to smoke cigarettes. This was not noticeable in the past when most Americans were cigarette smokers. Today, smokers are a declining minority in our population. Despite this, most alcoholics continue to be cigarette smokers, many more than would be expected from statistics. Even after successfully recovering from addiction to crack and alcohol, most addicts continue to smoke! Unfortunately, many people have turned their lives around through their recovery from alcohol, heroin or crack only to die prematurely from heart disease or cancer caused by smoking.

There is both medical and observational data to indicate a clear link between nicotine addiction and other addictions. Fortunately, today some drug treatment centers are offering assistance in smoking cessation concurrently with alcohol and drug addiction treatment. Other people recovering from addiction will wait a few months until their recovery is stable before attempting to deal with their nicotine addiction. There is no clear-cut answer as to the best time and way to quit, but there is no reason for the recovering man or woman to be condemned to a lifetime of smoking. Today, in many parts of the United States, the smoke-filled rooms of A.A. and N.A. meetings of the past have been replaced by smoke-free rooms. The smoking itself is neither an A.A. nor an N.A. issue, for those now smoke-free meetings are only a reflection of their own members personal growth in recovery.

■■

IS "ADDICTION" USED TOO EASILY?

What about addictions to thing other than drugs? My dictionary tells me that it is appropriate to talk about an "addiction to fast cars." However acceptable such use of language is, there is a danger in confusing drug addiction with other forms of addiction. It may be appropriate to think of some forms of behavior as addictive because they follow a pattern that is similar to drug addiction. Self-help groups, such as Overeaters Anonymous and Gamblers Anonymous modeled after Alcoholics Anonymous, lend some credence to this idea. However, some commercial treatment centers have created a serious dilemma by finding a profitable niche treating these addictions. Conflict occurs because resources are scarce and there is not enough available treatment for alcohol and cocaine addiction. The fashion of treating all troubled behaviors as addictions may or may not be right but it reduces the limited resources available for drug treatment.

The National Council on Alcoholism and Other Drug Addictions objects to the use of such words as "chocaholic" or "workaholic." These recent additions to our language may seem cute to the media, but minimizes drug addiction as a deadly disease. Describing someone who enjoys an occasional chocolate bar in a term modeled after someone suffering from a deadly disease is silly. Imagine how a patient fighting cancer would feel if the media foolishly joked about malignancy?

Drug addiction is a biological problem first. Drug use distorts the way the brain functions occur before any patterns of behavior can emerge. Prior to the discovery of many brain receptors, some scientists argued that addiction was solely a behavioral disorder. Now we understand that there is a strong chemical basis for much of this behavior in drug addiction. How do we classify these non-drug addictions? Can someone really become addicted to food, gambling or relationships? If you ask many who have overcome these problems with a self-help group the answer will be a resounding "Yes." Ask the parents of a young women who has died because of one of the deadly eating disorders such as anorexia nervosa. While they are right to ask that more attention be paid to these problems, are these addictions? Perhaps there are common biochemical pathways in the brain. Perhaps these behaviors trigger such powerful feeling that they cause an imbalance in brain chemistry. These are questions without current answers.

The best way to avoid this confusion is to avoid the overuse of the concept of addiction and dependency. Finally, when the concept of addiction is overused, it should not imply that treatment is required. Some would describe most residents of the United States as addicted to freedom, responsibility, running water and the electric light. If these are addictions, I hope no one attempts to change them.

7

RECOVERY AND THINKING

===

Powerful events take place in the mind and body during recovery, a process which appears beautiful when viewed after the fact, however, the metamorphosis of recovery is not always pleasant to watch. Followed through its full course, recovery can be compared to the emergence of a butterfly from a cocoon. Unless you know that a colorful butterfly will emerge when you see a plain caterpillar spin it's cocoon you would never suspect this could happen. Similarly, if you have not seen the process in action, it is difficult to believe the person well into recovery is the same person you saw in early recovery.

The changes that take place in recovery influence all aspects of a person's life. There are biological changes in the brain that affect the way a person thinks and feels. This chapter describes how these changes affected one man.

MARK'S STORY

Recovery has a special meaning to those who experience it. Abstinence from the addicting drug is a necessary and important step, but it is only a part of the process. Abstinence by itself can initiate many changes, but the new lifestyle associated with recovery allows the full expression of these changes.

Mark, a thirty-eight-year-old plumber, had asked for help because he could not stop drinking. He had not, however, asked for "sobriety." It was in his treatment program that he first heard about living a clean and sober life, as opposed to merely remaining abstinent. Now he calls his sobriety the most important thing in his life.

Mark had been working for the same contractor for many years and knew his job well. Most of his time was spent on new construction. His employer tolerated drinking as long as workers were doing their job. Mark was drinking daily but was able to put in a full day's work for many years. Eventually, however, he began to make mistakes that were obvious to the people around him. A formal Employee Assistance Program (E.A.P.) had been negotiated several years earlier as part of the collective bargaining agreement between the contractors and the local union. His foreman and his union steward discussed the situation and, rather than firing him, he was given the chance to get help. The shop steward brought in an E.A.P. representative named John–an older man who had worked in the building trades for forty years–to help Mark get started on a recovery program.

Mark was willing to go along with whatever he was told to do because he wanted to keep his job. John explained that since Mark had been drinking heavily every day for so many years he might not be able to stop without medical help. The first step was to enter a local community hospital for detoxification. This needed detoxification (or "detox" as John called it) would take just a few days, but would only be the beginning of Mark's recovery.

Following detox, Mark would be transferred directly to the rehabilitation program ("rehab"), where he was expected to stay for a month. After that, he could go home, but his return to work would depend on his continued monitoring by John. Abstinence alone would be sufficient to begin the biological changes that would allow him to do his job as well as he had in the past. However the likelihood of remaining abstinent without a recovery program were slim. A recovery program meant lifestyle changes that would begin in rehab and would continue after his return to work. Sobriety meant that the biologic improvements that would begin with abstinence would be likely to become permanent changes.

After this was explained to him, Mark said he was willing to accept John's offer to drive him to the hospital, if he could have one last drink. He was surprised when John readily agreed. He knew that if Mark began withdrawal during the drive to the hospital, he was very likely to become anxious and confused and could easily change his mind when he got there. John had learned that this last drink was ceremonial to some people–a way to say goodbye to their old way of life. This last drink also had biologic soundness by slowing down Mark's withdrawal until he was under medical care in a controlled setting.

Once Mark was admitted to the hospital, John arranged for a physician who was familiar with detox to see him. John stayed with Mark until all the red tape of the hospital admission was finally complete and his doctor arrived. By that time, Mark's body had eliminated much of the alcohol from his blood. His heart was beating faster and his blood pressure was up. He was anxious, and his hand shook when he extended it to greet the doctor. If this were a normal day for Mark, he would have stopped for the usual "one or two beers" on the way home from work. His wife had learned many years earlier that, no matter how sincere he may have been about his intention to do so, he never stopped at one or two. Tonight, for the first time in years, he was feeling the impact of truly stopping.

WITHDRAWAL AND THE MIND

The first process the brain goes through when beginning abstinence is withdrawal–part of the High-Low Trap. If the withdrawal is from a sedative, especially alcohol, it can be quite severe. Once the brain has accustomed itself to operating in the presence of a sedative, it may become overactive as the sedative is taken away. An electroencephalogram (EEG) is an electrical recording of brain activity. It is used to detect or analyze certain types of disease that exhibit unusual patterns of activity. An EEG taken during this stage of withdrawal will show a diffuse, disorganized activity occurring across the brain.

If withdrawal is very rapid, this electrical activity can cause an epileptic seizure. If there has also been a head injury at some time in the past–as many drinkers are likely to have had–this puts them doubly at risk. To help prevent a possible seizure Mark's doctor treated his withdrawal by substituting a tranquilizer for the alcohol and then slowly tapering him off the tranquilizer, over several days. He may not have had a severe reaction without being treated, but his doctor wisely chose not to take that chance. Mark was safer because his doctor used this supervised form of medical detoxification.

The need for medical services during detoxification can be compared to the situation of childbirth. Until this century, most births were handled at home. Some women used medical doctors, but most were attended by midwives or by family. This was sufficient in most cases but both the mother and the child were at a high risk of dying if there were complications. The situation with detox is similar. There is a cost-saving concept called "non-medical detox" and most people that go through it will be fine. But for those who do have difficulties the experience can turn into a life-threatening emergency.

Another effect of excessive electrical activity within the brain during withdrawal is visual hallucinations. This withdrawal symptom–seeing things that are not there–can be a frightening experience. Thankfully, it is not often seen in milder cases of withdrawal, if medical detoxification is carried out.

Hallucinations can occur even when a patient appears to be thinking quite clearly and does not have to be a herd of pink elephants to qualify. When Mark was in detox, he shared a room with a patient about his age who had arrived a few days earlier but was in far worse condition. The day after Mark got there, his roommate started talking to him about the priest who had visited the room earlier that day. Mark had been a bit sleepy that morning and assumed he had missed the visitor. As the conversation progressed, he realized his new friend was talking about the priest as if he were still in the room. When Mark tried to clarify what he meant, his roommate pointed to a bare wall in a shadowy corner. Mark realized the man was hallucinating, excused himself, slid out the door and caught the attention of a passing nurse. She was grateful to get this information and notified his roommate's doctor. Mark was amazed, that although she appeared concerned, she did not seem at all surprised.

Mark did not have hallucinations but he did experience anxiety, excessive activity of his autonomic nervous system and an altered sleep pattern. Most people experiencing the alcohol withdrawal syndrome will have these symptoms. Those withdrawing from other sedatives may experience this same pattern as well to a greater or lesser degree. Because he was taking detox medication the worst of his anxiety and sleep disturbance was over in a few days.

However, a rebound of excessive anxiety and irritability is common, often making the person in early withdrawal a very unpopular soul. This rebound reflects the High-Low Trap. It is one of the effects of sedative use that helps to reinforce the addiction in the first place. Anxiousness and irritability temporarily disappear when a person takes another drink or another pill. Normality then shifts to a chemically-supported world. During detox (and later) the body must shift back to its own regulation of anxiety and irritability. This natural regulation is lost during addiction and reestablished during recovery.

▪▪

In addition to anxiety and irritability, increased activity of the autonomic nervous system is common during the earliest phase of withdrawal. This excess activity can vary from mild to extremely dangerous. Since the autonomic nervous system can alter a person's heart rate and blood pressure, these are often higher than normal during withdrawal. These increases can sometimes be severe in an untreated withdrawal. Mark experienced this as he waded through the red-tape of the hospital admission. By the time he was seen by his doctor, his heart was beating fast and his blood pressure was up. His physician realized this was part of his withdrawal and he saw to it that the detox drugs he ordered were given promptly. Later, when the doctor returned home, he phoned the hospital to check on Mark's condition, to be sure that the medication had done its job. Mark's nurse reported that his blood pressure and heart rate were back to normal and he was sleeping.

▪▪

The normalization of Mark's sleeping pattern took much longer. Sleep patterns are complex and appear to be necessary for good mental health. There is a delicate balance between phases of sleep, known as rapid-eye movement (REM sleep) and non-REM sleep. Abuse of alcohol or other sedatives (even those sold as "sleeping pills") changes this balance. Withdrawal, once again, changes this balance. This can cause difficulty sleeping and may result in daytime drowsiness because a "good night's sleep" was not possible. The brain's serotonin levels play a large part in the regulation of sleeping patterns. Since these levels may be poorly regulated for some time following withdrawal, it is not surprising that many people experience repeated episodes of insomnia followed by daytime drowsiness. Mark found this problem continuing months after treatment. He sought additional help and was given advice on diet and sleep habits and told to be patient. Eventually, and to his great relief, he finally reached a point where he could take a good night's sleep for granted.

His sleeping difficulties during recovery were an annoyance. He certainly did not recall having insomnia when he was drinking. "Sleep" often meant passing out in an alcoholic fog. His wife was used to letting him "sleep it off" on the sofa or the floor of the den where he had passed out. This change in sleep patterns is one more example of the High-Low Trap. I have seen people return to their addiction just because they wanted one drink (or one tranquilizer) to get a decent night's sleep.

The early changes that Mark experienced are typical for an alcoholic. If he had also been addicted to another sedative, such as a benzodiazepine tranquilizer, the first phase of withdrawal would have been slower. Dealing with a dual addiction extends detoxification well beyond the three to five days the alcoholic may need. People who have been taking high doses of a long-acting tranquilizer may exhibit a milder form of withdrawal, continuing for several weeks.

COGNITIVE ABILITY

Over the next few months, Mark experienced changes in every organ system of his body, but the change he was most aware of was in his ability to think more clearly. Early in the process of recovery there is a gradual and increasing improvement in cognitive ability. Heavy and prolonged use of alcohol can permanently damage the brain, but people who stop early enough can avoid this damage. A few, unfortunately, will stop too late and remain severely impaired. Mark was lucky to have stopped in time. Except for some subtle memory weaknesses, most recovering alcoholics who have been abstinent for a reasonable period will appear normal on most tests that measure the ability to think and reason. In fact, many people have achieved business and academic success in recovery after years of devastating alcoholism and drug addiction.

During and after this initial withdrawal, changes in other parts of the body affect the brain. Alcohol may have caused nutritional deficiencies and liver problems which changes the composition of the blood. In Mark's case blood tests showed that his blood was diluted, causing many organs of his body, including his brain, to become somewhat bloated. During the first few weeks of his recovery, the composition of his blood improved and the bloating rapidly disappeared. Mark found he was able to think more clearly and this process probably played a role in that continued improvement.

VITAMIN DEFICIENCIES

Many alcoholics experience multiple vitamin deficiencies that affect the nervous system. Physicians will usually give at least one injection of thiamine (Vitamin B1) to any alcoholic in withdrawal. This is to prevent a severe and irreversible form of brain damage that occurs if this vitamin is not present. Other addictions do not cause such severe nutritional deficiencies directly, but drug addicts may be dually addicted to alcohol, or may have nutritional problems because they have been eating poorly.

Mark received a single injection of thiamine the first evening he was hospitalized. His wife had over-extended herself to see that he ate something every day, but Mark still had developed mild vitamin deficiencies. The alcohol itself had been very hard on his gastrointestinal tract. It had interfered with his ability to absorb all the vitamins that were present in his food. Mark probably had deficiencies of niacin, pyridoxine (vitamin B6), cyanocobalamin (vitamin B12), folate, zinc and other nutrients. Specific tests were not done for all of these because the test results would not have changed the treatment his doctor was already providing him. Shortages of all of these nutrients can cause problems with the nervous system, both within the brain and the nerves of the body. Once Mark stopped drinking, a normal diet was enough to rapidly restore these nutrients. His doctor added a daily therapeutic multi-vitamin tablet, just to be sure. This is usually the only medication given under these circumstances. Restoring the proper nutrient levels does not produce instantaneous results, but changes do gradually take place in the nervous system.

Whatever improvement is seen in the brain, it takes much longer to see changes in parts of the nervous system outside the brain. The peripheral nerves are the communication link between the brain and various parts of the body. The nerves to these parts of the body most distant from the brain are the slowest to heal. For example, the nerves carrying signals to and from the feet may take over a year to recover from some injuries. Alcoholics who have damaged their nerves badly (peripheral neuropathies) may have permanent problems walking.

MOOD FLUCTUATIONS

While all of these changes were taking place in Mark's body, his brain was gradually trying to restore its normal balance of neuro-transmitters. Mark was fortunate that he had not been involved with other drugs. How quickly this balance is restored varies depending on whether someone was taking alcohol, other drugs, or some combination. Periods of changes in mood and anxiety level are common during early recovery. Addicts who have used both alcohol and cocaine heavily are in for the worst time if they are not prepared for these mood fluctuations. People who are suddenly feeling better then they ever felt before often assume the recovery process is over and they can become complacent. They are like the riders on a roller coaster, which slows as its car reaches the top of the biggest hill. In that seeming period of calm, they might believe they have reached the smooth track at the end of the ride, not realizing that you are about to suddenly experience the most monstrous drop. Just having a friend along for the ride who gently warns you that it is not over yet can make quite a difference. In Mark's case, John warned him to expect these mood changes. This up and down experience is not all bad, but its inconsistency can be frightening.

THE PINK CLOUD

As Mark's recovery progressed, he began to experience a feeling of well-being. This was fortunate, because his newly-found sobriety was not a panacea for solving all his problems at work and with his family. While he worked at his recovery, he felt a certain internal serenity. He was able to act and react more rationally, neither over nor underreacting to the environment around him.

Many recovering addicts have this extremely pleasant period. This "honeymoon" of well-being is referred to as their "pink cloud." Little research has been done to explain this commonly reported phenomenon. It is probably the result of a rebound of natural functions, causing the body to produce high levels of neurotransmitters and endogenous tranquilizers. Ironically, many people report that this continued feeling of well-being is a state they have never experienced before and they had to get clean and sober to enjoy a natural "high" they could never achieve using drugs or alcohol.

A strong emotional factor is evident in people who reach this natural high–a positive and continued belief in their own recovery. It is not restricted to those who recover through treatment centers or self-help groups. I have heard it described in the same way by people who felt positive about their abstinence, despite differences in the methods used. I have also heard it from people who do not use alcohol or drugs, but have become heavily involved with religious programs or other causes.

They all report that they now can react to experiences that reinforce these good feelings. These experiences–whether a session of meditation, attendance at an AA meeting or a positive experience at work or with family–produce similar results. The feeling of well-being far outlasts the individual experience. Many AA members talk about going to a daily meeting to "recharge their batteries." Positive experiences such as this may flood the brain with endogenous tranquilizers. Perhaps, in a few years, research will provide a better understanding of how this happens.

Mark felt this natural high continue for much of his first year of recovery. Most people who have experienced this pink cloud phenomena find that it ends after several months. Again, this is probably the result of a process of brain chemistry self-regulation. Once the brain is able to produce enough neurotransmitters, it may begin the process of adjusting the level produced to suit the needs of the occasion. This fine-tuning allows the brain to respond normally to outside events; so people once again are faced with dealing with emotionally painful situations.

When this "pink cloud" ends, people in early stages of recovery face a crucial period. After getting used to feeling good about themselves, normal uncertainties and fears reappear. A large percentage of people who have been very enthusiastic about their own recovery are confused about these biochemical changes. Some will relapse into drinking or using drugs again.

If a personal program of recovery has been established during these initial months a relapse is much less likely. Simply being able to respond to feelings of anxiety or depression in a healthier way is a revealing experience for many. Dealing with situations that would have caused problems in the past helps them to recognize the true value of their recovery from addiction.

Because they are reacting to life in a different manner, they are less vulnerable to developing problems in response to everyday events. This new reaction is a change in behavior, but it makes a difference biologically. The old pattern of behavior could have produced either anxiety or depression, not warranted by the events. Either of these old reactions represents an internal chemical change to the brain.

By practicing the new behavior of a recovery program, they no longer have to deal with these old biochemical brain responses. This is when the recovery has come full circle. This is the time that recovering people look at an event in their own life and realize they have handled it on their own. They did not think about using a drug or taking a drink.

For Mark, a potentially disastrous event helped him to recognize this. Several months into his recovery, he discovered he had more time on his hands because he was no longer devoting hours a day to drinking. He started using this extra time by taking on small jobs as an independent contractor. He was using some of his employer's equipment without authorization when an expensive tool disappeared. He was upset but realized the best approach was for him to explain the situation immediately and pay for a replacement tool. Mark received a mild reprimand from his boss but was given permission to continue to borrow special tools. His directness and honesty had solved the problem and impressed his employer. Mark still had the burden of replacing the tool, but he was able to handle that from his earnings on the moonlighting job.

This was a turning point for Mark. He realized that he probably could not have faced this conflict in the past and may have gotten drunk, called in sick and created greater difficulties. The problem of the lost tool was one of the kind of minor life events everyone faces. Mark's reaction, as a sober and mature adult, felt new but comfortable. That day, Mark recognized that he was thinking and acting in new ways, *sobriety* took on a different meaning to him.

8

RECOVERY AND THE BODY

Addiction and recovery affects both the body and the mind. Changes in the body eventually affect thinking and behavior, as much as thinking and behavior cause changes in physical health. During recovery improvements mentally and physically support each other so closely that they cannot be fully separated. This chapter emphasizes how the physical side of recovery was experienced by a few people.

PHYLLIS' STORY

Physical appearance can change tremendously in early recovery. Phyllis, a woman who entered treatment a few days after Mark, appeared to be considerably older then he was, perhaps approaching fifty. As she began to get better, he realized she was in her mid-thirties! The first noticeable change is often in the skin. Because the skin may have been bloated before, it now quickly begins to resume a normal tone. The composition of sweat and fatty acids may effect the "skin flora," those bacteria and fungi that are usually present on the skin surface. As these change, skin improvements are supported up the resolution of vitamin deficiencies as well as improvements in personal hygiene.

Almost magically, recurrent skin problems often begin to clear up. Phyllis had looked heavily made-up for several years, as many cosmetics were used to conceal her bad skin. At the rehab, patients were not encouraged to dress in flashy outfits or use excessive makeup. Despite the lack of makeup, Phyllis began to look better.

Not only did her skin begin to improve, but her posture changed as well. Initially, she was probably standing straighter due to her new-found self-esteem. She quickly began to feel positive about having entered treatment, recognizing that this could be a turning point in her life. Smiling, laughing and holding her head up were all natural consequences of this new belief in herself. However, the changes in her bearing quickly went beyond those due just to an improvement in her self-esteem.

Alcohol may damage those parts of the nervous system that aid in controlling movement, thereby interfering with the ability to exercise. Alcohol may also work directly on the muscles, causing a condition (alcoholic myopathy) that injures and weakens them. Muscle strength may also decline because of low levels of the hormones that are important to muscle growth. Also a shortage of glycogen–the quick energy storage battery of the body–may make prolonged exercise difficult. But long before these negative biological effects have taken place, the sedative effect of alcohol (and many other drugs) will blunt the desire to exercise in most addicts.

During recovery most patients who have been using alcohol or other sedatives begin to experience an increased energy level and often want to exercise, despite being in poor physical condition. As their health improves patients frequently become more active, sometimes taking up recreational sports or a regular exercise program. In many rehabilitation programs, the most frequent medical complaints have to do with minor sprains and strains from impromptu softball or volleyball games. Over time, this physical activity brings about a change in body tone, movement and posture.

Phyllis enjoyed the workout she got from the informal volleyball games, and soon began other forms of exercise. By her third week of rehab, she was getting up early to jog, before beginning her daily routine. The way she walked, the way she moved gave Phyllis a new, younger look. At thirty-six, she had a spring in her step that told people she felt good about herself. Now no one could mistake her for a woman of fifty.

NUTRITIONAL DEFICIENCIES

Some of the physical improvements that Phyllis and Mark experience were the indirect result of the resolution of nutritional deficiencies originally caused by alcohol. The type of nutritional problems that addicts and alcoholics develop differs depending upon what drugs were used as well as social factors that might be related to their use. For many reasons, alcohol can cause the most complex nutritional problems. The solvent nature of alcohol enables it to enter and disrupt many cells of the human body, while other drugs can only influence cells that have specific receptors that they match. The digestive system is exposed to alcohol at a concentrated level from the moment a drink passes a person's lips. Mild alcohol use is tolerated well by most people, but heavy and frequent use is not. The risk of developing cancer of the mouth or esophagus is increased substantially by the heavy use of alcohol, even in the non-alcoholic. After alcohol passes through the esophagus it reaches the stomach and then the small intestine. Here, alcohol can act as an irritant and aggravate existing problems, such as gastritis and ulcers.

At the same time that alcohol is irritating the organs of digestion, it is being used by the body as food. Pure alcohol contains about seven kilocalories (commonly called calories) in each gram. This is one of the most concentrated forms of energy the body can take in, more concentrated than sugar, and containing almost as much energy as pure fat. A "standard" drink usually contains about 100 calories just from the alcohol alone, without counting any other ingredients. If you have ever struggled with a weight reduction diet of 1,000 calories or so a day, you will understand what this means. A social drinker need not worry about this, but an alcoholic may easily receive over half of his or her energy needs from alcohol. This can be very dangerous. In its most severe form, it can result in a deficiency of other nutrients usually seen only in times of famine. When we see pictures of starving children with pencil thin arms and legs but swollen bellies, we are often looking at the result of kwashiorkor or protein-calorie malnutrition. The alcoholic can create this same degree of malnutrition by receiving all of his or her energy from the calories in alcohol.

Usually alcoholics, except for the most severe cases, continue to eat. Some even take large amounts of vitamin supplements while still drinking. In fact, health food stores often feature special vitamin mixtures and other dietary supplements specifically for the drinking alcoholic. Even by taking these "drinker's" vitamin supplements the alcoholic who is imbibing heavily will not correct the underlying problem. Mark's wife saw to it that he continued to eat while he was drinking. What she did not know was that his body was unable to use many of the nutrients in his diet.

Mark's digestive tract was irritated by alcohol, interfering with its ability to pick up many nutrients. Normally his digestion process would have been aided by enzymes created in his pancreas. Mark's pancreas was often inflamed by alcohol, which, among other things, interfered with the production of pancreatic enzymes that help in the digestion of fats. This often caused Mark to experience very loose and foul-smelling bowel movements. Along with the fats that passed undigested through his body were a large portion of the "fat-soluble vitamins" that were in his diet. Fat-soluble vitamins (A, D, E, and K) are absorbed by the body along with other fats. Since he could not digest fats well, those particular vitamins were flushed down the toilet.

H.A.L.T.

The information on nutrition was extremely important to Mark and Phyllis in early recovery because they needed to learn how to react to hunger. It seems silly to have to teach adults that they must eat food when hungry, but not learning this can often lead to a relapse.

This important concept was often reiterated both in treatment and in the AA groups they would later join, and was based upon experiences that many people faced in recovery. The underlying biological causes for this are sound, but that was never really explained. Instead it was simply treated as a fact, to be accepted and heeded. Mark heard again and again that he must remember "H.A.L.T." He should never allow himself to become Hungry, Angry, Lonely or Tired. He was told that when alcoholics in early recovery experienced one or more of these four feelings, the desire to drink returned, and often resulted in a relapse to drinking–a "slip."

For the recovering alcoholic, never becoming hungry, angry, lonely or tired, is excellent advice. Fortunately, it was not necessary for Mark to fully understand this advice in order to follow it. Understanding that there are powerful biological and behavioral reasons for H.A.L.T. however, might have saved the life of a fellow patient.

CARL'S STORY

Carl was a former newspaper editor. He held a Master's degree in English literature and his newspaper experience had given him the equivalent of a Doctor of Philosophy degree in "advanced skepticism." He treated much of what he heard in rehab as ridiculous folklore, and he repeatedly asked the counselors questions about how a particular recommendation would help him. It seemed he would only follow those recommendations he understood and when a counselor was unable to answer Carl's objections satisfactorily, he simply decided to reject the advice in question. This intellectualization was a psychological defense mechanism that became a barrier to learning new behaviors.

Perhaps understanding the reasons why H.A.L.T. was actually very good advice would have helped Carl accept it. In any case, when he completed rehab–at about the same time as Phyllis and Mark–he appeared to be a new person. Four months later, he was drinking again. He had been warned before, by several doctors, that he was lucky to still be alive. His body could not take the abuse of continued drinking. This time, he was not so lucky. He died three weeks later.

▪▪

How could following the simple advice about hunger have prevented Carl's death? Carl's pancreas, like Mark's, had been repeatedly inflamed by his drinking. In addition to interfering with the ability to produce pancreatic enzymes, which helped him digest food, it also had interfered with the production of two important chemicals used in metabolic control, insulin and glucagon.

Insulin is vital in maintaining the right blood sugar level. It helps the cells of the body take in the sugar (glucose) circulating in the blood and use it for energy. If the cells cannot do this properly, the blood sugar level rises while the cells are starved for energy. The excess sugar in the blood is often spilled out by the kidneys, resulting in sugar in the urine. This condition, of course, is known as "diabetes mellitus" or commonly referred to as diabetes.

Glucagon is not as well known as insulin but is the companion to it. It, too, is created within the pancreas. Just as insulin production is needed to bring the blood level of insulin down, glucagon production is needed to bring it up. The right level of sugar in the bloodstream is the body's power-line of energy. When the body uses too much sugar from the bloodstream because of activity, more energy must be created from storage reserves. Normally, this is the job of glucagon. Created in the pancreas, it is the chemical signal for the liver to quickly break down a storage reserve of another chemical, glycogen, into sugar and pump it into the bloodstream. Insulin and glucagon, working together in a healthy body, keep the level of sugar in the blood from getting either too high or too low.

The liver, a main storage depot for glycogen, is severely attacked by the continued use of high levels of alcohol. For many alcoholics, this results in inflammation of the liver and the formation of fat deposits there. When this occurs, the stored glycogen often disappears, resulting in poorly regulated energy levels. That is, the combined problems of the liver and the pancreas create swings in blood sugar level not found in healthy people.

This blood sugar level swing to a low level is known as hypoglycemia, which, by itself, simply means "low glucose level in the blood." Recently, much has been written for the general public regarding hypoglycemia that has led some to believe it is an underlying cause of many of the problems of the civilized world. In a healthy person, hypoglycemia is rarely a problem. When the liver and pancreas are working properly, the body regulates its blood sugar level well, even under stressful conditions. Diabetics who take too much insulin or lower their blood sugar levels through strenuous exercise or by skipping a meal may experience a hypoglycemic episode. In the diabetic, such an event is an extreme emergency and they may faint or even go into a coma as a result. As an emergency measure, diabetics have been taught to quickly consume an easily digested source of sugar, such as a candy bar or a glass of sweetened orange juice. This quick jolt of sugar is then followed by more nutritious food that will sustain the increased sugar level. Hypoglycemic episodes in newly sober alcoholics are not as severe but can be a cause for concern. They are not going to produce the fainting or coma that the diabetic who has taken too much insulin will experience. These milder hypoglycemic episodes can still produce difficulty in thinking clearly as the brain becomes mildly starved for energy. At the same time, the body, due to increased activity of the autonomic nervous system, is producing physical reactions in response to the low sugar level.

Newly recovering people may suddenly find themselves confused, sweating, trembling and anxious. This unwanted stimulation is exactly as they felt between drinks or pills, when their bodies were beginning to go into withdrawal. The High-Low Trap feelings are occurring without any connection to actual alcohol or drugs. If the person was a cocaine addict, this may be the way she felt after using cocaine all night, when a "downer" was needed to be able to function.

The normal response of a healthy person during a hypo-glycemic episode would be to eat. The alcoholic or addict may have forgotten this and the mild confusion and autonomic activity can be misunderstood. In the past, the response to anxiety, was to take a drink or a tranquilizer. What would be a simple biologic event for a normal person instead takes on an insidious meaning as a powerful behavioral cue. The recovering person can interpret this feeling as "wanting a drink" or "needing a pill."

॥

This experience can be extremely stressful because the person knows that he does not want to drink or use again. Despite this, the body is sending out a powerful signal that it "needs" a drink or a pill. The recently sober person remembers the positive feeling he would get from taking a drink under these circumstances. This memory is biologically sound as well, for if alcohol were used now, it would not only temporarily relieve the anxiety, but it could also be used as a rapid energy source by the starving cells.

If he does not realize that he is dealing with a simple, chemical phenomena and has accidentally triggered the High-Low Trap, the person may feel there is something wrong with him. Self-esteem is usually very fragile at this stage. After doing well for several weeks, this feeling that is mistaken for an urge to drink can easily cause one to lose hope in their own recovery. Remember the advice not to let yourself get too hungry. No wonder that one of the orig-inal AA "tricks" for the newly sober was to carry some candy with them and take a "sweet" at the thought of taking a drink.

"Never let yourself get too hungry, angry, lonely or tired" was repeated again and again to Mark, Phyllis and Carl. None of them totally understood why, but Mark and Phyllis chose to follow this advice–Carl ignored it. We will never know why he returned to drinking. Perhaps, despite his desire to remain sober, Carl had felt compelled to pick up a drink again–a behavioral response to a powerful biological signal that he could not understand.

9

RECOVERY AND SEX

William Shakespeare used a porter suffering from a hangover to deliver the definitive description of alcohol's effect on sex.

Lechery, sir, it provokes, and unprovokes; it provokes the desire, but it takes away the performance: therefore, much drink may be said to be an equivocator with lechery: it makes him, and it mars him; it sets him on, and it takes him off; it persuades him, and disheartens him; makes him stand to, and not stand to; in conclusion, equivocates him in a sleep, and, giving him the lie, leaves him.

–Act II, Scene 3 of MacBeth

The Porter's speech elucidates how alcohol can create the desire for sex while destroying sexual ability through temporary impotence or unconsciousness. This is only one of the sexual problems caused by addiction. Alcohol and drugs have changed relationships and recovery does not necessarily mean that one's sexual problems are resolved. Recovery from addiction, however, is a necessary step in solving these problems. Often, sexual problems become obvious only after recovery begins.

When sexual difficulties are faced in early recovery, answers are not always obvious to the newly sober person. A common mistake is the belief that there is one right answer. Relationships that have withstood stormy years where one (or both) partners drink and/or do drugs are frequently shattered during the first year of recovery. Misunderstanding biological and emotional changes in sexuality is a common problem.

Recovery of "normal" sexual drive and sexual function is rarely considered a priority issue in alcoholism treatment. Discussion of

95

it is often totally avoided. Similarly, it is a topic not often brought up at AA or NA meetings. When a recovering person has the courage or desperation to bring up this subject, he or she may find the topic rejected because of a powerful societal taboo about honest discussions of sexual problems. Generally, other topics are never rejected as inappropriate for discussion within an AA or NA meeting as long as the people bringing it up directly relate it to their staying sober.

Alcohol has been called the "lubricant of social intercourse." The ability of alcohol and drugs to relax people in awkward and anxiety-generating social circumstances is considered by many people as a blessing. As Bill admitted, alcohol gave him the confidence to talk to women in a social setting. Bill's first sexual encounters were all related to these social contacts. Bill, as do many other young men and women, drank alcohol for social intercourse, which then led to sexual intercourse.

Until his recovery from addiction, Bill never experienced sex when he was not intoxicated. Because his drinking experience developed in the same time-frame as his early sexual development, this comes as no surprise. Many men and women report that they have rarely, if ever, had sexual intercourse without alcohol or some other drug in their system.

The porter's complaint in *Macbeth* was that alcohol increased sexual desire while it interfered with sexual ability. Since he was able to make this observation, the porter may have been a social drinker. Many an alcoholic has faced this dilemma without the porter's insight. When a person believes that alcohol or another drug must be present to have sex, it is difficult for them to accept that the alcohol or other drug is also responsible for the sexual dysfunction.

There are three major reasons that drugs (including alcohol) are closely associated with sex:

1. Prostitution: If an addict can't afford to buy drugs he or she will often resort to prostitution. They are not necessarily career prostitutes, but often it is the only avenue for a person addicted to an expensive drug. In the past, prostitution was usually associated with heroin use but cocaine addiction has created a new "crack prostitute" or "rock star." Younger women have more opportunities for this type of "employment." Young men find their choices are more limited unless they are willing to engage in homosexual sex. There is, however, a much more subtle form of prostitution connected to drug and alcohol use. Is a man or woman a prostitute when he/she always allows a lover to supply them with drugs? Is it solicitation if a woman goes to a singles bar and lets a new acquaintance know that she will leave with him if he has cocaine to share? There are many people–even career women such as Lisa–who admit to having done this on occasion, but do not see this as a form of prostitution. The true commercial nature of this type of sex becomes more evident once the addict is in recovery.

2. Sexual Stimulation: Drugs are sometimes used to enhance sexual sensation, by attempting to coincide the high of a drug with the natural high of a sexual orgasm, thereby intensifying both. This form of sex is most commonly tried with stimulants or mixtures of stimulants and opiates. Using the combination of injected amphetamine or cocaine and heroin (a speedball), a couple faces the additional risk of exposure to AIDS. They are exposed to this disease through a shared needle and sexual contact. The combined "rush" may indeed alter the perception of a sexual orgasm and the addict may confuse the two experiences so that the sensation can be experienced without the niceties of sexual contact–a form of chemical masturbation.

3. Sexual Inhibitions: Alcohol is commonly used by men and women to lessen their social and sexual inhibitions. The tranquilizing effect of alcohol allows many people to feel more relaxed, while its effect on judgment may change the way a person views a possible sexual partner. As one country western singer pointed out, "The girls all get prettier at closing time."

You do not have to be an alcoholic to experience this. Even social drinkers, find that "girls get prettier" after only one or two drinks. Alcohol has been considered an aphrodisiac, since it was first used. Why is that so? Physically, alcohol does nothing to enhance sexuality. What alcohol does do–at a low level–is relax those mechanisms that would normally suppress inappropriate sex. Very few people who have stayed sober the night before wake up in bed with a stranger and wonder why.

RELATIONSHIPS

Unfortunately, a great number of people have excessive fears about relationships. The "positive" relationship between sex and alcohol is not restricted to those with alcohol or drug problems.

Many otherwise normal people have difficulty having sex, even in a committed relationship, without alcohol or another drug. This does not make them addicts.

As recovering addicts become clean and sober, they may find that their old fears return. Phyllis, the woman who changed from looking like an older shopworn person to a healthy younger woman experienced this. Despite her new, fresh appearance she suppressed her sexuality for the first year of her recovery. When she entered rehab, most men would not have given her a second glance, but now, she had a vibrant, healthy glow and men began to notice her.

Phyllis sensed this, and it scared her. She reacted to the increased attention as a threat to her sobriety–and it may have been. When she finally did talk about it, her fear was obvious. "I have been in enough relationships in the past, including two bad marriages. I feel loved in AA. I needed sex to feel loved before. Now, I know that I was looking for the wrong thing in my relationships. Having sex, I felt loved. I was using men and using sex to make me feel wanted. Since I have been in recovery, I don't need it.

"I know the people around me love me. I have friends, both men and women, and it has nothing to do with sex. Why screw it up? I have women who are my friends now; something I have never had before. All my friends were always men. I was even using the men with whom I was not having sex. My sexuality was a way I tried to control them.

"The funny thing is, by having women as friends, I am learning to be friends with men, too. I mean, platonic friends. There are some men here that I really care about–men I do not think about sexually. If I did have sex with any of them, it would threaten the closeness and trust we have for each other. I know now when a friend hugs me that I am loved."

Phyllis was reacting in a way that was safe for her. She joked (or was she joking?) about changing her religion so that she could become a nun. Later Phyllis would reveal her deeper problems. She had an alcoholic father. As a young child, his erratic behavior had made her feel unloved. Like many children brought up in alcoholic or dysfunctional families, she blamed herself for this.

As a child, Phyllis had a desperate need to be loved by an older man but found that substitute for parental love in the wrong way. She had an affair at age twelve with a married neighbor. Sex became the way to feel "loved" and provided the kindness and hugs she could not find any other way. She knew the situation was wrong but she had a powerful, unmet need. As an adult, this conflict prevented her from having true friendships as well as from enjoying her sexuality. Alcohol, by easing the conflict, quickly became a necessary part of all her relationships, including both of her marriages.

It is little wonder that Phyllis was chaste in her first year of recovery. She realized that she was loved as a person, and that was enough. This healthy, spirited woman chose to exclude sex from her life rather then confuse these good feelings. She was a survivor and guarded her newly found sobriety.

Later in her recovery, Phyllis began to learn about relationships. While she could be called a mature women in terms of her past physical sexual experience, she was still a teenager in terms of relationships.

Jerry was a member of AA with about three years of sobriety when Phyllis began coming to his group. He was two years younger than she, and had also been married and divorced twice. He thought she was pretty, but he had no intention of dating her. He knew enough to understand that dating a person who had just gotten sober could be bad for both people. As he talked to her at the meetings, they became good friends and he sincerely appreciated the platonic nature of their friendship.

After that first year, Phyllis began to date but found it threatening and uncomfortable. She could joke with Jerry about it, again talking of becoming a nun. Rather then date, she preferred going out with friends, both men and women in a group. More and more frequently, she found herself out with Jerry. But as a friend, she had no interest in him sexually, so that never counted as a date. Gradually, they both realized that they liked being together more than being with any other friends. After taking a new look at each other, the relationship changed. Today they are married, and continue to be friends. They have discovered that, in recovery, sexuality and true friendship are completely compatible.

JERRY'S STORY

Phyllis and Jerry now have no difficulty with sexuality. Jerry had dealt with his own issues earlier, issues that were just as confusing and devastating to him as Phyllis' were to her. Perhaps it was his own bad experiences that had given him the understanding and sensitivity that Phyllis discovered in him. In Jerry, Phyllis found both kindness and strength.

Kindness and strength would not have been traits thought of by his second wife. Jerry was younger than Phyllis but had gone further downhill before getting sober. Shakespeare exploring the down side of alcohol and sex wrote, it "makes him stand to and not stand to." Many men, not just alcoholics, have found this to be true. High levels of alcohol may cause impotence. The desire may have been there, and the alcohol seemed to make everything go right, but just at the required moment–more often then he cared to remember–Jerry had been unable to perform.

Impotence is very threatening to men. It is often dealt with through shame, anger and denial. The same high levels of alcohol that brought on the episode of impotence may also subsequently, bring on an episode of amnesia or an alcoholic blackout. "Did we make love last night?" may sound like a funny question, but many heavy drinkers have had the experience of wondering this. Sometimes, neither partner can answer the question. Among some couples, this question goes unasked because it seems better to just assume then to appear foolish.

The inability to perform sexually is not restricted to men. Male impotence makes a normal sexual act virtually impossible, but women are often unable to have sex due to being intoxicated. "...in conclusion, equivocates him in a sleep, and, giving him the lie, leaves him." So said the wise porter.

As Jerry slipped deeper into his alcoholism, he became virtually asexual. The later stages of his alcoholism had chemically neutered him. Alcohol, at prolonged high levels, causes the testes to shrink. Continued liver inflammation creates problems in the production of the chemical precursors of sexual hormones. Both men and women have male and female hormones in their bloodstream. It is the correct balance of the levels of these sex hormones that cause the body to develop normal sexual characteristics.

Jerry did not understand what was happening when the desire for sex left him. He had not gone through a rehab, but because he was in such poor condition he had a long stay in detox when he first got sober. Sex was the last thing on his mind then, but his doctor had pointed out several changes. This is a subject that Jerry had discussed with few other men, but the doctor wanted him to understand the full extent of his illness.

Jerry is a little hazy about what happened during detox, but he recalled, "The doctor told me that alcohol was changing my sex! I had little thought of sex at that time, but hearing this from the doctor scared me. He pointed out to me how small my balls were and said that booze had made them atrophy. They had shaved me my first day in detox, and a few days later I still didn't need a shave. The doc told me my beard had stopped growing because of my reduced male hormones. Then he had me look in the mirror at my chest. I thought my chest was looking more pronounced because of fat. He told me to take a closer look. I had tits that would have been passable on a slender women. He told me that this was a condition (gynecomastia) of my body responding to female hormones instead of male hormones.

"I think I would have been ready to end it right there. Fortunately, he went on to say these changes were temporary. Over the next few months the doctor said everything should get back to normal provided I did not pick up a drink. If I started to drink again, I would get permanent liver damage and these changes would not go away so quickly."

Jerry then described what happened to him in early recovery. "I noticed my body changing, just like I had been told. When I had reached the point where I looked like I needed a shave every evening, I also began to feel differently. I felt myself stirring as a man and decided to try dating again."

Jerry, like Bill, had never before experienced sex while sober. He walked right into a common trap. "I had a few months sober and began dating a woman I had met at work. She was a pleasant person and a social drinker. After a few dates, we tried to get together, but I couldn't do anything. I did what I could to try to please her, but I really felt embarrassed. I knew I was capable of getting an erection, but I was very nervous about how I did. I figured it was just my nerves, so I decided that if it happened again, I would try a different tactic.

"Well, she must have liked me because we did date again. I had the same problem! I knew what I had to do. I suggested we have a drink. She didn't know about my past. It worked. I was able to satisfy her and felt good about myself. Of course, I knew I was cheating on my sobriety, but I thought that this one little indiscretion was worth it. The next date, I had two drinks before we went to her place, and it was great. Sobriety had given me my manhood back. Two little drinks were not going to hurt me."

Jerry had quickly found out the truth in this common trap. The

"L" for "Lonely" in H.A.L.T. had been responsible for another slip. "I was still going to my AA meeting and didn't tell anyone about my drinking. I didn't even consider it a slip, at the time. The next date was a disaster. This time, after two drinks I found myself having more. Back at her place, I could see that she was not thrilled with seeing me in this shape. That alcohol really hit me. We went to bed, but I was too drunk to perform. She had been patient with me before. Now, she seemed disgusted.

"I had lost everything! I had traded my sobriety for a piece of ass. Now, I had neither. I went back to my home group and told them about my slip. I could not talk about the sexual part of it. I did tell people that I had been drinking when I went out on a date with a social drinker. I was advised that I would be less likely to slip if I stayed out of slippery places. The slippery places that they meant were the clubs to which I had taken my date. They were right; except the slippery place was not the club but the bedroom.

"That slip was the last time I took a drink. I have been dead scared about sex since then. It was only after I had known Phyllis a long time that I seriously thought of dating her. I don't know what happened in the years between, but let me just say that I feel I have grown as a man."

ALCOHOL AND PREGNANCY

Jerry and Phyllis have grown as people. They are both healthy, emotionally and sexually. As evidence of this, Phyllis is now pregnant. She was pregnant once as a teenager and had an abortion. In her past marriages and relationships she was careless about birth control but never thought she was pregnant.

Actually, Phyllis might have been pregnant several times when she was drinking without knowing it. Women who drink heavily have difficulty conceiving. The reason for this stems from the same reason that men like Jerry notice sexual changes. The toxic effects of alcohol, as well as the hormonal changes, may cause irregular menstrual cycles. Women who drink heavily also have an increased risk of giving birth to a baby with defects. If an egg is fertilized, the body may reject the pregnancy early. This "spontaneous abortion" or miscarriage may just seem like a period that is late. For a woman already having irregular periods, it may not seem unusual. The body may have a built-in mechanism for aborting a fetus with the "fetal alcohol syndrome" thereby rejecting pregnancies that appear to have gone wrong.

Phyllis had not thought about pregnancy. After years of not using birth control, becoming pregnant as she approached forty didn't even seem like a remote possibility. Both Jerry and Phyllis, although surprised, seem to be ecstatic.

HEALING PAST WOUNDS

Everyone seems to react differently to sexuality and recovery. There are few absolute guidelines, but solid reasons exist to proceed cautiously. With time and patience, sexuality in recovery may take on a new meaning for many.

For some, long-ignored problems have to be faced again. This is especially true for men and women who were abused as children. Recovery from addiction can evoke memories that were too painful to face in childhood. This is true whether the abuse was physical, sexual or emotional. Recovery from addiction does not always make those scars go away.

Recovery does allow many people suffering from deep emotional scars of abuse to admit their need for further help. With that help–usually from a professional–recovery from addiction often provides the additional strength and ability to deal with other problems. This help in healing past wounds, coupled with the new skills of friendship and trust learned in recovery, opens the door to experiencing healthy and enriched relationships.

10
FINDING RECOVERY

▆▆▆ Recovery is a process, not an event. For some, the process begins with an event, such as entering treatment. For others, the exact start of their recovery is hard to pin down. This chapter examines different pathways to recovery that have worked for many and explains some common pitfalls.

Many people recover from addiction without expert help. Others require extensive assistance from professionals. Many people benefit from a little professional help to bolster their own program of recovery. Because of this variety, almost anyone can find examples of ways that have worked for others. The most important question is "What is best for you?"

Not everyone can afford professional treatment. Moralistic or archaic insurance regulations in some states continue to allow insurers to deny addiction treatment coverage to people who thought they had coverage for any disease. Fortunately, many insurers know that although treatment is a short-term expense, their company will benefit from long-term savings. Others may not have any health insurance and public programs may be over-crowded or unavailable.

Not being able to afford a treatment program should not prevent most people from getting better. There are two key steps, however, that, if not taken, can and do prevent people from getting well. These are abstinence and the desire to change. Strange as it may seem to the non-addict, many addicted people want to quit, but are only willing to try once things get better in their lives. A program of recovery can do nothing for the person still using. The lack of a desire to change is also part of the disease. Until this is present, the sick person will not have begun the active phase of their recovery program.

Later in this chapter I will discuss how someone can still get better even when one of these two crucial elements is missing. Many people who originally lacked any desire to change have been helped and now would give up their lives rather then return to the misery of their addiction. Still, it is the person who reaches out and asks for help who stands the best chance of finding recovery. This is also the person least likely to need complex care.

The cornerstone of recovery was based upon self-help for all the people discussed earlier except Alice. (Alice was an "innocent addict" and was able to abstain from drugs and alcohol without Alcoholics Anonymous or Narcotics Anonymous.) Jim, Bill, Lisa, Don, Mark, Jerry and Phyllis all used either AA or NA as a key part of their recovery program. For many people a self-help group is enough.

ALCOHOLICS ANONYMOUS

Before these self-help programs existed, a wide variety of psychiatric, physical, social and other treatments were used. William Menninger, M.D., former President of The American Psychiatric Association, was involved in giving these types of treatment. As he describes it, these various forms of therapy made the patients feel better temporarily but didn't help their addictions. In 1938, Dr. Menninger wrote about the treatment of chronic alcohol addiction in the Bulletin of the Menninger Clinic (2:101–112, July 1938). "We regard psychotherapy as probably the most important part of the treatment program...Our experience with less intensive measures has occasionally produced very satisfying results, but in more instances, very disappointing results...the majority of patients received minimal benefit..."

Once Alcoholics Anonymous was founded in 1935 people joined who had been unable to recover before and many began to get better. Doctor Menninger recognized the success of Alcoholics Anonymous and the earlier failure of psychiatry when in 1955 he addressed the Annual Meeting of the National Council on Alcoholism. He stated, "Alcoholics Anonymous has been far more effective in helping thousands of people than has psychiatry. This group has grown from a few people to more than 200,000 members. I think they have been successful because they made a direct attack on the problem. Their devotion, their persistence and dedication, to helping others ought to be an example for the rest of us."

Despite such strong praise from knowledgeable psychiatrists, Alcoholics Anonymous is careful to make no claims about itself. AA calls itself "a fellowship of men and women," not a treatment program and AA has wisely chosen to limit itself to what it does best.

The AA program itself is reminiscent of an older program–the Washingtonian Movement–which began in the 1830s. The Washingtonian Movement program helped thousands of people in the United States find recovery from alcoholism before the Civil War, but was destroyed by its own success and popularity. The Washingtonian Movement diversified in an attempt to deal with additional social and political issues. It lost direction. It stopped being an effective force to help alcoholics find recovery less than twenty years after it was formed.

When AA was established, its founders were unaware they were repeating history. During its early days there was a move to expand its role beyond a fellowship of men and women helping each other become and remain sober. Fortunately, the founders and early members of AA chose to limit the role of the fellowship so that the focus of one alcoholic helping another would remain its sole purpose. These principles were embodied as formal traditions followed by all AA groups. The result of this is evident today. AA neither owns nor operates any treatment programs. Members do not publicly identify themselves or attempt to make public proclamations on behalf of the fellowship. AA has no dues or fees and declines any outside payments, contributions, grants or endowments. It relies totally on the contributions of its active members for all its operating expenses, usually collected by passing a basket at AA meetings. Fortunately, its expenses are very low. AA employs no counselors. Its sole paid staff are a handful of administrative employees hired to answer telephones and coordinate central and headquarter offices. Alcoholics Anonymous is able to do this by relying upon the voluntary efforts of a majority of its members. This true voluntary spirit gives the organization a sincerity that makes it believable to many alcoholics who have previously scorned professional help.

AA works. Other groups, closely patterned after AA, such as Narcotics Anonymous or Cocaine Anonymous, are also effective. Many of these other groups have obtained permission to copy and use the AA twelve-step program of recovery. Because of this similarity, treatment centers often refer to AA, NA, CA and similar groups generically as "twelve-step" groups. Most successful addiction treatment centers in the United States today emphasize continuing participation in twelve-step programs to their patients.

ıı

The success of a chemical dependency program of any sort can never be measured during the early phase of recovery. Effective treatment can only be measured by the continued right behavior, and sobriety of patients long after they have left the controlled environment of inpatient treatment. Some treatment centers have done this. They have followed their patients after discharge in an attempt to determine what factors predict relapse or treatment success. In an attempt to do this objectively, treatment centers across the United States have turned to the Ramsey Clinic in St. Paul, Minnesota. This clinic operates the Chemical Abuse Treatment Outcome Registry (CATOR). When clinics join this service, CATOR remains in contact with all their patients for several years. This has allowed them to study how well treatment programs are working and provides these clinics with a tool to determine ways to improve their programs. According to Doctor Norman Hoffman–the psychologist who heads this major effort that has studied thousands of patients treated at centers across the country–the single most important variable in predicting whether a patient would do well or relapse was the patient's participation in AA.

Some experts argue that perhaps those who would do well anyway are more likely to go to AA, so the numbers appear distorted. To refute this, return to what Doctor Menninger had to say. Before AA existed, no matter how good the patients seemed during treatment, an eventual relapse was almost a certainty. After AA came into being, many that would have been doomed were able to recover. Treatment programs and professionals are valuable and useful, but the good that they perform is synergistic with the work of twelve-step groups. Professionals who do not accept the value of self-help groups may simply want to give themselves credit for the work of others.

ıı

Accepting the fact that AA and NA work, some may question why treatment programs are needed at all. There are sound reasons for their coexistence. Alcoholics Anonymous and other twelve-step fellowships are not enough for many people. Addiction is a deadly disease. If by doing more a person's chance of surviving increases, why not do it? One of the toughest problems for any health professional is determining whether their patient needs only the minimum treatment, or maximum therapy.

Twelve-Step groups, by themselves, seem to be enough for about one-third of the people who try them. This estimate is based upon surveys of people who have done well in AA compared to the total number of people who have attended groups. These people are sometimes called "first-nighters" because they appear to do well and maintain continuous sobriety from that very first meeting, even if they have suffered from addiction for years. Professionals and treatment programs can play a very important role, however, even with people who might have eventually recovered without professional help. They can speed up the recovery process, eliminating years of suffering, and often preventing economic losses to the patient and the patient's family and employer.

An equal number of people need considerably more time to get better using a twelve-step program alone. This includes individuals who seem to do well at first and then relapse, as well as those who at first cannot seem to stay sober at all. Eventually, these people will get better, but only after a very rocky course. Two years of continuous sobriety is the best indication that their recovery is stable. These people are survivors and once they become stable, the outlook for them is excellent.

This is the group that treatment programs often can and do help. They can recover, but they need every bit of assistance they can get. The difference between an addiction remaining in remission from the moment it is first dealt with and an addiction characterized by repetitive relapses can be years of unnecessary suffering. If there is any doubt, just ask the family of anyone who has had years of addiction without continuous sobriety. Less than effective treatment hurts the patient, his family and, indirectly, the community. This second group needs professional treatment programs that are synergistic with self-help groups, in order to help shorten the time from when they first seek help until their sobriety can be considered stable.

A third group, however, does not get better using twelve-step groups alone. They may intensely dislike AA. Although they want help for their addiction, they may be continuously sabotaged in their recovery by factors not addressed in self-help groups.

This third group is the hardest to treat, but requires more help.

They may be repetitive failures–even in the best treatment programs–and may foster the unsavory reputation of the addict or alcoholic as a person who cannot be successfully treated. They may use a disproportionate share of limited health care resources by going in and out of treatment and may be trapped in a revolving door–continually passing in and out of jobs, jails, hospitals and treatment programs.

Despite this, this group is not beyond hope. Many can and do get better. Although they seem incapable of benefitting from twelve-step groups on their own, they often embrace NA, or AA as part of their recovery once they are clean and sober. Treatment for this third group is never optional. They will simply not get better on their own.

THE SPIRITUAL ASPECT OF AA

Sometimes, the newcomer will be frightened away thinking he or she has walked into a religious cult. AA and similar self-help groups are not religious organizations. Many of their members return to earlier religious beliefs or find comfort in a belief in God. This is the "spiritual" aspect of recovery. It has worked just as well for agnostics and atheists as it has for the ministers, priests and rabbis who have joined AA. Spirituality means that a person accepts there are forces in the universe beyond their own self-will.

Religious approaches to recovery will be discussed in Chapter Twelve, as one of several alternate paths to recovery. The founders of AA once had strong ties to the Oxford Groups–a Protestant renewal movement. The program they developed benefitted many who were offended by the affiliation with a particular denomination. AA severed all formal ties to organized religion but not its need for members to believe in "a power greater than themselves." This definition, defined as "spiritual," not "religious" has allowed each member to practice a program of recovery that does not conflict with either religious or humanist beliefs.

This non-religious approach has allowed men and women embracing Catholic, Jewish, Moslem, Hindu, Baha'i, and Native American beliefs to accept a program of fellowship developed from a Protestant movement. This approach has allowed atheists, agnostics and secular humanists to benefit from a program based upon traditional Judaic-Christian values.

ⅠⅠ

HOW TO GET HELP

What is the simplest path to recovery for someone who thinks they may be addicted to alcohol or drugs? Anyone who wants help and is able to remain abstinent for one day can try attending an AA or NA meeting. There are no charges, and there is no obligation. If this person knows someone in recovery, asking this person for help may eliminate the fear of reaching out to a group of strangers. If not, a telephone call to Alcoholics Anonymous (or Narcotics Anonymous) will be all that is required. Volunteers will explain how to get to a meeting or may offer to meet the person and take him or her there. The phone numbers of AA and other groups will often be in the local telephone directory. Appendix D contains information on the "World Service Offices" of the self-help groups, as well as local phone numbers that will help locate a nearby meeting.

▥

As the word "Anonymous" in the name implies, these groups maintain personal anonymity, so there are no repercussions for attending. Of course, going to the meeting is an introduction to the program. What most first-nighters have reported is an immediate feeling of belonging. Members do not lecture or analyze each other. Instead, there is a sharing of personal experiences that help newcomers realize these are people with feelings and problems just like they have. The first-nighter often says, "They seemed so happy and appeared to be doing so well. I wanted what they appeared to have."

The new person who is interested is quickly encouraged to get to know people who have been clean and sober for a few years. Before and after the meeting, members will greet the new-comer. The twelve steps of the recovery program will be explained. Newcomers will be encouraged to attend as many meetings as possible. This encouragement may frighten off some people, especially when they are told to "attend ninety meetings in ninety days." This may sound like a sentence to some but frequent twelve-step group attendance is associated with fewer relapses. No right or wrong prescriptions are available for the use of a self-help group. People who do well seem to "work the program well" and attend frequent meetings. This may be too intense for other people, and if they can stay sober at a less intense level, that may be the right way for them, at the time.

■

If someone is ready to get help for his addiction, using AA or NA by itself can be the quickest and easiest path to recovery, however, this will not work for everyone. Many people fear or mistrust doctors and counselors. Because of this, they are reluctant to see a professional or enter a treatment program and find that going to AA without additional help, is the most desirable alternative. There are AA meetings every day in almost every city in the United States and most large cities of many other countries. NA and CA meetings are not quite as common, but they are available. There are enough recovering drinkers and users around that it is hard to find a place where there are no meetings.

RELAPSE

The pitfall in using the self-help approach is that not everyone will be a first-nighter. Some people will do well from the beginning, but others may relapse. Some of those who relapse will bounce back and having learned from the experience, return to a twelve-step group with a greater understanding of their disease. These people will do well. Others who relapse will not do well and some may die. Rather than recognize their own relapse as a common event, they will look upon it as a personal failure, as a proof of their inability to get better. It is this group that is in the most danger, because, having tried sobriety and failed, they may not attempt it again.

Anyone who is trying to get sober needs to be warned that relapses can and do occur. A person feeling good in the early glow of recovery should recognize that he or she may drink or use once again. The High-Low Trap can undermine the sobriety of sensible and well-meaning people in early recovery. The disease of addiction is never totally cured, but with time, relapse becomes less and less likely.

A person pursuing the direct path to sobriety by using a twelve-step group must follow the path correctly. The newcomer needs to establish contacts with other members, find a sponsor and create a network of people all interested in keeping him sober. This works. Like a novice mountain climber, these "safety ropes" connect him to more experienced climbers–people who will steady him and prevent a fall. If the novice does slip, he or she can quickly return to the program, beginning again with greater understanding and motivation.

Many people are loners. Even those who are married, have family and are active in a social circle never develop true close relationships and trust in other people. That one who has been this isolated is able to turn to strangers and trust them seems remarkable to those who have never seen the magical power of a group of recovering people working to help others.

However, many will not reach out to others. Relapse for such a person is devastating. Just going to a self-help group is not the shortest path for these people. Instead, it is one they will continue to slip and fall on. If you were attempting to climb a mountain and found the shortest path too slippery for you, you would look for another way. The novice climber would be foolish to continue on a path too slippery to be tackled alone. The alternate path might seem to take longer but he would probably reach his goal sooner, because on the short path he would have lost ground each time he slipped or was injured and unable to complete the climb. So it is, too, for the loner who goes to a self-help group but does not reach out to others for help. The shortest path becomes the longest–perhaps one that is never completed. This person requires more and needs to follow one of the other established paths to recovery.

INPATIENT PROGRAMS

One of the seemingly longer paths to sobriety is entering an inpatient chemical dependency program for a month. These programs are often called "Minnesota Model" programs because they use many techniques developed at Hazelden, one of several pioneering institutions in the vicinity of Minneapolis, Minnesota. Mark and Phyllis went to such an institution for inpatient treatment. Success rates tend to be higher for people who go through inpatient treatment. At some centers, about two-thirds of the patients who complete treatment will achieve that magical two years of remaining continuously clean and sober. These high success rates sound wonderful, but sometimes they are achieved because many inpatient programs take only the easiest patients–the ones with the best insurance, and those who are most likely to do well following any path to recovery.

Inpatient rehabilitation programs were described in several of the earlier cases. At the heart of inpatient rehabilitation is intensive alcoholism counseling, much of it in a group setting. Far from being a summer camp or country club, good treatment at an inpa-tient rehab is an intense experience, and has planned therapeutic activities for most of a patient's day, seven days a week.

Inpatient rehabs bear little resemblance to psychiatric hospitals. Even those rehabs that are operated as part of a psychiatric insti-tution usually maintain their own identity and physical separation from the psychiatric programs. Few inpatient rehabs treat psychi-atric disorders. Instead, they attempt to identify and screen out patients with apparent psychiatric diagnoses that require other forms of immediate care. Bill is a typical patient, one with an apparent psychiatric diagnosis but whose well-being is not threat-ened if psychiatric treatment is delayed. Once the addiction is in remission for a few months, many of the psychiatric symptoms will disappear. A psychiatric evaluation of a patient who has been free of alcohol and other drugs for several months may produce very different results then one does prior to detox. The majority of people going through rehab will have no psychiatric diagnosis other than their addiction, once they are sober and drug-free.

An important part of inpatient rehabilitation involves the fami-ly. People with intact families are less likely to relapse after treat-ment. Many patients' families have been strained by crises that came before treatment, and are no longer able to remain together. The family members may have protected themselves from the mis-ery the patient caused by their own defense mechanisms. Now that the patient is recovering, the family too must begin to recover.

Family programs are available at many rehab centers. They may be conducted on weekends, in conjunction with visiting, or they may be entirely separate. Some of the more intense centers even have week-long residential programs for spouses and other family. Most clinicians agree that patients are better off if the reha-bilitation program they pick has a strong family program.

Many inpatient rehabilitation programs also use a wide assort-ment of techniques and therapies borrowed from mental health programs. These may include supervised activities such as crafts, music, art and exercise. Exercise and activity level do seem to be important for the treatment of many patients, but more research is needed to determine if this is actually true. Proponents of the inclusion of special activities have done reasonable studies that show how each of these additions makes the patient feel better about him or herself. However, there is still a lack of sufficient evi-dence that patients actually are less prone to relapse because of these additions to treatment. These activities are not harmful, as long as emphasis is on treatment and not on the extras. Rehabilitation programs that utilize a wide variety of activities but minimize the treatment of the addiction are reminiscent of the programs of the 1930s described by Doctor Menninger. As discussed earlier, the programs made people feel better, but they failed to put a lasting dent in the patient's addiction.

Far more important than any special activities, is the fact that the patient will be introduced to AA or NA at virtually all rehabilitation programs. This is helpful for most patients. The few that recoil from the thought of a self-help group are often the people who expected to go away for four weeks and be cured. Since addiction is never totally cured, but instead can be successfully held in life-long remission, four week cures are impossible. Inpatient rehabilitation is a giant step in the process of recovery. Further treatment for months after discharge strengthens that process. Acceptance of the need for a personal program of recovery is crucial. As previously noted, the Chemical Abuse Treatment Outcome Registry showed that patients who chose self-help group involvement after they left treatment did far better then those who did not.

OUTPATIENT TREATMENT

There are several intermediate choices, offering paths to recovery other than just going to AA or NA or into an inpatient rehabilitation center for a month. Outpatient treatment is available in many areas. It is very good for some, but not for everyone. Outpatient treatment has so many variations that the programs in your area may be significantly different from the ones described here. In addition to being a substitute for inpatient rehabilitation, people who have just left rehab often are helped by outpatient treatment, used as an "aftercare" or continuing care program.

The most intense form of outpatient care, the "day rehabilitation program," is designed to be exactly the same as an inpatient program, except the patient returns home every night. It costs less and it does not separate the patient from his or her family. This is not an advantage for everyone because often an addicted person needs to get better before returning to the stresses of the family. There is also the risk of the patient using drugs or drinking at home. Also, some employers feel that time off or sick-leave is not justified for this type of program.

The day rehabilitation program is different from custodial types of day programs, which are sometimes also referred to as "rehab" programs. These are modeled after programs for people with chronic problems. The custodial day program has lower expectations and bears little resemblance to an intense inpatient rehabilitation center program.

A more workable model is a part-time intensive outpatient program where patients continue to live at home and go to work or school. Treatment takes place mainly through counseling and group sessions for several evenings a week.

In some programs I have run and others that I think work well, patients are expected to do about half of what they would do in an inpatient rehab. Instead of the four weeks that would be required in rehab, completion in two months or longer is typical. After this phase of treatment, transition to a less intense continuing care program is typical. Since our patients are at home, they are expected to learn how to practice a personal program of recovery under normal conditions. This is probably the greatest single advantage to this type of program.

Next, there is the most common type of outpatient program–a one-hour session, meeting one evening a week. It works for people who, like Bill, are well motivated. For others lacking Bill's motivation, this is a steep, rocky path. I have seen patients do very well at this level of treatment only when they have spent their other free evenings at self-help groups. Since the time spent in this program is only about one-tenth of the time spent in an intensive program, the reasons should be clear. A week between brief contacts can be an eternity for the newly sober addict. In many areas, insurance companies pay only for the least expensive form of care, so this type is very common. Many people have difficulty maintaining early sobriety in these less intensive groups.

On the other hand, this less intense outpatient care can be very useful as a part of a continuing care program. After completing intensive treatment, whether inpatient or outpatient, this is a good way to continue progress while allowing a person time to start developing a healthy and sober lifestyle. Many good outpatient programs have different phases of and reserve this less intense treatment for those who have already gotten through some of the more slippery early portions of the path to sobriety. Treatment in this less intensive group often can continue for a year or more.

Another alternative is individual treatment by an independent, qualified therapist. Using individual treatment is like hiring an experienced professional mountain guide. If the guide understands the mountain, the climber is shown the path and assisted in the climb. This does not mean that other paths are followed. The patient will use the same path, whether it includes just twelve-step groups or also includes inpatient treatment or outpatient groups. This is often helpful because the practitioner works with the patient and assists in the recovery process. Many times, the professional can quickly deal with issues that cannot be dealt with in AA or in group counseling. Additionally, the independent professional has a broader view and does not gain financially by suggesting additional treatment.

FINDING A QUALIFIED PROFESSIONAL

Unfortunately, the person suffering from addiction is in a poor position to locate a qualified professional. Even today, after years of effort to change the situation, most physicians, psychologists and social workers receive little training in addictions. In some states, addictions counselors who have been trained only to work under supervision in multi-disciplinary programs, instead attempt individual care on a private basis.

A well meaning but inexperienced professional unfortunately may prolong the addiction by attempting to cure a problem caused by alcohol or drugs. This can be true whether the professional is a physician dealing with a medical problem, a psychologist dealing with an emotional problem or a social worker dealing with a family problem. When the addict or alcoholic reaches out for help, that is a golden time. If a correct diagnosis is made, the alcoholic may, at that moment, be receptive and agree to treatment. If instead the addict is told that the other "problems" she is experiencing need attention first, that golden moment may be lost.

On the other hand, experienced addiction counselors, rarely miss diagnosing an addiction. However, a counselor trained to work as part of a team who tries to work independently presents another danger to the patient. Counselors should adhere to a professional code of ethics and not attempt to exceed their capabilities. An independent counselor with limited training may be unable to recognize individual variations or the need for referral. The patient may be told, wrongly, that he or she has no need to deal with other problems. This may result in financial loss, medical problems, breakup of families and even suicide. "When someone is trained only to use a hammer, every problem looks like a nail."

Individual care can be the best treatment choice for some. Although individual sessions often appear expensive, the addicted person may find just the help he or she needs. When this happens, recovery is helped and the total cost of treatment is lower. Through objective case management, the knowledgeable professional can steer the patient's recovery through the maze of addiction–treatment options. The difficulty is in determining who is a well-qualified guide. First, they must be a professional, licensed to practice independently. Whether a physician, psychologist or social worker, this assures a particular basis from which to assume this type of responsibility. Secondly, they must have demonstrated knowledge and experience in working with addictions. Depending upon their field, this experience and knowledge may be shown by positions held, special training completed and certification through special examination. Suggestions to help you recognize a specialist are included in Appendix B at the back of this book. Other appendices give information about finding self-help groups and treatment programs. None of these are guarantees, but they will help you exclude those who would be poor guides on the path to recovery.

This general guide to paths to recovery assumes that the journey has begun. At the beginning of this chapter, two necessary conditions to beginning this journey were mentioned. These are abstinence and the desire to change.

ABSTINENCE

What about abstinence? The process of recovery cannot begin without it. Many people simply are unable to remain abstinent, even for one day. This is not a flaw in their character. The biological basis for addiction is powerful. If someone has been able to stop at will, without serious problems, he or she usually does not require professional help for detoxification. Others, like Mark, must get help. A heavy daily drinker coming off alcohol may be risking deadly complications without medical help. Withdrawing from most other drugs is not as dangerous as withdrawing from alcohol, but can be even more uncomfortable. The extreme is the daily heroin user who is in such discomfort during withdrawal that the experience of "kicking" the habit is feared and avoided. If such powerful withdrawal is not treated, the willingness to become abstinent can quickly disappear.

Mark and Bill both required detoxification. Detoxification is done most safely and conveniently in a hospital or other institution. Often, detoxification is done in the same institution that is doing the rehabilitation. However, local customs and regulations sometimes limit which institutions regularly allow detoxification. A call to the local AA office or a rehabilitation program or a local hospital emergency room is all that is required to find a detox program. If there is no local detox program, a physician who understands addictions may detox the patient as a medical treatment in a local hospital.

One other way exists to handle detoxification. It is possible to detox some patients on an outpatient basis. This is appropriate only in milder cases, such as Bill's, and it has its pitfalls. It usually is done much more slowly than inpatient and the failure rate may be higher. Patients have to be extremely motivated and understand what is going on. They should be seen daily, and someone should be available at all times, both for professional help and for support. One reason outpatient detox is important to know about is that lower cost and availability may make it the only alternative. At other times, a fear of hospitals may prevent someone who wants to quit from entering a hospital-based program. If an addict needs detoxification and there is a reasonable choice, inpatient detoxification is preferable.

Detoxification is not recovery. It is preparation for the journey of recovery. It is important that detoxification is followed by a program of recovery. If it is not it is a waste of effort, time and money. Worse, it is a waste of hope. A person entering a hospital for therapy has hope that they will improve. If they go through detox without a further program of recovery they will usually drink or use again. Anyone who believes that detoxification will cure their disease will be disappointed. Anyone willing to change should not have their hopes of recovering destroyed by an ineffective treatment program. No addicted person is ever truly beyond hope.

DESIRE TO CHANGE

The other key element is the desire to change. This is necessary before true recovery can begin. Despite this, many people who originally lacked any desire to change have been helped. This makes the treatment of addiction unlike the treatment of many other diseases. The process of the disease itself can work against the patient wanting to get well. The professional must be willing to treat some people who only seek help because they are coerced by a concerned family member, employer or court.

When AA was first formed, the early members almost made a terrible error. People were told that they had to suffer more before they could get well. A "sincere desire to stop drinking" was debated as a requirement for membership. When these early AA members realized that many of their most sober members had initially lacked that very sincerity, they quickly compromised. AA now states, "The only requirement for membership is a desire to stop drinking." By dropping the requirement for sincerity, they opened the door for many to get help.

Waiting for some to "suffer enough" or to "hit bottom" is a common pitfall. It is a myth of treatment that has added years to the misery that addicts have to suffer. The dilemma is that the person lacking the desire to change will, at first, seem like a hopeless case. When programs or professionals have been unable to help a patient recover, they will often explain away this failure by blaming the patient's unwillingness to cooperate. Blaming an addicted patient for this lack of a sincere desire to change is like blaming a smoker for developing lung cancer.

Addiction is a real disease. Despite this, in treating addictions, the patients who are the toughest cases are often mistreated in just this way. In fact, it is in dealing with these "tough" cases that there can be real differences in outcome with good treatment. Many programs will work for some of the easier cases. Programs that reject the tougher cases or blame the victim for treatment failures are all too common. It is in dealing with these very difficult cases that the highly structured treatment programs and capable professionals can do the most good.

The person who fails to see his or her own addiction and cooperate in treatment is often chastised for being in denial. Yet, denial is a basic psychological defense mechanism that is often encountered in a case of addiction. The person that has repeatedly failed at sobriety after several attempts is often characterized as lacking the willpower or sincerity to get better. But willpower is not the key to sobriety. Effective treatment requires that these barriers to treatment are understood to be an inherent part of the victims disease.

Helping someone who does not sincerely want help is inherently repulsive to some. It seems to smack of big-brotherism, coerciveness and interference with individual freedoms. This perception may make people hesitate in trying to help others seek treatment. This is unfortunate, because the addict may need a firm approach to admit his or her own need for help. Mark was coerced into treatment. He agreed to cooperate first because he had to and later because he wanted to.

This coercive approach works for many who do not initially feel they need treatment. It defies the folk belief that "you cannot help someone who does not want help" or the AA belief that someone has to "hit bottom" before they are ready to get sober. A psychologist might explain it as belief following behavior. An AA member might say "just bring the body and the mind will eventually follow." In fact, "raising the bottom" to force a crisis requiring someone to enter treatment proves its worth every day.

In Mark's case, it was an employee assistance program that forced the issue. Employee assistance programs do this work every day. For those who have crossed paths with the law during a drunken escapade, it is often a judge or a probation officer that persuades someone to seek treatment. These are situations that people may refuse. They are rarely forced to go to treatment. Yet, they are strongly persuaded. In the words of the "Godfather," they are given an offer they cannot refuse.

One method, originally popularized by Vernon Johnson, is often used by family members with the assistance of an experienced professional. This is the structured confrontation. Those of you who have seen the television dramatization of the life of former First Lady Betty Ford have seen an example of this. This is not something that can be done easily. Often, without the assistance and guidance of a professional, it will not work. A family that attempts to force someone to get better usually will fail because they will revert to anger and destructive patterns of relating to one another. Yet, it is the resolve of the family to help someone they love that can be the crucial factor in such a confrontation.

Those of you trying to get someone into treatment who is unwilling may need to get professional help. It may take many calls to treatment programs and health professionals to get the assistance you need in doing this.

Coercing an addicted person into treatment can be worth it. Despite the tension and strain a family goes through during a confrontation, it is a loving act. The person entering treatment may not see it as a loving act at first, but as he or she begins to get sober, that view should change. It is important that this manipulation, this coercion, be recognized for what it is. It should never be continued beyond its original purpose. Once someone accepts the need for sobriety and cooperates with treatment, continued coercion can have a negative effect.

The person who needs to be coerced into sobriety might eventually get better without this extra effort but at a later date. Those extra years would represent a painful journey on a long and treacherous road. Starting them on the path to recovery can be lifesaving. Treatment works and recovery works.

11

FOLLOWING THE
TWELVE-STEP PATH

▰▰ The twelve-step method is the path followed by those who seriously work the program advocated by Alcoholics Anonymous or any of the numerous self-help programs that have followed their model. This chapter is intended to help you if you are interested in following such a program. This program is one of action, not of intellectual pursuit. Those who benefit from it are those who do it, not those who merely study it.

All of this emphasis on action rather than study has led to the impression that this simple twelve-step path is merely an unscientific home-spun American folk remedy. In fact, when first developed in 1939, it drew upon not only the collective experience of the earliest members in AA but also upon the wisdom of psychiatry, religion and other movements.

The society now known as Alcoholics Anonymous started in 1935 in Akron, Ohio. In 1939 that small group published the book *Alcoholics Anonymous* and took as it's name the title of the book. In those few years, the early members codified the process they were using for recovery into twelve easy to follow (but not easy) steps that anyone could use. These were suggested as a program of recovery. Those founding members built the twelve steps of AA upon a foundation blending the ideas of the father of American psychology William James, and the internationally renowned Swiss psychiatrist Doctor Carl Jung as well as the religious leaders Doctor Frank Buchman and Reverend Samuel Shoemaker.

Since publication of the twelve steps in 1939, AA has given permission for many self-help groups to utilize these twelve steps in their own programs of recovery. Therefore, the program of Alcoholics Anonymous has been successfully modified for use by such diverse groups as Narcotics Anonymous, Gamblers

Anonymous, Overeaters Anonymous and a host of others. Each of these groups uses essentially the same program. Only a few words are changed to make it appropriate for each. Because of this similarity, it has become common to call all of these programs twelve-step programs.

The twelve steps of Alcoholics Anonymous are:

1. We admitted that we were powerless over alcohol–that our lives had become unmanageable.
2. Came to believe that a power greater than ourselves could restore us to sanity.
3. Made a decision to turn our will and our lives over to the care of God *as we understood Him.*
4. Made a searching and fearless moral inventory of ourselves.
5. Admitted to God, to ourselves, and to another human being the exact nature of our wrongs.
6. Were entirely ready to have God remove all these defects of character.
7. Humbly asked Him to remove our shortcomings.
8. Made a list of all persons we had harmed, and became willing to make amends to them all.
9. Made direct amends to such people whenever possible, except when to do so would injure them or others.
10. Continued to take personal inventory and when we were wrong promptly admitted it.
11. Sought through prayer and meditation to improve our conscious contact with God *as we understood Him*, praying only for knowledge of His will for us and the power to carry that out.
12. Having had a spiritual awakening as a result of these steps, we tried to carry this message to alcoholics, and to practice these principles in all our affairs.

The Twelve Steps are reprinted with permission of Alcoholics Anonymous World Services, Inc. Permission to reprint the Twelve Steps does not mean that AA has reviewed or approved the contents of this publication, nor that AA agrees with the views expressed herein. AA is a program of recovery from alcoholism – use of the Twelve Steps in connection with programs and activities which are patterned after AA, but which address other problems, does not imply otherwise.

These steps, looked at in their entirety, seem formidable. Some people, upon first review, consider them to be a religious program. Yet, taken individually, they can be done by anyone. The absence of religious belief is not a barrier to successfully using these AA twelve steps, any more than atheism is a barrier to following the moral precepts contained in the Ten Commandments.

There are only three guidelines to the correct use of a twelve-step program.

First, take each step in order. Consider these steps the assembly directions for a child's toy or a barbecue grill. If you skip a step because you think you see how the parts connect, invariably you will discover that you must go back to the beginning before it all fits together. In the same way, this program only works when done in sequence, since each step relies upon the execution of the preceding one.

Second, use all the steps. Trying to light your barbecue or have your child ride her bicycle when you have only completed half of the assembly would be futile and could prove dangerous. Similarly, half an AA program is no program at all.

Third, do each step to the best of your ability at that moment, but do not be a perfectionist. Do not try to add more than is suggested. Overworking any one step will prevent you from moving on to the next.

STEP ONE

Keeping these guides in mind, consider and do each step individually. The first step is the entryway to this path. **"We admitted that we were powerless over alcohol–that our lives had become unmanageable."** This requires the admission of the problem, and dropping the pretense that you can control it. This admission can be difficult for most, yet once done it is a weight lifted off your shoulders. It means opening your eyes not only to your addiction but to the chaos it has caused in your life.

Taking the first step is easier than you may imagine. If you are reading this book for yourself, or if you have turned to anyone for help, you have already started to do this. Having done it, please don't let some well-meaning person convince you that you need to be tough and fight it. You have probably already been fighting it for years without success. It is time to admit that your addiction is a formidable foe.

STEP TWO

Having taken the first step, it is time to move to the second. **"Came to believe that a power greater than ourselves could** restore us to sanity." This step may come as a relief to you. First of all, it gives you hope that help is available. Secondly, it tells you more than that you will simply stop drinking. If you have been afraid that some of your thoughts or deeds were odd, this step allows you to accept that you can return to normal. The phrase "power greater than ourselves" troubles some. Those with religious beliefs may immediately interpret this as meaning God. This interpretation is acceptable, but this step works equally well for the atheist who chooses to believe in the power of the group or the power of the process. The important thing is to recognize that this healing does not come from within. It requires you to accept that, somewhere in this universe there is some power greater than yourself. It also promises that you are important enough for this power to help you.

(As you read this chapter, addict or not, try to actually do these steps yourself. They can be powerful.)

STEP THREE

The third step definitely sounds religious. **"Made a decision to turn our will and our lives over to the care of God as we understood Him."** God is an acceptable concept to most Americans, but not to all. This step is carefully worded, with the phrase *"as we understood Him"* broadening it to anyone with a personal concept of God. Whether your concept of a Higher Power in the universe is a religious one or a philosophical one, this wording should not be offensive. Many atheists can agree that there are forces in the universe greater than that of an individual human being. For those of you who are uneasy when others mention a deity, substitution of the term "higher power" for the word God may help you to understand the content of the message.

The important part of the third step is not what you choose to call your higher power. The important part is the "decision to turn our will and our lives over." This is truly the process of surrender of self-will and independence. In exchange, you gain trust and interdependence. This is not surrender to your enemy. In the first step, you recognized that the enemy was addiction. In the third step you are now putting your future in the hands of a powerful and trusted ally. This alliance gives you the guidance and strength you have needed all along. By accepting it, you recognize that many good things can happen as a result of acceptance of events and decisions that may not have been entirely of your making. Many AA members call this "turning it over."

▪▪

These first three steps have a common theme. Taken together, they allow you to admit that you have an illness, that you are ready to accept help and that you are willing to accept the help that is offered. This seems like such a simple process, yet it is often the barrier to getting well. Turning it over does not imply being passive. You now have to begin to work on recovery. You must work without making excuses or giving up because you can not see the end point. If you are religious you may find it easier to turn it over to God. If you choose to turn it over to another higher power, trust the steps and those clean and sober people around you that you have come to trust. Whether it is in God or in your fellow humans, in these first three steps you must develop faith and trust. Looking around at the people who have been clean and sober for many years, you must accept that you are as good as they are. You must believe that you too can achieve the peace that they have found in sobriety.

These are the steps of early recovery. Some people who only get this far will feel good for a few months, perhaps longer. However, these first three steps are only the beginning. When you take the steps, do not hesitate. The next six steps on this path are better than the first three. Steps four through nine are the middle steps of recovery. These do not deal with alcoholism or addiction. These are concerned with living. If you fail to change how you deal with life, you will return to being unhappy with the world around you. It is you, not the world who must change if the world is to be a different place for you. The time to change is when you are basking in the comfortable glow of early recovery. However, it is at precisely this time that you may feel content and not understand why it is necessary to do more.

If you deceive yourself that it can work in any other way, disappointment, despair and inevitably relapse to your addiction will follow. Think of yourself as the pioneer who arrives in a new land in the warmth of summer. You must begin to build your shelter now, for you recognize that the cold winds of winter will eventually arrive. These middle steps of recovery will become your shelter from the unexpected but inevitable storms. Begin them now and you will be secure in your recovery.

STEP FOUR

Step Four sounds formidable: **"Made a searching and fearless moral inventory of ourselves."** Many of you who try these steps will hesitate here. Don't pause now! Think of entering a swimming pool when the water is cool. If you stand on the edge and test the water with your toe, the pool will not warm up. As you procrastinate, it will intimidate you and seem worse than it is. Jump in and enjoy your swim and you will find it is quite comfortable. Step Four does not ask you to be a perfect person. It does ask you to find your faults and honestly describe them. Any complete accounting lists assets as well as liabilities, accounts receivable as well as accounts payable. Some of you may have difficulty finding the faults in yourself. Others may see only the faults and not the strengths. Each of you has both. No one can honestly take this step and not find faults. No one cannot find strengths.

This fourth step may require help. Some of you will be able to take a pencil and paper and do this in hours or days. Others, who are in treatment may find that the exercises of treatment give you the framework for this. Those of you who are getting individual professional help will often be able to draw upon what you have discovered about yourself.

You may not feel ready. The idea of a searching and fearless inventory of yourself seems impossible, almost ludicrous. You are absolutely right. Do it anyway.

Earlier, I suggested that you do each step in order and to the best of your ability at that moment, but do not be a perfectionist. Nowhere is this more important than now, at the Fourth Step. It is normal for your vision of yourself to change as you recover physically, mentally and spiritually. You can repeat these steps if new insights come to you later. Now you must work these steps for today.

STEP FIVE

Step Five **"Admitted to God, to ourselves, and to another human being the exact nature of our wrongs"** can now be done. Most people find that while they were completing Step Four they were already admitting these wrongs to themselves and to the higher power of their understanding. Completion of Step Five requires discussion with another person. It should be with a person who understands why you are doing this. If you have an AA or NA sponsor, this is the ideal person to trust to listen. If you are seeing a psychologist or psychiatrist, particularly one who understands the self-help process, use her. The only caution is to use an individual, do not use the group for this Fifth Step. "Another human being" does not mean all humanity. The group is often trusted with many secrets but there are other personal items that you can only frankly discuss with a single individual.

As you take this Fifth Step, you will begin to feel a burden lifted. The Fourth Step was painful, for you identified some things you were not proud of. The Fifth Step allows you to air out this dirty linen which was previously mildewing in a lonely dark closet of your mind. This Fifth Step allows you to share those secrets and lose the loneliness they created. The next steps provide more relief.

STEP SIX

Step Six **"Were entirely ready to have God remove all these defects of character"** does not explain how. It merely asks that since you have acknowledged ownership of the problems you also acknowledge the need for help in correcting them. You have already said "This is my dirty linen" and now you agree that you would prefer if it were cleaned.

STEP SEVEN

"Humbly asked Him to remove our shortcomings" tells you how to begin. A simple request or prayer is enough, whether it is directed to God or another personal higher power.

STEP EIGHT

These last two steps were quick and easy, but not complete. Your higher power needs your help. Now that you have expressed a willingness to change and asked for help, you must do your share. The Eighth Step **"Made a list of all persons we had harmed, and became willing to make amends to them all"** is a major turning point, but one you will be able to do and will actually be anticipating. In Step Four, you acknowledged much. Step Eight asks you to be ready to make up for the harm you have caused. Now, the atheist in you can come out, for here prayer will not work. God can not work alone. You must be willing to take responsibility for your own actions.

This also is a focusing step. Be clear about this. Recognize those you genuinely have harmed. That list is long enough. Do not take personal responsibility for the earthquakes in California nor the droughts in Africa. Those items are on God's list. Stick to your list, it is the one you own. In the past, writing a check (or even personally volunteering) for earthquake or famine relief may have seemed easier than making amends to those close to you. In taking this Eighth Step you have focused on accepting responsibility for your own actions.

STEP NINE

The Ninth Step **"Made direct amends to such people whenever possible, except when to do so would injure them or others"** completes the action started in the Eighth Step. They are separated for good reason. A positive act of "making amends" to right a prior wrong may not always be possible. You have taken full responsibility for identifying all those you have harmed in Step Eight even though you may not be able to make amends to them all. There may be valid reasons that you cannot right every wrong. This Ninth Step should be done to the best of your ability at the moment. Taking this action does not erase what wrong you may have done, but when you have done it correctly, you will know that there is no more you can do and you can move on with your life.

There will be times that attempting to repay a debt or confess a wrong would do great harm to another person. If that is the case, don't do it. There is no reason an innocent person should be further harmed by your need to lift this burden of guilt and shame. There will be other times that a victim of your mistreatment cannot be reached. Perhaps they cannot be identified or have moved or died. There are many creative and genuine ways to make amends. You may wish to write a lengthy letter of apology and burn it, so that the spirit of your apology may symbolically reach them. You may wish to devote your time and energy to helping others who have been wronged in similar circumstances.

However you proceed on Step Nine, this is not a *pro forma* step. The response you will receive from some will startle you, because it will be well received. Others will not accept your gesture, whether it is a simple apology or includes substantial restitution. This is natural, for there may be mistrust or bitterness that is not easily erased. You will find that if you have sincerely and honestly done all that is within your power to do, your burden has been lightened. It is your responsibility to make a sincere act of contrition to another person. Whether or not it can or will be accepted is not within your control.

Having completed Steps Four through Nine, you are through the middle steps of recovery. None of these steps mentioned alcohol or drugs. In your individual inventory, you may have included some or many things related to your addiction, but these steps related to all aspects of your life.

Now it is time to move out of the past and on to the present day. The final three steps are the maintenance steps of any twelve step program. At the completion of the Ninth Step, you felt very good. Maintaining that good feeling will require you to dedicate your life to a new way of living. This new life, embodied in these maintenance steps, is remarkably easy, provided you have thoroughly carried out the first nine steps.

STEP TEN

The Tenth Step **"Continued to take personal inventory and when we were wrong promptly admitted it"** is remarkably simple. If you are able to do this at least once a day, you will not backslide. If you do not, you will gradually regain the burden of an accumulation of old resentments and fears that guide your current life. The humility of admitting a mistake promptly prevents the complications and convolutions that occur when we try to justify or excuse our own errors. The people you deal with may be disarmed by this simple honesty. Their response will be rewarding.

STEP ELEVEN

The Eleventh Step **"Sought through prayer and meditation to improve our conscious contact with God *as we understood Him*, praying only for knowledge of His will for us and the power to carry that out"** bring to the follower of a twelve-step path the wisdom of the ages. Prayer is not a greedy call to a higher power to ask for more. Instead, prayer and meditation mean a recognition of and gratitude for the blessings of life, including the gift of your own recovery. Those of you who choose to use a spiritual defini-tion of a higher power will find this concept embodied in the following eleventh century prayer, which has been attributed to Saint Francis of Assisi:

> "Lord, make me an instrument of your peace!
> Where there is hatred–let me sow love
> Where there is injury–pardon
> Where there is doubt–faith
> Where there is despair–hope
> Where there is darkness—light
> Where there is sadness–joy.
> ...Grant that I may not so much seek
> To be consoled–as to console
> To be understood–as to understand
> To be loved–as to love,
> For it is in giving–that we receive;
> And it is in pardoning–that we are pardoned..."

The Third Step was the one in which you acknowledged that you had gotten lost being in the drivers seat, trying to steer an uncharted course. You had said you were willing to turn control over to another. This Eleventh Step is a reminder that now that your life is on course, you must continue to trust the pilot.

The Eleventh Step is simple. Despite the reference to a saint, I do not personally know anyone who has taken this step and immediately adorned either a nun's or a monk's habit. This con-cept of following the right path is found in both the Old and New Testaments, but is not unique to religion nor to solely western beliefs. Buddhists believe that you will follow "The Good Way of Behavior" if you remove all greed, anger and false judgement from your mind. Even in the science fiction world of *Star Wars* the novice knight learns that he intuitively makes the correct choices only when he allows "The Force" to be with him.

STEP TWELVE

The Twelfth Step **"Having had a spiritual awakening as a result of these steps, we tried to carry this message to alcoholics, and to practice these principles in all our affairs"** closes the cir-cle. It has two distinct parts. In carrying it out, you now recognize that to stay sober, you must live a program of sobriety in all your affairs. Sobriety involves far more than the end of your addiction, for it has given you a whole new way of living. Carrying the message to alcoholics requires you to explain your personal experience to another. Each time you do this, it reminds you of what you were like and how you have changed. It helps prevent your own relapse by noting the contrast between who you are today and the still suffering person who resembles the you of only a few months or years before.

▪

It should be obvious that if these steps are done in order, you must complete one through eleven before attempting twelve. Such obvious logic has not stopped a few who hold on to the grandiose logic of their drinking days. Please be sure you have actually taken these steps, not merely read them, before you attempt to use this last step and share your experience with another. They will tell you in AA or NA "You can't give away what you don't have." Conversely, if you wish to follow an experienced guide down this Twelve-Step Path, do not ask a novice. All of the twelve-step groups suggest that a newcomer ask an experienced member to act as a sponsor and give them any guidance they request. Be sure you ask someone who has actually followed this path. "Stick with the winners" is the advice you may have heard at a meeting. It is good advice and the winners are usually easy to spot.

Remembering all of these twelve steps during your first sober weeks can be difficult. If you are facing a hard decision and forget what you are supposed to do, remember the "Serenity Prayer" quoted by many twelve-step group members.

"God, grant me
the **Serenity** to accept the things I cannot change,
the **Courage** to change the things I can and
the **Wisdom** to know the difference."

12
OTHER PATHS TO RECOVERY

In Chapter Ten I described some of the most common paths to recovery. Other paths have been followed; other techniques have been tried. Some are helpful, some work poorly. This chapter provides you some idea of what these other paths offer. As a friend or relative trying to help a suffering addict find the best route to recovery, you have the choice of using one of these alternative paths. Knowing what each is and where it may lead should aid you in deciding what is most appropriate.

These alternate paths include:

> Simple Abstinence
> Acupuncture (and it's variations)
> Aversion Therapy
> Brain Wave Training
> Transcendental Meditation®
> Aversive and Blocking Drugs
> Religious Approaches
> Charismatic Groups
> Educational Approaches
> Maintenance Therapy
> Therapeutic Communities

Simple Abstinence is often overlooked as a legitimate choice for many people. In earlier chapters, much was said about "white knuckle sobriety" and "undiagnosed alcoholism in remission." Many alcoholics and other addicts have tried simply abstaining from any use of alcohol or addictive drugs, only to fail many times. These people who have failed can and do eventually recover with the help of a twelve-step group or professional treatment or both.

What of the people who try and **do not fail**? They are never seen in treatment centers and so many experts do not realize that they exist. Recently, I was interviewed on a talk show. The station had asked me to talk about addiction. I had not met Hal, the host of the program, before that day. Fifteen minutes before going on the air we were alone in the studio discussing the subject when he suddenly said "I don't tell anyone this but I was addicted to drugs." Hal explained to me how, in his twenties, he had realized that he had become a drug addict. He made a decision to quit and turn his life around. He was dating a woman who supported that decision. They are now happily married and he has a successful career. Hal has not used alcohol or drugs for over ten years. I questioned him regarding treatment and self-help groups and found he had used neither. Although he was knowledgeable regarding addiction through his own experience, he had no knowledge of any formal principles of recovery. Yet, Hal was practicing an excellent program of personal recovery.

I have met many men and women like Hal. Not knowing how impossible it is to quit without help, they simply did it and were successful. Some people who were addicted have been successful quitting on their own for as long as there have been addictive drugs.

Are these people **real** alcoholics or addicts, if they can quit on their own? Of course they are. Look at how many people addicted to the drug nicotine quit smoking on their own. We cannot judge whether someone was "really addicted" because they can quit without help. Simple abstinence can and does work for some people. If someone can quit on his own, let him. There is nothing magical about recovery programs.

The people who need help the most cannot practice simple abstinence. If someone attempts to remain abstinent without help and finds he cannot, that is a solid reason to go to AA or a treatment program. If someone is abstinent and finds she is miserable, that too is reason to go beyond simple abstinence. I have seen people who had quit without help enter a treatment program or seek the help of a twelve-step group years after quitting. They went from white-knuckled abstinence to a full program of recovery years after the last drink or drug use.

■■

Acupuncture, an Oriental technique, uses needles placed in the skin to block the sensation of pain. The placement of these needles follows ancient traditions that modern science has been unable to explain. Acupuncture may work by setting up signals that block specific gateways for pain in the nervous system. A number of practitioners of acupuncture claim that it has worked to cure addiction. The limited research done on acupuncture does not substantiate such broad claims. On the other hand, it has been repeatedly demonstrated that for some people it can relieve the discomfort of withdrawal and reduce cravings. I have witnessed it being used effectively to reduce anxiety and cravings for drugs in conjunction with more conventional medical detoxification. It impressed me to see the rapid improvement in symptoms. Few physicians skilled in addiction treatment are trained to use acupuncture. If you happen to receive treatment from such a person, acupuncture may prove a useful aid in recovery. These experts may be distinguished by the fact they will not make outlandish claims for the technique. Instead, they may offer it as one more technique to bolster an effective recovery program. Claims for cures for addiction that rely solely on *any* one technique should be regarded skeptically.

There is a variation of such signal blocking that bears watching. When western medicine realized that acupuncture did work to block some types of pain, modern technology created a western version of signal blocking. This western method of pain relief is used to allow physicians to help many patients without embracing Oriental systems of philosophy or belief. That pain relief method is called Trans-Cutaneous Nerve Stimulation, or T.E.N.S. Jim, the veteran with the chronic pain, was finally given the benefit of T.E.N.S. to help relieve his pain and to replace the addictive medicines that had harmed him so much.

T.E.N.S. uses a small box containing electronic circuits to send a high frequency electrical signal to wires attached to a patient's skin. This special signal is supposed to offer blocking through the same type of counter stimulation that makes acupuncture work. Some physicians have suggested that if acupuncture helps in addictions, perhaps T.E.N.S. could also help. Since T.E.N.S. is a medical device requiring a doctor's prescription, the United States Food and Drug Administration (FDA) regulates unproven claims by manufacturers or distributors. Recent research has not demonstrated the effectiveness of this technique. If you encounter this therapy, be aware that it is an experimental treatment. As with acupuncture, if it does work, its value is the reduction of discomfort and craving, used in conjunction with more conventional treatment.

Alpha-theta brain wave training is an advanced form of

biofeedback. Primarily an advanced relaxation technique, it uses electronic monitoring to assist in teaching how to reach the equivalent of a deep meditative state. Meditation itself is not a new technique, both Eastern and Western religions have practiced it for thousands of years. The Eleventh Step of Alcoholics Anonymous has always suggested the use of meditation. Whether alpha-theta training proves that it is an improved way reach a meditative state remains to be seen. It is costly, with the few psychologists offering it charging several thousand dollars for a complete course of treatment. The initial research done was very promising but not rigorously controlled. Whether it helps the recovering alcoholic remains to be determined. It is completely compatible with conventional treatment, as long as its appropriate place is as an adjunct, to strengthen conventional programs.

Transcendental Meditation (TM)® is often thought of as a 1960's "New Age" fad and was proposed at that time as a "cure" for addiction. No critical research was done and, as our culture changed, it faded from view. Recently, it has been revived with some very solid research (using severe hardcore alcoholics) to demonstrate that it is a useful technique. TM is a specific, non-religious variation of Eastern meditation. Taught in a simple but highly structured way, it requires no equipment and is relatively inexpensive. Based upon this new research, I expect to see new interest in using this method as an adjunct to conventional treatment.

Aversion Therapy is an old and controversial technique based upon principles of behavioral psychology. In its present form in the United States it is usually conducted in an inpatient setting. It is more likely to be encountered on the West Coast than on the East Coast, where its use is rare. Aversion therapy is not pleasant. It consists of giving a patient an unpleasant experience in association with their favorite drug. As an example, a patient may be given a drink of bourbon whiskey at the same time he is given a painful electric shock or chemically forced to vomit.

Addictions are very complex. Aversion therapy may be useful in a purely behavioral aspect, but that is only one part of addiction. In the past, aversion therapy has been tried as the mainstay of treatment.

One man traveled to California for such treatment. He was not given any other program to work. He maintained abstinence for a year, then began drinking again. He returned to California for further treatment. On the way home, he got drunk at the airport bar. He had discovered that he cringed at the taste or smell of bourbon, so he switched to vodka. Fortunately, he recovered later with a more conventional program.

These past problems do not mean that aversion therapy has no value. Today, those few institutions that offer it use it in conjunction with a more traditional program. Used in this manner, it may be of value to some people who have been difficult to treat. Remember Lisa and Jane? Despite working a good recovery program, they still had cravings when they saw objects that had been associated with cocaine use. This is a common problem, rooted in the strong psychological reward of cocaine, crack and other stimulants. In the future, if the two sides in this controversy could communicate more, perhaps there will be an acceptable niche for this therapy. In spite of its bad history, it may prove a useful tool in the future.

Aversive drugs and blocking drugs are two interesting but different categories of treatment that many physicians believe have a useful place in therapy. In the United States, disulfiram (also commonly known by its trade name, Antabuse®) is a drug often used as an aid to help people recover from alcoholism. If you take disulfiram and you drink, you get sick. If you drink a lot, you get very sick. Most people cannot get beyond their first drink without getting violently ill. Disulfiram works because of the way the body breaks alcohol down to eliminate it. One of the chemicals that it becomes, acetaldehyde, is very toxic. Normally, chemical reactions in the body quickly convert this acetaldehyde to another chemical. Disulfiram blocks this from happening. Instead, within minutes after drinking alcohol, this toxic chemical builds up in the bloodstream. A headache, vomiting, sweating, fainting and other unpleasant symptoms quickly replace any good feeling that may have accompanied that first drink.

When this drug first was introduced, it was used indiscriminately. People who had little desire to remain abstinent were encouraged to take it. There were bad results. Some people drank anyway and became very ill. Others, lacking any other program of recovery, simply stopped taking disulfiram first and went back to drinking. Many physicians stopped using it, feeling it was of little value.

Today, it is used in a different way. People who are motivated and receiving treatment often ask to be given this medication. It has no psychoactive effect. It does nothing unless someone drinks alcohol. Some people relapse in recovery because of what they claim is impulsive behavior. No sane person taking disulfiram will drink impulsively. Instead, he or she will stop taking the drug and wait the several days to two weeks that it takes them to return to normal. During these two weeks, people in treatment or self-help groups will have time to reconsider their action before a relapse can take place. Patients who want this drug have to be warned of its risks and educated about its use. The physician prescribing the drug must decide whether any potential risk of the medication is outweighed by the potential risk of the patient returning to drinking.

Despite its earlier failures in poorly motivated patients, it remains useful in selective cases where motivation is questionable. An alcoholic who needs to demonstrate sobriety to a spouse, an employer or a parole officer may choose to take disulfiram. Even though the sincerity may be questionable, with time, a positive feeling about sobriety often results. Disulfiram is of no value if the patient is likely to use another addictive drug. Disulfiram is only effective against impulsive use of alcohol.

Another type of drug is also useful–in certain limited cases. This is the blocking drug introduced a few years ago in the United States called naltrexone (trade name Trexan®). Naltrexone blocks narcotics. If it is taken regularly, a person who injects heroin or any similar opiate will feel nothing. It works by blocking the opiate receptors in the brain. The theory is that if an addict knows that he or she will not get high, that will be enough to stop their use. In practice, the original experiments were dismal failures. Chemical blockade did not stop the desire to use.

Now, naltrexone is used in a very different way. Like disulfiram, it works best in motivated people. Addicts who have been treated and want to stay drug free may ask for it as an aid to their program of recovery. If they suddenly decide to stop taking it, that act is a strong signal to get to an NA meeting or talk to a counselor. They are buying time and avoiding the risk of using impulsively.

Naltrexone probably has no value except in the treatment of opiate addiction. One drawback is that it also blocks the brain's natural opiates. This means that if you hurt yourself, your body cannot use its natural system to moderate the pain. Some people also report that they don't feel quite as good when they take the drug. Joggers report that they do not feel their natural "runners high." These changes are probably the result of its action of blocking natural opiates. Most people taking the drug accept these as minor drawbacks, compared to the risk of using again.

There has been some recent publicity claiming Naltrexone worked for alcoholics. The actual research results do not support this claim, because the "cured" alcoholics were still drinking. Unless further research demonstrates otherwise, the only role for Naltrexone is treating heroin and other opiate addictions.

In 1995, a major marketing campaign was kicked off by the makers of naltrexone. Newspapers and television broadcasts featured the startling news that there was a new breakthrough in alcoholism treatment. The director of the National Institute of Alcoholism and Alcohol Abuse even sent out a letter to professionals (at taxpayer expense) announcing this wondrous development. Professionals were curious as to what this could be, since scientists and physicians usually try to keep track of research that might benefit their patients.

This startling "new" development proved to be a disappointment. DuPont® had increased the price of naltrexone, renamed it Revia® and received government approval to advertise and market it as useful in helping alcoholics achieve abstinence. Was there a new and startling development that no one had seen before? No, only a change in the Federal government's use of the English language. The supporting research for this new development was research that had been published three years earlier. It showed a slight difference in drinking patterns between a group getting this medication and a group who did not.

It did not show any difference in abstinence, if we all use the common English language meaning of that term. The researchers involved chose to define abstinence as not showing up to the appointment highly intoxicated, not admitting to drinking on more than four out of seven days, and not admitting to drinking five or more drinks at one sitting. In other words, the average person could become legally intoxicated on four days of each week and still be doing fine under this definition! Most families of alcoholics would be very disappointed at this behavior. Most judges, police officers and families of victims of intoxicated drivers would not be pleased with this loose definition of a "cure."

This research is of value to scientists exploring how the brain regulates drinking behavior but of questionable, practical value. Experienced physicians must always put the health and safety of their patients first. This means being skeptical and attempting to learn all the facts before accepting any claims of a miraculous cure. The actual research containing the standards used was published in November

1992 by Doctor Volpicelli in the *Archives of General Psychiatry* (page 877). Most of the papers and press releases since that time have quoted his results without bothering to disclose the definitions used. If your physician recommends this treatment, be sure he or she has seen the actual research, not just a press release or a salesman's brochure!

Religious approaches to sobriety are as old as the recorded use of alcohol and other addictive drugs. Many addicted people have at some time taken an interest in an organized religious group without any beneficial change. Some who had turned to religion and not found the answer they sought became bitter towards religious groups.

Despite these failures some people do become clean and sober through a religious experience. Many religious organizations remain interested in "saving" addicts and alcoholics. Alcoholics Anonymous exists only because Doctor Carl Jung, one of the world's great psychiatrists, told a wealthy American patient he had treated that he was beyond his help. Roland H., the alcoholic patient, was told that some alcoholics who were beyond the help of psychiatry had found help in religion. Roland did become sober through a religious experience. He in turn carried this message to another suffering alcoholic–Edwin Thatcher, who in turn carried it to Bill Wilson–who went on to become one of the founders of Alcoholics Anonymous.

Alcoholics Anonymous broadened the recovery program practiced by Bill Wilson by removing the ties to organized religion. This enabled many people to benefit from AA who could not have benefitted from a religious program. Yet, without the religious conversions of Edwin Thatcher and Bill Wilson, none of this would have taken place.

Today, many respectable religious organizations such as the Salvation Army continue to devote a large part of their time and energy to helping the suffering alcoholic and addict. However, this work is done with the recognition of the benefits of both AA and treatment programs. Most religious organizations see their efforts as complementing other tools of recovery and support. No single religious group has a monopoly on recovery, but those that seem to have the most attraction are those with a message that reaches out to the non-believer. These groups seem to have a simple, positive and spiritually uplifting message regarding the relationship between God and man. Such a message can be found in common among groups that seem to be as diverse as Protestant

Fundamental Christians and Orthodox Hasidic Jews.

Those that take a religious path to recovery often make one common error. Religion, by itself, does not provide a sufficient answer for continued sobriety for most people. This is true even for people who seem to do quite well at first. Edwin Thatcher, the man whose religious conversion brought sobriety to Bill Wilson, died tragically after returning to drinking. Religious groups do not provide the proper framework to discuss feelings that result from the physical aspect of addiction. The High-Low Trap can cause powerful cravings for a drink or a drug. A person who has undergone a religious conversion can still need to go to an AA meeting to talk about dreaming about drinking or to an NA meeting to talk about a cocaine craving. Religious groups experienced in dealing with recovering people recognize this and will encourage simultaneous participation in a self-help group or treatment program.

Charismatic Groups seem to pop up every few years in our culture, offering a "cure" for addictions. These take many forms. Their one common feature is a strong belief in the teaching of one central figure. Another name for such groups is "cults."

The self-help groups have, so far, avoided becoming cults. Although their founders are admired, they are very human. The self-help movement relies heavily on what it calls "the group conscience." In this way, there is no central authority figure to run amok.

Cults, on the other hand, often run amok. The greatest example is Synanon. This organization was founded in the 1950s to help the recovering drug addict. It has helped some people and many effective treatment programs were started by grateful addicts who first got clean in Synanon. Unfortunately, the parent organization was focused on one individual and as the organization grew, its leader underwent profound changes. As he changed so did the program, yet the program continued to control the lives of its adherents.

By the 1970s, Synanon had lost all effectiveness and was torn by scandal. Not only did it no longer help the addict, its members were not expected to remain clean and sober.

Other cults are more subtle. Some believe in novel religions, others are built around single ideas. Many are thinly disguised profit-making organizations. They always seem to evolve around a single individual and demand a high degree of control over the life and finances of the members. Joining such a cult is dangerous for any addict. Often, an addicted newcomer will be able to remain free of alcohol and drugs in the sheltered environment of the cult community. However, unlike the person joining a self-help group or an established treatment program, the person in the cult does not experience personal growth and learn to become a recovering person in a normal world. Instead, the member of a cult may behave like the trapped victim of an abusive relationship. The longer the relationship goes on, the greater the loss of self-esteem and the more difficult it becomes to leave. The addict looking for an emotional shelter may be lured by the outside appearance of a cult. Looking in from the outside, the path into a cult may at first appear to lead to recovery. The addict entering a cult is similar to a person following a blind path into a maze, a path that can seem to lead to recovery but instead leads to bewilderment and isolation.

The cults are useful in one way. They may represent a response to a need not being dealt with by established groups or institutions. The bizarre behavior of the cults should make the mainstream programs and institutions realize that there are people who need something that the mainstream is not dealing with.

Educational approaches can mean many things. In this discussion, I am talking about treatment programs that primarily educate patients. Most good treatment programs do some education, but that is just part of the process. Some programs limit themselves to education and do little counseling or group therapy. These may prove useful to the frightened social drinker who has been found guilty of driving while intoxicated (DWI) and required to go into treatment. The person who is already addicted is less likely to benefit. Although the alcoholic or addict may leave such a program knowing much more than when he or she started, this is rarely enough to cause a change in behavior. These programs are popular with some agencies because they can "treat" large numbers of people cheaply and often be paid well for this.

Counseling, both group and individual, is much harder than education. The presence of educational programs as a substitute for treatment, differs based upon state regulations and local custom. They are a blind path for anyone interested in recovering from addiction. If there are such programs in your city, you will have to recognize them in order to avoid them or the opportunity to get better may be lost.

Recognizing these non-treatment programs is comparatively easy. They will avoid confronting people who need help. Instead, they offer a faster, easier way for those who need to regain their driving privileges or meet other requirements to demonstrate that they have been "treated." Some will routinely do rapid evaluations in order to produce reports that someone is not addicted despite multiple alcohol related driving offenses. Others will offer group therapy that amounts to little more than showing traffic safety films to a large audience. A few may offer solely individual counseling for those people who state that they know they are not alcoholic and resent having to attend groups with those who are alcoholic or addicted.

In each case, these programs exist primarily to meet a consumer demand. They short-circuit the efforts of government and citizens groups to break the cycle of the addicted driver. If you are trying to help a relative or friend locate a good treatment program, call the program first. Ask questions as if you are a driver who has lost his or her license and who wants to get it back rapidly. If you receive sympathetic answers and an indication that your needs will be accommodated, this is not a program to recommend to a friend.

Maintenance therapy takes several forms, but the underlying principle is the same. In contrast to programs that stress abstinence, maintenance therapy programs stress that abstinence is an unrealistic goal for some people. Much of such therapy involves issues of control. For alcoholics, this means teaching techniques of controlled drinking rather then stressing abstinence. Since it is perfectly natural for an alcoholic to drink, experiments with these programs can report short-term "success." Unfortunately, when long-term follow-up is done, some of these "successes" are dead, and others are drinking alcoholically again. There seems to be a very strong intuitive appeal to these programs. Many addicted people enter treatment hoping to find a way to go "back" to social drinking or "moderate drug use." Most find out, as Lisa described, that once a cucumber has been pickled, it never becomes a cucumber again.

Another subtle form of maintenance therapy is providing the alcoholic with benzodiazepine tranquilizers. Although this is different from the drug alcohol, we have seen that it can effect the brain at many of the same points. The alcoholic taking benzodiazepines never truly learns what it feels like to be alcohol free. The result, all too often, is that the alcoholic begins to drink again, frequently on top of the tranquilizer. In either of these two forms of treatment, the risks are high and the rewards are few. The proba-

144 ··   ADDICTION: The High-Low Trap

bility of achieving a stable, successful outcome is low, and the benefits, if achieved, are dubious. On the other hand, the probability of failure is extremely high and the risks include continued suffering and death. Leading an alcoholic down this path is a cruel and deceiving hoax for most.

The third form of maintenance therapy, methadone maintenance, is the most controversial. Methadone maintenance has been praised as the salvation of the hopeless and incurable heroin addict. It has equally been damned as a cruel hoax, trapping thousands who could otherwise recover deeper into addiction. The truth is somewhere between these two extremes. When all the claims and hysteria are swept away, methadone maintenance is no panacea. It is to the heroin addict what tranquilizer use or controlled drinking is to the alcoholic.

Methadone is swallowed. Once in the body, it lasts for many days. Because of this, the high achieved is different than the heroin addict gets by shooting up. Remember the difference discussed earlier between the sports car and the heavy truck? Both may get the driver to the same cruising speed, but the sports car driver feels the acceleration that the truck driver does not. So it is with methadone.

Methadone is an opiate, a narcotic. In fact, methadone is quite an effective narcotic in some cases of pain control. Because of its effectiveness and long lasting nature, it has been used at times for for someone who is dying. For a patient dying of the late stages of a painful illness, this can be a blessing.

Any claims that methadone is not a narcotic are wrong. Methadone has a "street value." It is sometimes traded and sold illegally on the street. There are opiate addicts who first got hooked on narcotics using street methadone before graduating to heroin.

Despite this, methadone programs have been of value to society. Some addicts have gotten their lives together while on methadone. Others have used methadone temporarily, as a respite from using street drugs, and as a step before becoming drug free. The use of methadone evolved in this country through programs related to the criminal justice system. Because of the relationship between narcotics and criminal behavior, methadone was once considered an anti-crime measure. Early methadone treatment programs considered themselves successful if their patients reported committing crimes on fewer days than before. The government encouraged this attitude, and many methadone programs became chemical warehouses–a place to put people in order to cut down on street crime.

Addicts who come into a center every day for their legal methadone may be committing fewer crimes, but if they receive no further treatment, they are not getting better. Most addicts can get better, if given a chance. Like other addicts, many heroin users in recovery return to school, get jobs and become productive citizens. This recovery has happened too often to tolerate the old stereotypes of the addict and deny them further treatment.

Some methadone programs encourage recovery. Addicts are given amounts of methadone that correspond to their heroin addiction. They receive counseling and are encouraged to become drug-free. These programs may be less able to control the person who is not interested in recovery, but those that want help can and do benefit.

Other methadone programs unfortunately are chemical prisons. Addicts in this second type of program are warehoused. They may actually be required to take larger doses of methadone than the amount of heroin they were using on the street. By becoming addicted to extremely high, nearly lethal doses of methadone, they can never leave the program, but they are unlikely to steal or commit prostitution to obtain heroin. Their brains are so saturated with methadone that if they shot up with heroin they could die but would not feel a "high." Since these patients receive little counseling and there is no emphasis on becoming drug-free, other non-narcotic drugs such as cocaine and alcohol often continue to be used by these unfortunate people. Unfortunately, many will go on to develop another addiction.

Methadone maintenance therapy is a tool. Used properly, it is useful for a phase in the treatment of some narcotic addicts. Used as a political and social tool to clear cities of junkies, it can enslave some addicts in a permanent cycle of addiction, crime and poverty. Take the time to visit the program you are interested in before starting a friend on this path. Look around at the patients visiting the program. Talk to them, if you can. Would you feel comfortable if they were your neighbors? Are they laughing, smiling and talking about having a job or being back in school? Often, these simple judgments can help you determine whether a program is one of recovery or one of social convenience.

Therapeutic communities offer another, very useful form of treatment. A therapeutic community is a drug-free residential treatment program that may often last for a year or longer. This extended treatment is very structured. A criticism of conventional rehabilitation programs is that they offer the most help to people who want to hold onto or regain some structure in their life. Adolescents and adults who became addicted early in life need more than this. Since they are not returning to their old lives before addiction, but instead are learning the skills of living as drug-free young adults, some counselors refer to this as "habilitation" instead of rehabilitation. Therapeutic communities have always offered this needed structure. The expense of this long-term care has prevented these programs from becoming very common.

Unfortunately, the good being done by therapeutic communities has often been overlooked in disputes about doctrine. The early therapeutic communities often had strong ties to charismatic programs–such as Synanon. Some programs emphasize behavioral psychology, at the expense of all other aspects of treatment. These approaches were useful to many people who were not helped by other programs. This rigidity, while useful for some, was a barrier for others. Additionally, some programs did not recognize the addicts' need for abstinence from all drugs, including alcohol. Finally, the bad reputation of a few programs overshadowed the good of other well-established ones.

Today, therapeutic communities such as Daytop Village and Phoenix House are an established and recognized part of the choices available in treatment. They have evolved and grown, just as the more conventional programs have. The therapeutic community movement has absorbed many concepts from other programs. Conversely, other programs, particularly those treating adolescents, have absorbed valuable concepts from the therapeutic community movement. Today, the therapeutic community should not be viewed as offering an opposing philosophy of treatment. It is an established and well-marked path to recovery for some who require its structure and long-term view. It should be considered one more option on a continuing scale of useful treatment choices.

This chapter has reviewed a number of alternative paths to recovery. Some of these paths are blind alleys leading nowhere. Others are useful and for some may be the only path to recovery. If you must lead a friend to a program and set their feet on the best path, be cautious. If a path is well trodden, if many people have walked that path before, seek them out. Look for success, because some paths lead to failure and failure in recovery may lead to death.

13
AVOIDING RELAPSE

▬▬▬▬

▬▬Relapse prevention is the underlying reason for treatment. Stopping drinking or drug use is only the first step in recovery. Detoxification programs help a person stop, but this is never enough. Once an addicted man or woman is alcohol and drug-free, going back to using, to any degree, is a relapse. Therefore, relapse prevention should not be treated as a separate issue, but must be an integral part of any recovery program.

Relapse is a natural part of addiction but it does not have to be a natural part of recovery. Relapse is such an integral part of addiction that it is often used in the definition of the addiction. That is too pessimistic a viewpoint. Addiction is a tough disease to deal with, and many will relapse one or more times before their recovery becomes permanent. On the other hand, many people successfully remain abstinent without ever having a relapse.

It is important that a recovering person and those around him or her understand relapse. Many can be prevented. If a relapse does occur, it does not necessarily mean that treatment has failed. Instead, it can point the way to needed improvements in a person's program of recovery. However, it needs to be immediately recognized and treated.

Relapses occur in different ways. I would like to separate people who relapse into two groups. There are people who have never truly had any recovery and those who had it and lost it. Looking at the time from their last drink or drug use these two groups may appear to be the same, but clinically the difference is like day and night.

This first group never had recovery, only abstinence. They may have been dry or drug-free for a long period, but often they continued to believe that there is some way to return to safe drinking or drug use. The psychological defense mechanism of denial was strong. They could intellectually understand their disease but had never accepted it emotionally. If they were using an AA or NA program, they probably were having difficulty with the first three of the twelve-steps. If they were being seen by a counselor, he or she would have noted that they were still in the earliest stage of recovery, despite being abstinent.

This first group is not hopeless, however. Often, time and the group process can achieve what no intellectual process can. Many people who continue to harbor denial will at some point identify with something revealed by another person and admit that they too had that feeling or experience. From this beginning, many people can suddenly change and accept their own need for recovery. Treatment programs will sometimes confront a person in an attempt to break down this defense of denial. This confrontation works well for some people but not for all. Self-help groups will often just let time work on these issues. If someone can remain clean and sober long enough and actively participate in the group, they are more likely to reach this stage, although it may take weeks or even months. Sometimes the newcomer will be told "Just continue to bring your body to meetings and eventually your mind will follow!"

The problem here is keeping someone abstinent when he or she is still equivocating. Professionals can help as well as families, employers and judges. Treatment programs that routinely test for drug and alcohol use may help. For some, the use of disulfiram or naltrexone may be helpful. Behavioral techniques, contracts between patient and therapist, highly structured programs all may help. Treatment programs cannot be passive with anyone who may have a less than sincere desire to remain abstinent, or the reluctant patient will not stay around long enough to benefit.

This patient may stay in treatment long enough to resolve a life crisis, then return to drinking or using after the first few months. If allowed, they can become caught in the revolving-door, repeatedly showing up for detoxification and short episodes of treatment but never getting better. This revolving-door cycle must be broken or prevented.

One way this can be done is by preparing the patient for relapse. Often, their family or employer must also be prepared. If not, relapse can be disastrous. Rather than admit to a relapse, he or she may secretly return to drinking or using. This person may have had very low self-esteem, even before starting to abuse drugs. Years of addiction would have worsened his opinion of himself. A return to drinking or using may serve as proof in his mind that he is not as good as everyone else and probably does not deserve to get better. He should have been prepared for the possibility of relapse, not with shame, but with acceptance.

I have seen people struggle with early recovery for months, only to find acceptance after they relapsed. A woman who has not accepted her own disease may suddenly change because of a relapse of only a day or two. Unfortunately, if she had not been prepared to return to her self-help group or therapist, guilt and shame could instead worsen her downward progression. When relapses are recognized for what they are and prepared for in advance, they are the turning point for some people.

••

The second group of people are often the greater disappointments. They are those who had recovered and then lost it. (Some professionals feel these are the only true relapses.) A man who was in a treatment program may have completed it and thought he had graduated. A woman who had been talking to a divorce attorney may be thrilled at the new harmony in her marriage. Someone in NA or AA may have stopped progressing through the steps of recovery somewhere between the fourth and ninth steps–the steps that require the greatest personal changes.

Sometimes losing recovery is more complex, however. Powerful biological and psychological forces can sabotage otherwise good recovery programs. The association of craving, euphoric recall and the powerful stimulus of an innocent object has played havoc with many recovering cocaine addicts. Attempting to follow a personal program of recovery while living or working or socializing in a chaotic environment has tripped up others. Misreading biological cues has confused many people. Repeating old patterns of behavior in response to biological signals has proved disastrous to many recovering men and women.

Most people at this stage are past the early biologic changes of recovery. This does not mean that they are beyond the grip of the High-Low Trap. Treatment programs have long recognized this and have borrowed the AA term of "dry drunk" to describe it. As an example, a man may have considered himself better and felt guilty about being a poor provider during his years of drinking. He may have gotten a new job or is even working two jobs. He seems obsessed with doing those jobs well. This has led to his skipping sleep, which in turn has led to physical exhaustion and neurotransmitter depletion. Pretty soon, he was back on the emotional roller coaster he had been on when he was using and drinking. The result is often a return to his old behavior pattern but without the alcohol or drugs—truly a dry drunk! This cycle needs to be recognized by family and friends. The recovering person must be made aware of it and quickly.

Overconfidence can be fatal. The power of recovery is limited. If a person had very low self-esteem and was in a destructive relationship or job before recovery, often, she will return to that very same situation after recovery with the mistaken belief that the problem was solely a result of her own faults and now everything will work well. Of course, this is wrong. The old psychological defense mechanism of denial has returned and is preventing her from seeing how hopeless the situation is. Some life situations will get stronger with recovery while others should be allowed to fade away. The healthy recovering person recognizes that he or she cannot stay in a destructive relationship without repeating the mistakes of the past.

JUDY'S STORY

Tom and Judy were married nineteen years and had two children in high school. Tom had inherited his father's business and built it into a leader in the local retail industry. Judy stayed home and ran the house while Tom ran around. His affairs would have been humiliating to her had she admitted she was aware of them. Instead, the defense mechanism of denial protected her from facing the truth. Over the years, Judy's drinking increased until she was unable to function as a wife and mother. Confronted by her family, she agreed to go to treatment. She admitted she was alcoholic and seemed to enjoy her newfound sobriety. Tom and the children were encouraged by the change in her. After Judy returned home, however, Tom continued his affairs. Sober and facing the truth, she confronted him. He not only denied the accusation but turned it around. He questioned her sexuality and fidelity. Confused and humiliated, she found some tranquilizers and took them. The next day she was drinking again. After a few days of playing the role of the old Judy, she rebelled. She returned to detox and when she was discharged moved into her parents home. She began attending AA meetings and seeing a psychologist. After a few weeks, she saw an attorney about a divorce, rented her own apartment and took the children with her. Her alcoholism had allowed her to be a victim of Tom's abuse. Her recovery was not compatible with remaining a victim.

ıı

Recovering people are often cautioned about "going into slippery places." They are told that they are less likely to slip if they avoid them. In early recovery, most people interpret this in very concrete terms–a slip or relapse is more likely to occur where drugs or alcohol are being used. It is good that they are cautioned to avoid such confrontations, because other people using may initiate powerful cravings. However, there is a more abstract but far more important meaning to this. Slippery places may include jobs, relationships and any other situations that could trigger a relapse. These will, of course, be highly personalized and individual.

This middle stage of recovery requires change and patience. This portion of a recovery program is not about drinking or using. It is about living. Recovery cannot stop events in life from occurring, but recovery can bring about new understandings and attitudes about those everyday events. Tom continued to have affairs. Judy could not change that, but she could admit that he was not being faithful without blaming herself for his behavior.

THE MIDDLE STAGE OF RECOVERY

It is in this middle stage of recovery that the most rewarding changes take place. If someone is following a twelve-step program, the action of carrying out steps four through nine is often enough to bring about such changes.

The fourth step involves a process of self-review or personal inventory. The fifth step requires the recovering person to share this inventory with another person. Six through nine require a person to recognize their effect on others in the past and to apologize or make amends to those whom they have harmed. Many recovering people have been helped by turning to a psychologist or psychiatrist who is familiar with addictions, to deal with issues or feelings brought out through these steps. Seeking such assistance is not working against the principles of a self-help group. In fact, it usually strengthens the recovery program.

Throughout this stage of middle recovery, the person needs to accept his or her own recovery as a process, not an event. Change and personal growth are taking place at a rapid-fire rate but there is no graduation day to indicate that recovery is complete. To say "This is enough. I am content with all the change that has already taken place. I do not need to continue this recovery process further," is a common mistake and can lead to relapse. The Chemical Abuse Treatment Outcome Registry (CATOR) studies discussed earlier show that continued participation in self-help groups is related to continued abstinence.

Unfortunately, after relapse many people have reported to counselors stories such as one woman who said "I was doing so well. My life had gotten better. I had completed my counseling and had been attending AA meetings. I never had gotten a sponsor nor finished my fourth step, but I had read the steps many times. I felt I was OK and this emphasis on recovery was taking too much time away from my career and family. Now that I was sober, I could enjoy them, but spending time working on my recovery program interfered with that. I thought I would just go to an AA meeting once a month and say `hello' to people. I had internalized the program, I didn't need to keep practicing it." The woman had found that she was wrong. She thought she had made enough progress to graduate, without realizing that recovery is an ongoing process. In her relapse, she may have lost the very career and family to which she had wanted to give more time.

THE FIRST TWO YEARS

The first two years of recovery are the most important. After two years of continuous sobriety, the average recovering person is well on his or her way to permanent abstinence. There is nothing magic about that length of time, but most people can reasonably deal with the middle stage of recovery during that time and move on to the later or maintenance stage. There can never be any graduation, however. Addiction is a disease that cannot ever be considered "cured." It is always in remission and can readily reappear if a man or woman turns back to old patterns of behavior.

People who slip in this stage frequently telegraph their intentions to those around them. There are no impulsive relapses at this point. I do not mean that they willfully intended to return to drinking or using. I do mean that they lose momentum in their program of recovery. Since this stage is about living, not about drinking or using, many people who relapse will exhibit old behavioral patterns first. Teaching people to recognize their return to these old patterns is a valuable aid to the prevention of relapse.

Although a slip during this period may have been avoidable, fear and shame should not keep someone from returning to recovery. If the person accepts that he or she will be welcomed back to treatment and/or the twelve-step group before a relapse actually happens, the relapse should it occur, can be brief. Again, some people, like Judy, will have to suffer the disappointment of a relapse to fully accept the need for a program of recovery.

Finally, I urge anyone having difficulty with relapse to recognize that they may need additional professional help.

14

PREVENTION IS POSSIBLE

Prevention of addictions is not only possible, it is necessary for renewal of our nation. In this chapter, we will see that prevention is often misunderstood or merely a slogan without substance. We can have realistic prevention programs, but they must be well coordinated and well planned. We will see that there are very different types of prevention efforts and each has its own place. Prevention is not merely education, in fact, it requires coordinated action in many forms at many levels. We will find that we have had uncoordinated and often unproductive efforts. In short, because prevention has been misunderstood, our nation has been doing a poor job of it. We have the capability to come together as a nation and support our prevention efforts, just as we found it within ourselves to support our military efforts in the Persian Gulf. Once our prevention objectives are achieved, we must have a plan to maintain them.

You need not be a scholar to recognize that our country is failing at prevention. Everyday, even in the smallest communities, we see the results of this failure. Newspapers describe automobile accidents in which whole families are wiped out. The article often ends with a statement such as "The police charged the driver of the other car, who was hospitalized with minor injuries, with traffic violations as well as driving while intoxicated." The President of the United States is interviewed and reporters question if he is worried about his personal safety because of terrorism by drug dealers. National television news programs on some days devote almost half of their air time to coverage of events related to drug problems.

These are the public stories. The private stories are often more painful. A son grows up, never knowing the love of his alcoholic father, even though his parents remained together. A small child is being brought up by his grandmother because his addicted mother has turned to prostitution. A young mother is stunned to learn that both she and her baby carry the deadly virus of AIDS because her husband had used intravenous drugs when he was a teenager. A grieving father and mother bury their daughter who died of an overdose, the one who was going to accomplish so much. Many readers will know of other examples that are more personal, more painful.

Why has this happened? Because addictions are a powerful biological threat. Can the United States, still the most powerful nation in the world, succumb to the epidemic from this biologic enemy? In the past, nations have disintegrated when they have not taken decisive actions against such threats. A century and a half ago, the British Prime Minister, Benjamin Disraeli made this observation: "The health of the people is really the foundation upon which all their happiness and all their powers depend."

It is ironic that Great Britain used this fact to dominate another nation. In a shameful episode of world history, Britain, a century and a half ago, became a leader in the drug trade. India, then a colony of the British Empire became a supplier of opium to China. British traders profited tremendously, using British ships. The government of China, which had existed and served the people for thousands of years, did not want to allow this drug trade. Great Britain, a much smaller country than China, was the world's leading military power at that time. It used it's military might to aggressively force the Chinese government to allow British merchants to continue the drug trade. This tragic period is known in history as the Opium War.

The Chinese government lost that war and any ability to protect it's people from the epidemic of opium addiction that followed. (Opium is the natural narcotic from which heroin and other newer narcotics are derived.) The flood of cheap opium meant that it could be used by the poorest Chinese. Smoking and eating opium quickly became synonymous with China. The ability of the Chinese to govern themselves further disintegrated. The British, joined by other nations, used bigoted theories of racial inferiority to explain the Chinese epidemic, and to justify their own military interference in Chinese affairs.

It took a century of war and internal strife before the Chinese rid themselves of this epidemic. The price they paid was a loss of liberty. It was the brutal Chinese communist government that showed no mercy to drug dealers within its borders and wiped out the internal epidemic. As that same government again allows some small measure of liberty, the old problems of addiction may resurface.

How can the drug addiction epidemic be stopped in a democratic society? It is possible if we, as a society, recognize and accept the need for an effective prevention program.

WHY HAVE PREVENTION EFFORTS NOT WORKED IN THE UNITED STATES?

We forget lessons of the past, including prevention efforts that have worked. Today some people advocate the legalization of illicit drugs. They may be unaware of the epidemic of drug use, including cocaine, that plagued the United States a century ago when many of today's illicit drugs were legal and freely available. They ignore the fact that the United States achieved and maintained its industrial and economic leadership during the time that those prevention efforts were proving effective.

We create contradictory programs, with one program undermining the results of another. As an example, the Federal Government created separate agencies to deal with alcoholism and drug addiction. At first, many states followed the federal example. This resulted in ambiguous treatment programs, with addicts being declared cured by one agency and in need of help by another. In this ambiguous and contradictory atmosphere, prevention programs could not define what it was they were preventing.

We allow government agencies to bicker over resources. In the 1980s the U.S. Department of Health and Human Services reported to the United States Congress on federal projects related to alcoholism. They reported on hundreds of activities spread across dozens of agencies. This effect is often multiplied at a state and local level, when local government agencies respond to uncoordinated regulations or competing funding opportunities resulting from these federal activities. Lacking coordination at the top, the agencies at the bottom are forced to compete for public attention and money.

We have taken prevention programs geared for people who have never used drugs and misapplied them to young men and women who were already in need of treatment. "Just Say No," the rallying cry of government programs for almost a decade, is an excellent message for the young. However, it has no effectiveness to a teenager who is already caught in the trap of addiction–a web of crime, prostitution, unintended and unwanted pregnancy and AIDS infection.

We mistake slogans and hyperbole for programs. We are fighting a War on Drugs and have a Federal Drug Czar. Today, there is more money being spent in this effort than ever before. Yet, this government war on drugs is about twenty years old. During many of those years campaign slogans instead of strategic plans characterized the war activity.

We are not using existing resources, including people, groups and facilities willing and able to help in the fight. As the Gulf War showed the world, the United States still has tremendous resources that can be enlisted in any fight, including the drug war. Instead, we have created an elitism that is defeating us. Few of our "generals" in the war on drugs have either training or experience. There are thousands, perhaps hundreds of thousands, of recovering people who would be willing to volunteer time and effort if they were asked, but we often shun and sometimes punish those who come forward to help. In a remarkable request for aid, the Russian government, while still under the repressive Soviet system, sought help from the United States for it's own addiction problems. They reached out to groups and institutions that form the backbone of recovery in America. While our government continues to fund and create new "experts" with every change in program, Russia quietly went outside its own bureaucracy. It is now taking advantage of American altruism, volunteerism and goodwill to try to deal with an epidemic of addiction that rivals our own.

There is no point belaboring past failures. The place from which we must start is to realize that some of these programs do work, but they need to be part of a well-planned, coordinated effort.

Doctors trained in stopping epidemics recognize three types of prevention that can be practiced: Primary, secondary, and tertiary prevention. All three may be used in the face of an epidemic; each one can strengthen the other.

PRIMARY PREVENTION: Attempts to prevent disease from being transmitted or from taking hold. Often, it concerns itself with issues that seem far removed from the healing of the sick. For instance, doctors practicing primary prevention may prevent epidemics of various diseases by working with educators to see that young children learn sanitary habits. They may work with clinics to see that immunizations are given to large numbers of people. They may work with engineers to see that water supplies are pure. They may work with agricultural groups to see that food products meet the health needs of the people. Primary prevention is extremely effective–whereby a few physicians or other workers are able to prevent many diseases that thousands of doctors could not cure. Today, around the world, many programs of primary prevention are routinely administered by government agencies. Often, the programs have been so effective that the original reasons for them have been forgotten by most people.

Unfortunately, there is no immunization or injection to protect a young person from the disease of addiction. There have been numerous attempts to protect people through education, but education, by itself, has never been effective in preventing addiction.

Effective primary prevention of addiction requires us to clean up our drug-infested environment. Reducing the pollution of drugs that our children, that all of us, are exposed to reduces the chance of becoming addicted. Just as we clean up our beaches so that we don't have to swim in a sea of sewage, we must clean up our communities for our children, indeed for everyone. Otherwise, people cannot swim in the sea of addiction without many becoming infected by the epidemic.

Therefore, primary prevention of addiction deals more with establishing effective public policy than dealing directly with potential victims. Helping the law enforcement system do its job is a vital part of this picture. The debate about enforcement or prevention is an exercise in futility. Since efforts to reduce or eliminate the supply of illicit drugs are a cornerstone of primary prevention, this choice can not be made.

In a free society, effective law enforcement requires community support. Having a community attitude of intolerance to illicit drugs is vital to the success of any program. This requires honest communication.

One example of what not to do happened in the United States. During the 1950s the Federal government conducted one of the worst anti-drug propaganda campaigns ever conceived. The messages, particularly about marijuana, were so exaggerated and poorly done that many people believed the effort to be a complete lie. Studies done later showed that many people exposed to that campaign became curious about drugs and skeptical about their danger. In other words, it completely backfired and may have done more harm than good.

The lesson for today is that the truth about the trap of drug addiction is enough to create strong public support for government efforts to control the problem. An anti-drug campaign that contains false, exaggerated or misleading information is never justified. Communities that were known as pro-drug during the turbulent 1960s are only now recognizing the true danger of addiction. The current efforts for providing public information regarding addiction require a new honest attitude in order to obtain public support.

Community support works in various ways. Education, by itself, is not effective in preventing addiction. Of the many reasons for this, the most important is the conflicting message that people hear. The parent that smokes marijuana can not tell a child about the dangers of drug use. The teacher that has had many DWI's will not be believable when talking about alcohol use. The mayor that is rumored to have drugs available at all his parties is laughed at when he makes speeches about drug addiction. These were some of the mixed messages that both adults and children heard. Is it any wonder that education has been an ineffective tool in prevention?

In spite of the mixed messages of the past, today there are some bright lights on the horizon. Education can and does help prevent addiction, if it is part of a consistent and ongoing community campaign. This depends totally on community support. As an example, one community found that they were far more successful in their program for students when they implemented an employee assistance program for teachers. Another community which had tried the usual road of safety campaigns for many years implemented a massive alcohol and drug free family New Year's celebration with great success. Smoking cessation programs are all far more effective now that many workplaces restrict smoking. Each of these examples is about a different type of effort, but they each have one point in common–the community banded together to establish a new norm. That new community norm created an environment in which a previously unbelievable message became both believable and acceptable.

Another powerful and believable source of information regarding addiction are the community members who have gone through it themselves. This requires the participation of people who are recovering that are seen everyday in the community, not someone giving an insincere speech because a judge has ordered him to perform a community service. Although treating those already addicted is not primary prevention for the person helped, it does help prevent the spread of the addiction epidemic by providing powerful sober role models for the community. A community that uses people who have been addicted and are now recovering as role models sends a powerful prevention message to young people.

None of these efforts are examples of comprehensive primary prevention of addiction, but each provides a building block for the future. Primary prevention can work, if it is a broadly based community effort.

SECONDARY PREVENTION: Attempts to thwart the normal disease process through early identification and intervention. This may mean locating people who might have a problem but are not yet suffering from the symptoms of a disease. Secondary prevention often involves screening people without apparent problems and usually includes some form of treatment. Doctors who practice preventive medicine usually do not practice secondary prevention on their own. Instead, they work in an advisory role teaching primary care practitioners and other institutions what they need to do.

Persuading others to practice secondary prevention takes a great deal of knowledge and understanding. People who are told they have an early stage of a disease may be skeptical. Their insurance companies are often reluctant to pay the costs of screening and any treatment that results. Sometimes, unscrupulous organizations may attempt to profit from peoples fears by offering excessive or unproven treatments. Despite these problems, secondary prevention is a bargain. It is often the most cost-effective method of saving lives and preventing human suffering.

Treating disease when it can be detected in it's earliest stages is far less costly than waiting for it to develop further. By detecting disease before people are symptomatic, those people are saved from having to suffer the consequences. Today in the United States, many physicians routinely practice secondary prevention by screening for early disease. Men and women have come to expect such screening as a routine part of their health care. Pap smears and mammography to detect cancer at an early stage in women are two excellent examples of secondary prevention. Physicians routinely give such tests as part of their preventive care. Cases of cancer are detected while they are still treatable and lives are saved. Cholesterol levels are routinely checked and if elevated, dietary advice is given. This is helping to reduce the number of people who will develop heart disease.

It took many years of research and public education to make these strategies widespread. Today, they are an expected part of routine medical care. Doctors do them and patients want to have them done. Insurance companies reimburse patients for having them done, because they are a cost-effective way to prevent disease and premature death.

Similarly, in addiction, secondary prevention works. Finding cases of addiction at their earliest stages can be done in many settings. Doctors do it, lawyers and judges do it, teachers do it, employers and co-workers do it. Friends, lovers, husbands and wives do it. Parents do it to their children and children do it to their parents.

Public education is important here. There is denial in society to addictions that go on all around us. The community that is acutely aware of the addictions around them can learn that it is an important link in recovery. People trained in addiction can help, but they can never totally do the job. The specialist usually only sees the addicted person *after* someone else has recognized that there might be a problem. Educating and training others to recognize problems, and seeing that there are good ways to deal with those problems, are important pieces of the secondary prevention picture.

Mark, the plumber, helped by his employee assistance program, is a good example of secondary prevention. His boss was not trained to be an expert on medicine or addiction but he knew plumbing. Mark's work had suffered and his boss turned to the union employee assistance program based upon his deteriorating work performance. Waiting for Mark to recognize and correct his own problem would have been futile. Instead his boss retained a good worker and may have saved Mark's life.

Certain programs are associated with the courts. This is natural, because some people will cross paths with the law due to their addictions. In fact, between half and three-quarters of the people in prison today can relate alcohol or drug use to the act that resulted in their conviction. It is important to remember that not all these people are addicted and most addicted people do not get in trouble with the law. However, for those who do, it may be the first time that anyone is able to recognize an alcohol or drug problem.

Judges and legislators have recognized this for years. Many programs now exist, based upon this simple relationship. Do they help? Many people are alive today, leading crime-free lives because of a treatment program suggested by a judge or probation officer. Some people will misuse these programs. Several times a year we read of a public figure accused of a crime who attempts to avoid a conviction by claiming to be addicted to alcohol or some other drug. These public performances overshadow the work being done with thousands of people who really are victims of their own disease.

How can secondary prevention work and not be misused by a few people attempting to avoid responsibility for their own actions? The answer, to borrow a phrase from religious friends, is to love the sinner but not the sin. An addicted person who commits criminal acts may not be responsible for his (or her) own addiction but is responsible for his actions. The sentencing laws are weak in this area, so the addicted criminal is often given a choice of either jail or treatment. This easy way out often does work, in that a person entering treatment rather than jail may recover and, in doing so, lead a crime-free life. However, it will not work for someone who sees it as a short-cut to freedom. Instead, they will play the game many times. The public sees these failures, and often finds it difficult to support the programs.

The answer to this dilemma is to both punish and rehabilitate. Addiction is a disease and requires treatment. A criminal act is a criminal act, even though the person committing it was intoxicated or stealing to support a drug habit. Interestingly, some people come to trial only after they have had a period of recovery. Unlike many criminals who espouse innocence or try to shift blame; these people usually accept the sentence they are given.

Secondary prevention attempts are often inadvertently derailed. One example is a state which adopted a system of "no-fault" automobile liability insurance. Anyone in an auto accident in this state is guaranteed the payment of their hospital bills arising from that accident, without waiting to see which driver was at fault in causing it. Anyone, that is, except an intoxicated person. A special exception was made in the law to "punish" the drunk driver. The result was that non-profit hospitals were getting stuck for the bill, frequently amounting to thousands of dollars, when they aided an injured accident victim who turned out to be intoxicated.

Hospitals were not supposed to be punished by the law. The result has been a shift in the policies of some hospitals, to encourage their doctors to not look for intoxication. If no one finds that a driver was intoxicated the hospitals are rapidly paid and the problem, as far as they are concerned, is solved. Unfortunately, the problem has instead been made worse both for the intoxicated driver and for the general public. The no-fault insurance law inadvertently undermined an important source of identification of people who needed help. Some of those people will leave the hospital and continue to harm themselves. Some will do harm to others.

An important point regarding secondary prevention is that there is often a blurring of primary and secondary prevention. Look at the example of the intoxicated driver who leaves the hospital only to repeat this act in several months. He may harm himself or another person. Secondary prevention through the early detection of his alcoholism would result in the prevention of trauma to another person–therefore primary prevention. In this way, secondary prevention of addiction often results in the direct prevention of another disease or injury. How important this is can be realized only when we see that trauma is the leading cause of death of young adults. Alcohol or other drugs play a role in over half of the cases of trauma leading to death. This means that dealing with addictions in their earliest stages can save many lives; lives of the young addicts and sometimes lives of innocent victims.

These few examples are not intended to represent all aspects of secondary prevention. Many programs have been proposed over the years and some have been implemented and work well. However, we live in an age of short-term profit and immediate results. Most government officials, insurance executives and others who make decisions on paying for such programs are not experts on preventive medicine. In some states, it took years of grass roots public lobbying to pass laws that required insurance companies to reimburse women who followed their doctors' advice and obtained routine mammograms and pap smears. Similarly, broad public support for other efforts of preventive medicine will be needed before we see additional effective secondary prevention used in addiction.

TERTIARY PREVENTION: Preventing as much damage as possible by treating a disease that has taken hold. This is the least efficient form of prevention. Often, it simply means providing the best available clinical care. Much of the acute health care given in the United States today is tertiary prevention. The people doing it are primary care and specialist physicians who are doing the jobs they are best prepared to do. Few stop to pause and reflect that what they are doing is also an important part of prevention. They are treating disease already present and trying to restore a person's health and normal function.

Tertiary prevention is important in addictions, too. Tragically, the majority of people treated for addiction could have been treated earlier. Despite this, as the examples in this work have shown, complete remission is possible. Anytime someone is able to stay clean and sober we are preventing further harm.

In treating a person with addiction, we are preventing the medical consequences of late stage alcoholism or addiction. We are preventing the psychological and social suffering of the family. We are preventing the transmission of the AIDS virus to an unborn child. We are preventing the accident or crime that would make a victim of an innocent person. Effective treatment programs must be an inseparable part of any addiction prevention plan, but the money spent for these would have been better spent preventing people from reaching this stage. In general, it often costs more to treat one person with a disease than to prevent many cases of that same disease.

It is worth understanding these prevention distinctions. They are important in preventing addictions because the prevention battle must be fought on all three fronts. The person new to this and perhaps even some of the experts are surprised to learn that most of our "new" prevention strategies are not new. The history of public addiction prevention in North America goes back over four hundred years, long before the founding of the United States. Colonial communities and governments had problems with alcoholism. Many laws and customs regulating taverns and public consumption of alcohol are today regarded as the result of colonial "puritanism." In fact, they were often the result of innovative attempts by communities to protect the health of their own citizens, in an atmosphere that was far from puritanical. As a nation, the United States has tried many of the strategies for the prevention of addictions at one time or another. What we haven't tried here has been tried elsewhere. Our public planners must understand what has been done before and the results achieved in order to develop a national plan.

HOW CAN WE PREVENT ADDICTION?

First, make no mistake about it, **prevention of addiction is a national problem.** Individuals must be involved, but the United States must learn to act as a community of neighbors, by adopting policies that protect the entire community and not a limited few.

The individual states have often progressed far beyond the Federal Government, yet are held back by lack of money and the regulations coming out of Washington. Federal policies are often based upon the loudest voices, often aimed at the squeaky wheels of communities that have done the poorest job. This must change. States and communities that have taken the initiative and are showing progress must be viewed as a source of new policies and ideas.

Second, prevention is for everyone. As a nation, we can not write off any group as beyond hope or as not needing help. The government has based too many programs on racial, ethnic, or economic assumptions. Our democracy can not exist based upon these stereotypes. Yet, programs that work for midwestern heroin users of Scandinavian descent are not tried in eastern cities because many of their heroin users are of African or Hispanic descent. Such assumptions carry the odor of institutional racism. Our nation can not afford to write off a large share of our population as beyond hope.

Similarly, our more privileged citizens carry no immunity from addiction. The sons and daughters of the middle-class and affluent suffer and die from addiction. Yet, many suburban communities refuse to acknowledge the problem in their midst and instead try to keep prevention programs focused on other communities.

Third, we must know what we are talking about. Prevention of addiction cannot just be a slogan, with different groups all fighting over whose brand of prevention deserves our tax dollars. Today, there are only a handful of doctors in the United States jointly trained and qualified in both Preventive Medicine and Addictions. About twenty years ago, there was a fledgling effort by the government to train people in this fight, but that plan was quickly lost to budget cuts. Few benefitted by those efforts. A few more people have taken it upon themselves to pursue the education and experience necessary to understand this complex problem. Except for this handful of people, many of the foot-soldiers who have to fight this battle have never been to basic training. As a nation, we need to see that those who are to fight the battle are trained to know what weapons are available and how to use them.

Fourth, we must have leadership. The problems with drug addictions have been compared to a war. During a war, the side without leadership will lose, no matter how well the individual soldiers fight. Our soldiers fought well during the Gulf War, but thankfully they did not have to fight for long. Much of the credit for that swift victory goes to the leaders. Every key leader during that fight impressed our entire nation as a professional. They knew what they had to do and they did it well. They had the backing of the President, the Congress and the Nation. Those who were not as capable stepped aside and let them do their job. Contrast this effectiveness with the War on Drugs. Over the years, there has been a succession of people appointed to coordinate these efforts. Many of these were capable people with accomplished records in their chosen fields, but none had the training or experience for this difficult job. The creation of a "Drug Czar" position with greater coordinating power does nothing to rectify this. Imagine what would have happened during the Gulf War had retired politicians replaced Generals Schwartzkopf and Powell. Many of our men and women would have been slaughtered.

The leadership in the continued war to prevent addiction will determine the future health and well-being of our citizens and effect the course of this nation.

In summary, what is clearly needed now is a national plan, one that resembles a great mosaic picture. Each small part of the mosaic must be done well, but all the parts are needed to create that picture. In order to do this, we need to firmly believe in two things:

The first is that it can be done. Half-hearted pursuit of ambitious plans will amount to nothing. Listening to those who say the United States lacks the ability to deal with addiction is folly.

The second is that it must be done. We must be sick of seeing our nation and our people destroyed by addiction and those who profit from it. We cannot do effective prevention if we wait until we are mourning the loss of our independence as a nation.

Prevention is possible. It will take a great effort and a great interest on all of our parts, but it will be worth it. It is much easier to prevent people from suffering than to remedy that suffering. Only by our working together as a nation, to turn individual and community efforts into a comprehensive national plan, will the next generation escape the suffering that has trapped many of our generation. It is vital for the survival and the rebirth of our nation.

Appendix A
WHAT YOUR DOCTOR
SHOULD KNOW

═══════

■■■**N**ot every doctor can be an expert on alcoholism but the American Medical Association believes that all physicians must be familiar enough with addiction to recognize it and its consequences.

They have established minimum guidelines for all physicians as well as additional guidelines for those physicians giving specific treatment for addiction. As a patient, you have every right to expect your doctor to know this much:

AMA Guidelines for Physician Involvement in the Care of Substance-Abusing Patients[1]

Level I. For All Physicians With Clinical Responsibility: Diagnosis and Referral

Recognize as early as possible alcohol- or drug-caused dysfunction.

Be aware of the medical complications, symptoms, and syndromes by which alcoholism (or drug abuse) is commonly presented.

Evaluate patient requirements and community resources so that an adequate level of care can be prescribed, with patients needs matched to appropriate resources.

Make a referral to a resource that provides appropriate medical care.

---

[1] As adopted by the AMA Council on Scientific Affairs Oct. 8-9, 1979. Copyright by the AMA.

In addition to the guideline for all physicians just given, the AMA goes on to recommend two additional levels of minimum requirements for physicians who treat a patient during detoxification as well as for those who will be responsible for long-term treatment.

Level II. –For Physicians Accepting Limited Responsibility (To Restore the Individual Patient to the Point of Being Capable of Participating in a Long-term Treatment Program)

Assist the patient in achieving a state free of alcohol and other drugs, including management of the acute withdrawal syndrome.

Recognize and treat, or refer, all associated or complicated diseases.

Apprise the patient of the nature of his disease and the requirements for recovery.

Evaluate resources–physical health, economic interpersonal, and social–to the degree necessary to formulate an initial recovery plan.

Determine the need for involving other persons in the initial recovery plan.

Develop a long-term recovery plan in consideration of the above standards and with the patient's participation.

Level III.–For Physicians Accepting Responsibility for Long-Term Treatment

Acquire knowledge, by training and/or experience, in the treatment of alcoholism (and other drug dependence).

The following responsibilities should be conducted or supervised by a physician:

Establish a supportive, therapeutic, and non-judgmental relationship with the patient.

Within the confine of this relationship, establish specific conditions and limits under which therapy will be conducted, and carefully explain them to the patient.

Periodically evaluate and update the recovery plan with the patients participation.

Involve the patient with an abstinent peer group when appropriate.

Become knowledgeable about and be able to utilize various health, social, vocational and spiritual support systems.

Evaluate directly or indirectly significant other persons and, unless clearly contra-indicated, involve in the treatment.

Continually monitor the patients medication needs. After treatment of acute withdrawal, use psychoactive drugs only if there is a clear-cut and specific psychiatric indication.

Be knowledgeable about the proper use of pharmacotherapy.

Throughout the course of treatment, continually monitor and treat, or refer for care, any complicating illness or treatment.

Be available to the patient as needed for an indefinite period of recovery.

These guidelines are clear and cover many important points. It is entirely reasonable for you to expect any physician treating you or your loved one for any illness to know something about addictions. The minimum standards given in Level I are necessary because addiction is so often the underlying or complicating factor in other diseases. The ability of your doctor to rapidly recognize addiction is just as important to your well being as his or her ability to recognize heart attacks. Levels II and III are additional qualifications for specialists, but Level I is intended for all physicians.

Talk to your own doctor about this. If you find that he or she cannot or will not discuss the subject of addiction with you, then you, as well as other patients, may suffer for extra years before being guided to the appropriate care. You may wish to consider finding another doctor. More constructively, you may wish to express your concern in the hope that your physician will become better acquainted with this deadly disease that costs so many lives and so much suffering.

Appendix B
HOW TO RECOGNIZE
A SPECIALIST

▅▅▅▅▅▅▅

▅▅**A**lthough your personal physician does not have to be an expert on alcoholism and other addictions, you may wish to be referred to a specialist. You may wish to consult a private physician, a specialized addiction clinic, or someone with other credentials who is a licensed specialist in mental health.

Physicians in the United States are easily recognized by their licenses. Most are Doctors of Medicine (M.D.) but there are also many equally qualified Doctors of Osteopathic Medicine (D.O.) in practice. In order to use such designation (M.D. or D.O.), physicians have to pass difficult licensure examinations after completing medical school and a prescribed amount of post-graduate residency training. Following their initial training, physicians often limit their practice to or develop particular skills in a highly specialized area of expertise. This may involve additional years of training and additional examinations of knowledge and competence.

Physicians who have undergone such additional specialization often identify themselves as "Board Certified" by a well recognized specialty board. Just a few examples of such specialties include Internal Medicine, Surgery, Family Practice and Psychiatry. A few states now have regulations to assure the public that physicians claiming special expertise have a recognized basis for those claims.

Further specialization exists beyond Board Certification. Sometimes this sub-specialization applies to a small number of experts all from one background. At other times, it applies to an area so broad it encompasses physicians from many branches of medicine.

Addiction Medicine is such a broad form of specialization. Physicians practicing addiction medicine have a variety of backgrounds. Whatever their background, physicians practicing Addiction Medicine should be able to render the care described by the AMA Guidelines (Appendix A) at both Level II and Level III. Several thousand physicians in the United States practice Addiction Medicine. Some call themselves "addictionologists." Many physicians who practice Addiction Medicine maintain membership in the American Society of Addiction Medicine (ASAM).

Over two thousand physicians have also passed a difficult examination regarding their knowledge in Addiction Medicine. Passing such an examination should not be sole criteria for claiming expertise, but it does certainly demonstrate a minimum level of knowledge that it is reasonable to expect. Before being allowed to take this examination, the American Society of Addiction Medicine requires a physician to be a licensed physician in good standing with at least one years experience in Addiction Medicine, as well as having completed either additional experience and post-graduate training leading to Board Certification in another specialty or a specialized "Fellowship" in Addiction Medicine.

The American Society on Addiction Medicine can provide further information. They may be reached by telephone at 301–656–3920 or by mail at:

American Society of Addiction Medicine
4601 North Park Ave.
Suite 101
Chevy Chase, MD 20815

Although physicians practicing Addiction Medicine come from many backgrounds, there are a large number who were initially trained in and are Board-Certified in Psychiatry. Many of these psychiatrists have passed the ASAM certification requirements. In the future, some of these psychiatrists may also qualify for additional sub-specialty certification in addiction by the American Board of Psychiatry and Neurology. For further information regarding the certification of psychiatrists call 708–945–7900 or write the:

American Board of Psychiatry and Neurology
500 Lake Cook Road, Suite 335
Deerfield, Illinois 60015

Many people will turn to specialized clinics claiming expertise in treating addiction. Addiction clinics vary widely from state to state, but are usually regulated by the state specifically for treatment of alcoholism and other drug addiction. These clinics should have physicians and psychologists who are experts in addiction supervising specialized addiction counselors. When done properly, this is a good arrangement, since the person needing treatment receives the benefit of dealing with a team of concerned and knowledgeable people.

Well trained and certified addiction counselors conduct much of the treatment at most addiction clinics. They are the backbone of many good treatment programs. Although a few counselors have training at a Masters Degree level, many have less than a year of training beyond high school. Many states require counselors working in addiction treatment programs to pass a certification examination. This career field of addiction counseling was intended to provide team members to work with professionals. Such supervision is vital, since an inexperienced addiction counselor may not recognize how limited his or her own knowledge is.

You may wish to ask about the degree of involvement of the physicians and psychologists working at the clinic. Never assume that the title "Doctor" signifies a physician or psychologist. There are doctoral degrees given in many fields and some individuals with Ph.D. degrees in other fields have chosen to become addiction counselors later in life. Don't be afraid to ask questions, to be sure that "Doctor Jones" is not actually a person with a few courses in counseling and a doctoral degree in chemistry, law, or art history.

You may wish to determine whether a clinic is licensed to specialize in addiction treatment. The best way to do so is to contact the appropriate state licensing agency listed in Appendix D.

Another source of care could be a licensed professional providing mental health care. Licensed Clinical Psychologists provide the best source of this type of care. Psychologists cannot deal with your physical problems and cannot prescribe medications. If you have either of these needs, be sure that your personal physician can coordinate your care with your psychologist. There are many college degrees in Psychology but a clinical psychologist is a highly trained professional with a doctoral degree (usually a Ph.D.) and additional training approved by the American Psychological Association. He or she has a state license to practice independently.

Unfortunately, there is no special credential that identifies a psychologist as a specialist in addictions. A small number psychologists are affiliated with the Society for Psychologists in Addictive Behavior. In some states, a clinical psychologist or certified social worker may also take the addiction counseling certification examination. If the psychologist or social worker is already properly licensed, this is a way of identifying an individual with special interest in addiction. Since the examination is below the level of training of either a psychologist or social worker, it does not signify expertise at that level. Either of these may indicate a strong interest in addictive diseases, but is not evidence of appropriate expertise. You should ask questions and seek the opinion of others. A good source of information regarding the qualifications of over 16,000 clinical psychologists is the National Register of Health Service Providers in Psychology. They can be reached by telephone at 202–833–2377 or write to the:

Council for The National Register
of Health Service Providers in Psychology
1730 Rhode Island Avenue, N.W., Suite 1200
Washington, D.C. 20036

Another group of professionals who sometimes are in private practice are social workers.   This can vary widely between states. Social workers sometimes provide counseling to people with addictive diseases. Although a social worker cannot fulfill your needs for either medical or psychological care, the care given by a properly trained social worker may meet your needs. There are different degrees in social work but a social worker doing this type of counseling should have a Master in Social Work (M.S.W.), have passed a certification examination (C.S.W.) and meet other special requirements in your state for private practice in mental health. Again, as is the case for psychologists, there are no credentials at this time that identifies a social worker as having special expertise in the treatment of addictive disease. Check with the appropriate state agencies if you are uncertain about his or her credentials. You should definitely ask questions and seek the opinion of others.

In some parts of the United States, you may find counselors in independent practice claiming to be specialists in addictions. Although in most states, addiction counselors cannot see or treat patients without supervision, loopholes exist and state laws vary. Use caution when seeking care in such situations and check with appropriate state agencies or professional groups if you have any doubt.

In summary, when seeking specialized care, take the time to determine that you are receiving the care you are paying for. Well qualified experts are never insulted by such questions and will be flattered that you have selected them on the basis of their reputation, experience and qualifications.

Appendix C
KNOWING WHO NEEDS TREATMENT

Today, commercial treatment centers peddle their services on television. Those fortunate enough to have complete health insurance coverage or unlimited funds can pick and choose among treatment centers costing between ten and thirty thousand dollars for a month of inpatient treatment. Often, recommendations to enter a particular treatment program are made on the basis of greed and profits, not on the basis of a professional evaluation of need.

This book cannot take the place of professional help. Seek expert help if it is available to you. Be cautious about free diagnostic services offered by institutions that would profit by finding new patients. Be extremely cautious of treatment centers that employ agents or representatives. Would you trust a surgeon who employed a commissioned salesman to locate patients who might need surgery? The best way to determine the type of treatment you require is by seeking help from an independent physician or other professional who is an expert on addiction and familiar with the options available in your area. If you cannot find such an expert, another objective source of help is usually the local agency affiliated with the National Council on Alcoholism and Drug Dependence. Appendix D will help you find such an agency. The third way to get some objective answers is to attend a local A.A. or N.A. meeting and ask some members for their opinions after the meeting. The self-help groups take a firm position on never endorsing anything, but the individual members will often tell you of their own experiences and lead you to local professionals they have found trustworthy.

Figure 1 depicts a pyramid which will help you understand who will need particular levels of treatment. Different levels may be needed, starting from Level A at the base to support the goal of mental health and serenity.

Level A **"Abstinence from Alcohol and All Other Drugs"** is the foundation which is always needed to support the pyramid. Attempting to build a treatment program without abstinence is equivalent to building a house in the sand without a first establishing a foundation. Having such a solid foundation is not a luxury or an extra, it is a necessity.

Level B **"Detoxification to Achieve Abstinence"** is needed for anyone without the ability to stop safely on their own. It is the preparation for the foundation that may be needed because of the soil on which you are starting your house. People can and do die from withdrawal, especially from alcohol. Detoxification under medical supervision is a necessity for anyone who has any medical condition, or for anyone who has suffered from any form of medical complication (such as high blood pressure, a fast heart rate or an epileptic seizure) or psychiatric complication (such as hallucinating or having a suicidal thought) when undergoing withdrawal in the past. It is also strongly recommended when someone has not gone through withdrawal recently. This would be the case when a person has been using alcohol or another drug virtually every day.

Mental Health & Serenity

Level H Structured Environment

Level G Psychiatric or Psychological Care

Level F Inpatient Addiction Rehabilitation

Level E Utilizing Addiction Counseling

Level D Following the Twelve-Step Path

Level C Comfortable Maintenance of Abstinence

Level B Detoxification to Achieve Abstinence

Level A Abstinence from Alcohol and All Other Drugs

Figure 1: Hierarchy of Treatment Needs

Some people will skip detoxification because they have learned how to gradually wean themselves from alcohol or other drugs over a period of several days without apparent harm. This can be an effective but highly dangerous procedure.

So-called "Social Detoxification" centers exist without medical supervision but their very name is a contradiction in terms. These are facilities to house alcoholics and addicts during withdrawal and offer an alternative to the old "drunk tank" in jail. They are a safe alternative when shelter and support rather than detoxification is needed.

Those who are already abstinent and have been for several days usually have no need for detoxification in any form although they may still need medical care for problems that are a result of their alcohol or other drug use.

Level C **"Comfortable Maintenance of Abstinence"** forms the support for the walls of the pyramid. Abstinence must be comfortable and maintainable to be effective. However, there are many people who, once they recognize their need to stop, successfully and comfortably maintain continuous abstinence without the need of either treatment programs or self-help groups.

Such a statement is heresy to those who claim that everyone needs treatment. Nevertheless, many people exist who are able to do this. Those who have done so show up in studies that survey the population. Since they are not seen in treatment centers, even the most experienced counselors make the mistake of believing that such people do not exist.

It may be appropriate for some people who have nothing to loose (if they fail) to see how comfortable they are with nothing further. However, this should only be tried once. Typically, people seeking help from a self-help group or treatment center have already found that they cannot maintain comfortable abstinence without further assistance.

The two critical elements here are comfort and maintenance. To support mental health and serenity, abstinence must be continuously maintained and comfortable. "Improvements," such as reduced use, switching to another drug or only using on holidays and special occasions are all failures to maintain abstinence. Similarly, irritability, depression, anxiety or malaise indicate a lack of comfort that is significant and means that more is required.

Level D **"Following the Twelve-Step Path"** is highly recommended to strengthen and complete the walls of the house you are building. Most people will find that this is what is needed for the comfortable maintenance of their abstinence. It costs nothing monetarily. The only cost is the commitment to the hard work of recovery and change. Following the Twelve-Step Path means joining and participating in the self-help group that is right for you, whether it is Alcoholics Anonymous, Narcotics Anonymous or one of the other groups built on similar principles. Appendix D explains how to locate a group near you. However, there is more. Chapter Eleven explained how merely attending these self-help groups is rarely enough. They work only if the you or your loved one actually works the twelve suggested steps of recovery.

Level E **"Utilizing Addiction Counseling"** will be needed by those who need the guidance and structure of a professional to show them how to build and strengthen the walls of their house of recovery. Counseling cannot substitute for these other steps. A counselor may be likened to an architect or a builder. You may hire such a person to show you what you must do and to help you do it. In the end, you must still build the supportive walls of your house. No one expects their builder to stay after the house is complete to help hold up the roof.

Addiction counseling may be individual, group or a combination. You may only require a few sessions but most agencies and counselors will recommend an extended course of counseling over several months that may cost thousands of dollars. One of the agencies listed in Appendix D may help guide you to such counseling. Do not despair regarding the cost. You may find that if you have health insurance, it will cover some or all of the costs involved. You may also find some tax-supported agencies that will charge you based upon your ability to pay.

Look where you are in this pyramid of treatment. You have progressed halfway before reaching one of the costly levels. Many people can be successful before reaching this level, saving this expense for those who truly need require it.

Level F **"Inpatient Addiction Rehabilitation"** is not needed by everyone. It offers the advantage of a safe environment for an individual to learn about and work on a program of sobriety. Some people will only be able to become clean and sober away from the distractions of work and home. Others have no stable environment and require inpatient treatment as much for the shelter and stabilization as for the treatment itself.

These inpatient programs are costly, although there seems to be little correlation between cost and quality. Some of the best known programs will cost a few thousand dollars while many lesser known programs may cost between ten and thirty thousand dollars. Fortunately, some employers will cover these costs through health insurance and some tax-supported programs exist. Be cautious if you or your loved one is referred to an expensive inpatient program by a counselor you do not know. A few profitable programs have muddied the waters for the reputable programs by employing sales agents offering "counseling" and who are paid on the basis of patients referred. Once again, one of the agencies listed in Appendix D may help you in locating an appropriate program.

Although inpatient rehabilitation is costly and not everyone will need it, if you have only one chance to do it right or face a major loss in your life (such as your job, your spouse or even your personal liberty) it may be the wisest course from the beginning.

Level G **"Psychiatric or Psychological Care"** is relatively high in the pyramid because it is needed for only about one person in ten. In an even smaller number of people, it is as important as abstinence and recovery and will have to be attended to first. This small number includes people who are acutely psychotic, severely depressed or suicidal when they are not intoxicated and not in withdrawal. These people are a very small percentage of those who need abstinence and recovery. Addiction counseling by itself is never enough and could even be harmful. There are special programs, often called "Dual Diagnosis" or "Mentally Ill Chemical Abuser (MICA)" programs, offered within large psychiatric hospitals and programs. These special programs can deal with these complex people who would otherwise find addiction treatment not helpful.

There is a much larger group of people who feel that they need mental health care because of very troubling thoughts and behaviors. Often, they have sought out such care and continued to use drugs, not thinking it important to disclose to their psychiatrist or psychologist their use of marijuana, cocaine or alcohol. For such people, if they have no life-threatening mental illness when they become abstinent, abstinence and an active program of recovery often works wonders.

After a period of abstinence, some of these people will continue to have mental health problems. Others, people without a history of psychological problems in the past because they had used alcohol or other drugs to escape dealing with issues, may first recog-

nize their need for help months or years after they become abstinent. These situations are beyond the scope of addiction counseling, but treatment by a psychologist or psychiatrist can be highly
effective. Such professional help should support and not conflict
with a program of abstinence and recovery. The role of the professional is often made clear because the veil of drug use has been
swept away.

Level H **"Structured Environment"** is a necessary step for a
small number of those in recovery. This covers a variety of envi-
ronments such as halfway houses and recovery homes. This is not
treatment, but an environment where someone who is newly sober
can live in a stable and supportive atmosphere, follow a recovery
program and return to work as a productive member of the community. This is usually a transitional step for people completing
inpatient rehabilitation who would be unlikely to remain clean
and sober immediately returning to the environment they had left.
Inpatient rehabilitation facilities will usually help in locating such
an environment for the few who may need it.

Progressing up through the pyramid, the walls now have sufficient strength to support the roof of mental health and serenity.
Mental health and serenity that can enable each individual to live
the good life that God or nature intended for each person on Earth.

Appendix D
LOCATING HELP

━━━

This section contains telephone numbers to assist you in locating help in most regions of the United States and Canada as well as selected foreign locations. The numbers listed for Alcoholics Anonymous and Narcotics Anonymous are hot-line numbers often answered twenty-four hours a day in larger metropolitan areas. These many local self-help groups provide direct help at no charge. The numbers for NCADD are non-profit organizations affiliated with the National Council on Alcoholism and Drug Dependence, which provide information about treatment and prevention programs. The state and provincial government offices listed can provide further information.

Use this list to find a nearby location checking your state, area code and city. You may contact the national headquarters for further information or to locate nearby help.

CAUTION: If you can not find what you need here, use care when checking your local telephone directory. Many ''free information services'' are sales representatives of expensive treatment facilities. Be wary if you find you are not dealing with one of the voluntary or non-profit organizations listed here.

National Headquarters

Alcoholics Anonymous General Service Office   (212) 870-3400
    or write to: P.O. Box 459
          Grand Central Station
          New York, NY 10017

Narcotics Anonymous World Service Office   (818) 780-3951
    or write to: P.O. Box 9999
          Van Nuys, CA 91409

National Council on Alcoholism and Drug Dependence
1-800-NCA-CALL   (1-800-622-2255)
    or write to: 12 West 21st Street
          New York, NY 10010

ALABAMA
State Agency: (205) 271-9253

Area Code & City	Alcoholics Anonymous	Narcotics Anonymous	NCADD
205 Birmingham	933-8964	320-8836	
Huntsville	534-8524	535-6671	
Mobile	478-1679	639-4156	471-1498**
Montgomery	281-2424	213-1847	262-7401

ALASKA
State Agency: (907) 586-6201

Area Code & City	Alcoholics Anonymous	Narcotics Anonymous	NCADD
800 Statewide			800-478-PREV**
907 Anchorage	272-2312	277-5483	349-6602**
Fairbanks	456-7501	452-7372	
Juneau	586-1161		463-3755

ALBERTA
Provincial Agency: (403) 427-7301

Area Code & City	Alcoholics Anonymous	Narcotics Anonymous
403 Calgary	265-8888	235-9901
Edmonton	482-6783 or 424-5900	235-9901

ARGENTINA

City	Alcoholicos Anonimos
Buenos Aires	97-6666 or 855-1813

ARIZONA
State Agencies: Alcohol (602) 220-6478 Other Drugs (602) 255-1152

Area Code & City	Alcoholics Anonymous	Narcotics Anonymous	NCADD
520 Flagstaff	779-3569	774-6779	
602 Phoenix	264-1341 (Español 273-6352)	784-4004 395-3468	264-6214
520 Tuscon	624-4183	881-8381	620-6615
520 Yuma	782-2605	783-5642	

ARKANSAS
State Agency: (501) 280-4501

Area Code & City	Alcoholics Anonymous	Narcotics Anonymous
501 Fort Smith	783-0123	441-6278
Little Rock	664-7303	373-8683
Pine Bluff	535-8427	

AUSTRALIA

Area Code & City	Alcoholics Anonymous	Narcotics Anonymous
Melbourne	429 1833	417 6472
Sidney	799 1199 or	212 3444
	008 442 947	

BAHAMAS

	Alcoholics Anonymous	Narcotics Anonymous
	322-1685	328-2294

BELGIUM

City	Alcooliques Anonymes
Brussels	513 23 26
	(English 537 82 84)

BRAZIL

City	Alcoolicos Anonimos
Sao Paulo	227-5601

BRITISH COLUMBIA

Provincial Agency: (604) 387-5870

Area Code & City	Alcoholics Anonymous	Narcotics Anonymous
604 Vancouver	434-3933	873-1018
Victoria	383-0415 or	383-3553
	383-7744	

CALIFORNIA

State Agency: (916) 445-0834

Area Code & City	Alcoholics Anonymous	Narcotics Anonymous	NCADD
209 Tulare	747-1277	688-2944	734-0403
Stockton	464-1594	464-9262	
213 Central LA area	936-4343		
East Los Angeles	(Español 722-4175)		
310 El Monte area	442-3933		
Hollywood		850-1624	
Los Angeles	777-9740	935-5395	384-0403
310 Santa Monica area	836-8716		
310 South Bay area	675-2624		
Southeast LA area	582-2439		
310 Central South Bay	644-1139		
Long Beach	493-5323	372-9666	

408 San Jose	297-3555	998-4200	
	(Español 259-6533)		
415 San Francisco	621-1326	621-8600	
510 Concord	685-4357		
Walnut Creek	939-4155	685-4357	
619 San Diego	265-8762	584-1007	696-7101
	(Español 280-7224)		
707 Vallejo	643-8217	428-4120	643-2715
714 Riverside	825-4700		
805 Santa Barbara	962-3332	569-1288	963-1433
818 Azus	(213) 777-9740	(310) 334-0212	
Covina	914-1861	584-6910	331-5316
	(213) 779-8006		
916 Sacramento	454-1100		(213) 936-4343

COLORADO
State Agency: (303) 331-8201

Area Code & City	Alcoholics Anonymous	Narcotics Anonymous	NCADD
303 Boulder	447-8201	441-7787	
Denver	322-4440		825-8113
719 Colorado Springs			633-4601

CONNECTICUT
State Agency: (203) 566-4145

Area Code & City	Alcoholics Anonymous	Narcotics Anonymous	NCADD
203 Danbury		1-800-627-3543	
		792-4515	
Hartford	282-5924	1-800-627-3543	
New Haven	624-6063	1-800-627-3543	787-2111
	(Español 773-3044)		
Norwalk/Westport	855-0075	1-800-627-3543	227-7644 or 226-0043
Waterbury	755-2124	1-800-627-3543	753-2153

DELAWARE
State Agency: (302) 421-6101

Area Code & City	Alcoholics Anonymous	Narcotics Anonymous
302 Dover	736-1567	1-800-229-7244
Southern Delaware	856-6542	1-800-229-7244
Wilmington	655-5113	429-8175

DENMARK

City	Anonyme Alkoholikerer
Copenhagen	01 42 79 16)

DISTRICT OF COLUMBIA

District Government Agency: (202) 673-8085

Area Code & City	Alcoholics Anonymous	Narcotics Anonymous	NCADD
202 Washington, D.C.	966-9115 (TDD 966-9782)	399-5316	783-1300

FLORIDA

State Agency: (904) 488-0900

Area Code & City	Alcoholics Anonymous	Narcotics Anonymous	NCADD
305 Ft. Lauderdale	462-0265	476-9297	
Miami	887-6762 (Español 642-2805)	662-0280 (south) 949-8809 (north)	
407 Orlando	521-0012		
West Palm Beach	883-0132 or 667-8800	863-2316	
813 Tampa	933-9123	879-4357	
904 Jacksonville	399-8535	723-5683	353-3454

FRANCE

City	Alcooliques Anonymes
Paris	(1) 48 06 43 68

GEORGIA

State Agency: (404) 657-6400

Area Code & City	Alcoholics Anonymous	Narcotics Anonymous	NCADD
404 Atlanta	525-3178	708-3219	351-1800
706 Augusta	860-8331	855-2419	
Columbus	327-6078	1-800-347-5304	
912 Macon	746-6652	741-8613	743-4611
Savannah	354-0993	233-4357	

GERMANY

City	Anonyme Alkoholiker
Berlin	4 53 71 53
Frankfurt am Main	5 97 42 52
Hamburg	271 33 53
Munich	55 56 85

GREAT BRITAIN

City/Region	Alcoholics Anonymous	Narcotics Anonymous
Aberdeen, Scot.	0224 582184	
Belfast, N.Ire.	681084	
Birmingham	773 3449	
Edinburgh, Scot.	225 2727	
Glasgow, Scot.	221 9027	
London	071-352 3001	071-351 6794
Manchester	236 6569	
York		
Stonebow	644026	
Leeds	454567	

HAWAII

State Agency: (808) 548-4280

Area Code & Island	Alcoholics Anonymous	Narcotics Anonymous
808 Hawaii Island	961-6133	969-6644 or 325-7609
Kauai	245-6677	533-4900 (call collect)
Maui	244-9673	242-6404
Oahu (Honolulu)	946-1438	734-4357

IDAHO

State Agency: (208) 334-5935

Area Code & City	Alcoholics Anonymous	Narcotics Anonymous
208 Boise	344-6611	887-4234
Idaho Falls	524-7717 or 525-1805	

ILLINOIS

State Agency: (312) 814-3840

Area Code & City	Alcoholics Anonymous	Narcotics Anonymous	NCADD
217 Springfield	525-9433		
309 Peoria	673-1456		792-0292
312 Chicago	346-1475	(708) 848-4884	
708 Waukegan	623-9660	848-4884	244-4434
815 Rockford	654-9990	964-5959	

INDIANA

State Agency: (317) 232-7816

Area Code & City	Alcoholics Anonymous	Narcotics Anonymous
219 Gary	980-3475	1-800-289-7879
Ft. Wayne	426-5721	

South Bend	234-7707		234-6024
317 Indianapolis	831-1156 or 632-7864	875-5459	542-7128
812 Bloomington	334-8191	1-800-339-8183	
Terre Haute	234-0827		

IOWA
State Agency: (515) 281-4417

Area Code & City	Alcoholics Anonymous	Narcotics Anonymous	NCADD
319 Cedar Rapids	365-5955		
Davenport	324-5665		
Dubuque	557-9196	557-6200 (ask for pager #418)	
515 Des Moines	282-8550	244-2277	244-2297
712 Council Bluffs	556-1880	(402) 449-1822	

IRELAND

City	Alcoholics Anonymous	Narcotics Anonymous
Dublin	538998 or 6795967	300944

ISRAEL

City	Alcoholics Anonymous
Tel Aviv	225 255

JAMAICA

	Alcoholics Anonymous
	952-0134 or 952-2481

KANSAS
State Agency: (913) 296-3925

Area Code & City	Alcoholics Anonymous	Narcotics Anonymous	NCADD
316 Arkansas City	442-5880		
Dodge City	225-4300		
Emporia	343-3455	342-8467	
Liberal	624-4214		
Ulysses	356-1733	356-3764	
Wichita	684-3661		
913 Junction City	238-1153	762-3861	
Kansas City, KS	384-2770		(816) 361-5900
Lawrence	842-0110	749-6631	
Manhattan		776-9933	
Salina	823-3338	823-1988	
Topeka	232-8914	232-5683	235-8622

KENTUCKY
State Agency: (502) 564-2880

Area Code & City	Alcoholics Anonymous	Narcotics Anonymous
502 Frankfort	227-4729	
Louisville	582-1849	566-6709
Owensboro	683-0371	
606 Lexington	276-2917	253-4673

LOUISIANA
State Agency: (504) 922-0730

Area Code & City	Alcoholics Anonymous	Narcotics Anonymous	NCADD
318 Lafayette	234-7814		
Shreveport	865-2172	677-4344	222-8511
504 Baton Rouge	924-0030	381-9609	343-8330
New Orleans	525-1178	899-6262	

MAINE
State Agency: (207) 287-2595

Area Code & City	Alcoholics Anonymous	Narcotics Anonymous	NCADD
207 Augusta		1-800-974-0062	626-3494**
Portland	774-3034	1-800-974-0062	

MANITOBA
Provincial Agency: (204) 944-6200

Area Code & City	Alcoholics Anonymous	Narcotics Anonymous
204 Winnipeg	942-0126	338-2370

MARYLAND
State Agency: (410) 225-6925

Area Code & City	Alcoholics Anonymous	Narcotics Anonymous	NCADD
301 D.C. Suburbs	(TDD 966-9782)		(202) 783-1300
Hagerstown		790-2171	
410 Aberdeen	272-4150		
Annapolis	268-5441		
Baltimore	433-4843		328-8444
Easton	822-4226		
Ocean City	289-6400		

MASSACHUSETTS
State Agency: (617) 727-8614

Area Code & City	Alcoholics Anonymous	Narcotics Anonymous	NCADD
413 Springfield	538-5822	538-7479	
508 New Bedford	997-9051	991-3360	675-0336
Worcester	752-9000	756-2284	
617 Boston	426-9444	884-7709	
		756-2284	755-7118

MEXICO

City	Alcoholicos Anonimos
Acapulo	3-7382
Mexico City	211-5871
Monterrey	71-86-77 (Northern Suburbs 44-98-21)

MICHIGAN
State Agency: (517) 335-8809

Area Code & City	Alcoholics Anonymous	Narcotics Anonymous	NCADD
313 Ann Arbor	482-5700		971-7900
810 Detroit	541-6565**		(810) 443-1676
or Wayne County	831-5550		
810 Flint		238-3636	767-0350
517 Lansing	321-8781	483-9101	887-0226
Saginaw/Bay City	776-1241		
616 Kalamazoo	349-4410	382-6262	382-9820
Grand Rapids	361-6010	452-5400	

MINNESOTA
State Agency: (612) 296-4610

Area Code & City	Alcoholics Anonymous	Narcotics Anonymous
612 Duluth/Superior		728-3119
Minneapolis	922-0880	822-7965
	(TDD 922-1061)	
St.Paul	227-5502	822-7965

MISSISSIPPI
State Agency: (601) 359-1288

Area Code & City	Alcoholics Anonymous	Narcotics Anonymous	NCADD
601 Jackson	366-2212	949-9499	366-6880
Gulfport	865-0156	868-8595	

MISSOURI
State Agency: (314) 751-4942

Area Code & City	Alcoholics Anonymous	Narcotics Anonymous	NCADD
314 Columbia	442-4424		
Jefferson City	642-6795	634-5123	
St. Louis	647-3677 (TDD 647-3683)	830-3232 or	962-3363
417 Springfield	862-9264	866-7392	831-4167
Joplin	673-8591	781-2210 or 800-955-3454	
816 Kansas City, MO	471-7229	531-2250	361-5900

MONTANA
State Agency: (406) 444-2827

Area Code & City	Alcoholics Anonymous
406 Billings	657-0776
Butte	782-8440
Great Falls	452-1234
Helena	443-0438

NEBRASKA
State Agency: (402) 471-2851 EXTENSION 5583

Area Code & City	Alcoholics Anonymous	Narcotics Anonymous	NCADD
308 Grand Island	384-7044	384-7365	
402 Freemont	721-0272 or 721-8667	721-9511	
Hastings	463-4110	463-0524	
Lincoln	438-5214	474-0405	474-0930**
Omaha	345-9916	593-4790	553-8000

NETHERLANDS

City	Anonieme Alcoholisten
Amsterdam	614 94 81

NEVADA
Stage Agency: (702) 687-4790

Area Code & City	Alcoholics Anonymous	Narcotics Anonymous
702 Carson City		883-5110
Las Vegas	(TDD 369-1888) (Español 796-5222)	369-3362
Reno	355-1151	322-4811

NEW BRUNSWICK
Provincial Agency: (506) 453-2136

Area Code & City	Alcoholics Anonymous
506 Saint John	693-9080

NEW HAMPSHIRE
State Agency: (603) 271-6100

Area Code & City	Alcoholics Anonymous	Narcotics Anonymous	NCADD
603 Concord	228-2558	1-432-0168	
Derry		432-0168	
Manchester	668-3326 or	1-432-0168	625-6980
	622-6967	225-3085**	
Nashua	882-2259	1-432-0168	

NEW JERSEY
State Agency: Alcohol (609) 292-8947 Other Drugs (609) 292-8947

Area Code & City	Alcoholics Anonymous	Narcotics Anonymous	NCADD
201 Jersey City	(Español 242-2848)	1-800-992-0401	451-2877
Newark		1-800-992-0401	
Morristown		1-800-992-0401	
Somerville		1-800-992-0401	
609 Long Beach Island	494-5130	1-800-992-0401	
Trenton	888-3333	1-800-992-0401	392-0644**
908 Asbury Park	668-1882	1-800-992-0401	
New Brunswick		1-800-992-0401	246-1450
Toms River		1-800-992-0401	

NEW MEXICO
State Agency: (505) 827-2658

Area Code & City	Alcoholics Anonymous	Narcotics Anonymous	NCADD
505 Albuquerque	266-1900	260-7195	256-8300
Las Cruces	527-1803	647-2094	
Santa Fe	982-8932	984-2098	

NEW YORK
State Agency: Alcohol (518) 474-5417 Other Drugs (518) 457-7629

Area Code & City	Alcoholics Anonymous	Narcotics Anonymous	NCADD
212 Manhattan		212-929-6262	979-6277
315 Syracuse	463-5011	472-5555	471-1359
Utica	732-6880	472-5555	
516 Nassau County	292-3040	937-6262	747-2606
Suffolk County	669-1124	937-6262	

518 Albany	489-6679	447-5776	
Troy	273-2225		
607 Binghamton	722-5983		723-7529
Corning	776-7321		937-5156
716 Buffalo	853-0388	878-2316	852-1781
Jamestown	484-1544		664-3608
Niagara Falls	285-5319		282-1228
Rochester	232-6720	264-7587	423-9490 ext. 690
718 Bronx	515-8481		
	(Español 212-781-4183)		
Brooklyn	339-4777		
Queens	520-5021		
Staten Island	212-683-3900		
914 Kingston	331-6360		691-2750
Newburgh	342-5757	1-452-8514	
Poughkeepsie	452-1111	452-8514	
White Plains	949-1200	212-929-6262	

NEW ZEALAND

City	Alcoholics Anonymous
Auckland	734 294
Christchurch	379 0860
Wellington	499 3681

NEWFOUNDLAND
Provincial Agency: (709) 737-3600

Area Code & City	Alcoholics Anonymous
709 St. John's	579-5215 or
	579-6091

NORTH CAROLINA
State Agency: (919) 733-4670

Area Code & City	Alcoholics Anonymous	Narcotics Anonymous	NCADD
704 Ashville	254-8539	258-4537	
Charlotte	332-4387	379-0440	376-7447
919 Durham	286-9499		688-7058**
910 Greensboro	854-4278	370-2199	
919 Greenville	758-0787		
910 High Point	885-8520	841-8600	
919 Raleigh	783-6144	755-5391 or	781-1072
		790-4153	
910 Wilmington	762-1230 or	452-6034	
	343-1034		
910 Winston-Salem	725-6031 or	607-8280	
	762-1230		

NORTH DAKOTA
State Agency: (701) 328-2769

Area Code & City	Alcoholics Anonymous	Narcotics Anonymous
701 Fargo	235-7335	234-9330

NORTHWEST TERRITORIES
Provincial Agency: (403) 873-7155

NOVA SCOTIA
Provincial Agency: (902) 424-4270

Area Code & City	Alcoholics Anonymous
902 Halifax	461-1119

OHIO
State Agency: Alcohol (614) 466-3445 Other Drugs (614) 466-7893

Area Code & City	Alcoholics Anonymous	Narcotics Anonymous	NCADD
216 Akron	253-8181		
Canton	456-9304		
Cleveland	241-7387		
Youngstown	783-5000	1-800-451-3000	
419 Toledo	472-8242	729-6007	
	(TDD 472-1582)		
513 Cincinnati	861-9966	820-2947	281-7880
	(TDD same #)		
Dayton	222-2211	278-2988	
614 Columbus	253-8501	274-0006	

OKLAHOMA
State Agency: (405) 271-7474

Area Code & City	Alcoholics Anonymous	Narcotics Anonymous	NCADD
405 Oklahoma City	524-1100	524-7068	
918 Tulsa	627-2224	747-0017	

ONTARIO
Provincial Agency: (416) 595-6000

Area Code & City	Alcoholics Anonymous	Narcotics Anonymous	NCADD
416 Niagara	685-0075		
Ottawa	523-9977	236-4674	
	(Fr. 243-2838)		
Toronto	487-5591	691-9519	
	(TDD 487-9450)		

OREGON
State Agency: (503) 945-5763

Area Code & City	Alcoholics Anonymous	Narcotics Anonymous	NCADD
503 Eugene	342-4113	341-6070	
Medford	773-4848	770-4885	
Portland	223-8569	233-2235	232-8083**
Salem	399-0599	370-2914	

PENNSYLVANIA
State Agency: (717) 783-8200

Area Code & City	Alcoholics Anonymous	Narcotics Anonymous	NCADD
610 Bethlehem	882-0558	439-1998	867-3986
610 Lebanon	1-800-232-4673		
610 Norristown	933-9674 or 323-3450		
215 Philadelphia	574-6900	934-3944	627-9640
412 Pittsburgh	471-7472 (north 935-7238)	391-5247	
717 Harrisburg	234-5390	233-3733	
Scranton	654-0488	1-800-464-4010	
York	854-4617	848-9988	
814 Erie	452-2675		

PRINCE EDWARD ISLAND
Provincial Agency: (902) 892-4265

Area Code & City	Alcoholics Anonymous
Charlottetown	892-5584

PUERTO RICO
Commonwealth Agency: (809) 764-3795

Area Code & City	Alcoholicos Anonimos
809 Bayamon	786-8287 or 786-8565
Rio Piedras	763-5919
Santurce	(English) 723-4187

QUEBEC
Provincial Agency: (418) 643-6024

Area Code & City	Alcoholics Anonymous	Narcotics Anonymous
418 Montreal	(Francais/English 376-9230) (Español 731-4188)	525-0333
Quebec	529-0015	649-0715

RHODE ISLAND
State Agency: (401) 464-2091

Area Code & City	Alcoholics Anonymous	Narcotics Anonymous
401 Pawtucket	725-0410**	
Providence		461-1110

SASKATCHEWAN
Provincial Agency: (306) 565-4085

Area Code & City	Alcoholics Anonymous	Narcotics Anonymous
306 Regina	545-9300	757-6600
Saskatoon	665-6727	652-5216

SOUTH AFRICA

City	Alcoholics Anonymous
Johannesburg	337 7870

SOUTH CAROLINA
State Agency: (803) 734-9520

Area Code & City	Alcoholics Anonymous	Narcotics Anonymous
803 Charleston	723-9633	
Columbia	254-5301	254-6662 or 1-800-922-6587
Greenville	233-6454	282-0109
Myrtle Beach	280-1476	449-6262

SOUTH DAKOTA
State Agency: (605) 773-3123

Area Code & City	Alcoholics Anonymous	Narcotics Anonymous
605 Aberdeen	229-7640	
Pierre	224-4570	
Rapid City		394-8008
Sioux Falls	339-4357	339-4357

SWEDEN

City	Alnonyma Alkoholister
Stockholm	42 26 0906 11 (English 328 92 86)

SWITZERLAND

City	Alcooliques Anonymes
Geneva	345 06 11
Lucerne	44 11 14

TAHITI
Alcoolique Anonyme
43.21.63

TENNESSEE
State Agency: (615) 741-1921

Area Code & City	Alcoholics Anonymous	Narcotics Anonymous	NCADD
615 Chattanooga	267-6277	899-6500	
Knoxville	522-9667	1-800-798-5560	
Nashville	298-1050	297-9762	269-0029
901 Memphis	454-1414		

TEXAS
State Agency: (512) 867-8700

Area Code & City	Alcoholics Anonymous	Narcotics Anonymous	NCADD
210 Brownsville	544-8530 (Español 542-7874)		
Laredo		726-4673	
San Antonio	828-6235	434-0665	
214 Dallas	239-4599 (Español 388-9630)	699-9306	
409 Beaumont	724-6501		
Galveston	740-1382	762-5605	
512 Austin	451-3071	480-0004	
Corpus Christi	853-0234	992-2113	851-8761
713 Houston	686-6300		520-5502
806 Amarillo	373-4600	379-2520	
Lubbock	799-0124	799-3950	763-8763
817 Fort Worth	332-3533 (Español 624-0927) (TDD 293-1434)	624-9525	332-6329
Waco	754-3336		753-7332
915 Abilene	673-2711	691-4280	673-2242
El Paso	562-4081 (Español 778-2334)	757-5410	772-0139

UTAH
State Agency: (801) 538-3939

Area Code & City	Alcoholics Anonymous	Narcotics Anonymous	NCADD
801 Ogden	393-4728	625-3311	
Provo	375-8620	379-3139	
Salt Lake City	484-7871	488-2141	
Provo	375-8620	379-3139	
Salt Lake City	484-7871	488-2141	

VERMONT
State Agency: (802) 241-2170 or 241-1000

Area Code & City	Alcoholics Anonymous	Narcotics Anonymous
802 Burlington	658-4221	862-4516
Middlebury	388-9284	862-4516
Montpelier	229-5100	862-4516

VIRGIN ISLANDS (U.S.)
Territorial Agency: (809) 773-1992

Area Code & City	Alcoholics Anonymous	Narcotics Anonymous
809 St.Thomas	776-5283	774-4358

VIRGINIA
State Agency: (804) 786-3906

Area Code & City	Alcoholics Anonymous	Narcotics Anonymous	NCADD
703 Northern Virginia	281-7501	(202) 399-5316	(202) 783-1300 or 682-1700
Roanoke	343-6857		
804 Norfolk/Va.Beach	490-3908	626-7685	
Newport News	877-0600	1-800-777-1515	
Richmond	355-1212	1-800-777-1515	

WASHINGTON (State)
State Agency: (360) 438-8200

Area Code & City	Alcoholics Anonymous	Narcotics Anonymous	NCADD
206 Bellevue	454-9192	329-1618	454-1505
Bremerton	479-9050 or 1-800-562-7455	698-5302	
Seattle	587-2838	329-1618 or 872-3494	854-6513
Tacoma	474-8897	531-8792	

WEST VIRGINIA
Stage Agency: (304) 558-2276

Area Code & City	Alcoholics Anonymous	Narcotics Anonymous	NCADD
304 Charleston	342-4315	344-4442	
Huntington	529-9820 or 1-800-443-2207	1-344-4442	
Wheeling	234-7511	234-7630	

Locating Help 199

WISCONSIN
Stage Agency: (608) 266-3442

Area Code & City	Alcoholics Anonymous	Narcotics Anonymous	NCADD
414 Appleton	731-4331	383-5855	
Green Bay	494-9904 or 469-9999	383-5855	
Milwaukee	771-9119		276-8487
608 Madison		258-1747	
715 Eau Claire	832-3234		

WYOMING
State Agency: (307) 777-6494

Area Code & City	Alcoholics Anonymous	Narcotics Anonymous
307 Casper	234-1447	266-7154
Cheyenne	632-7706	

YUKON
Provincial Agency: (403) 667-5777

Area Code & City	Alcoholics Anonymous
403 Whitehorse	668-5878

The telephone numbers listed come from many public sources. If any have been changed, are in error or if you wish to suggest additions, please notify the author or the publisher for correction in later printings. Thank You.

FOR FURTHER READING

Chapter 1: Innocent Addicts

Vaillant, George E., M.D. *The Natural History of Alcoholism; Causes, Patterns and Paths to Recovery.* Cambridge, Massachusetts: Harvard University Press, 1983. This book is the result of a landmark study. It is the result of 45 years of work by Dr. Vaillant and his predecessors and provides both insight and a scientifically sound understanding of lifelong patterns of alcoholism. It is based upon a study of people over many years, starting long before it was evident which of them might develop drinking problems.

Stimmel, Barry, M.D. *Pain, Analgesia and Addiction: The Pharmacologic Treatment of Pain.* New York, New York: Raven Press, 1983. This is an excellent book for professionals dealing with either pain control or addictions in a person with chronic pain. Its author is a well-known authority on the pharmacology of addiction.

Darcy, P.F. and Griffin, J.P., editors. *Iatrogenic Diseases.* Third Edition. Oxford, England: Oxford Medical Publications, 1986. This encyclopedic work discusses many forms of iatrogenic disease (those induced by a physician's words or actions), including iatrogenic addiction.

Chapter 2: The Addictive Sedative

Alcoholics Anonymous. Third Edition. New York, New York: Alcoholics Anonymous World Services, 1976. Commonly called the A.A. Big Book and first published in 1939 this widely read book is available at local A.A. meetings or through local A.A. groups if it is not available at your local bookstore or library. It contains many varied personal stories of despair turning into recovery and explains briefly the history and philosophy of Alcoholics Anonymous.

Chapter 3: The Pill Person

Narcotics Anonymous. Third Edition. Van Nuys, California: Narcotics Anonymous World Service Office, 1986. First published in 1983 and referred to as the N.A. Basic Text. This short book is available at local N.A. meetings or through local N.A. groups if it is not available at your local bookstore or library. Similar in purpose to A.A.'s Big Book, it contains varied personal stories and explains the history and philosophy of Narcotics Anonymous.

Chapter 4: Cocaine Addiction

Nuckols, Cardwell C. *Cocaine: From Dependency to Recovery.* Second Edition. Sulzberger & Graham, 1989. An understandable introduction to cocaine dependence.

Chapter 5: Dual Addiction

Stimmel, Barry, M.D. *The Facts About Drug Use.* Binghamton, New York. Hayworth Medical Press, 1993. Chapter 16 **Multiple Drug Use** provides a short, easily understandable discussion about dual addiction.

Chapter 6: Other Addiction

Stimmel, Barry, M.D. *The Facts About Drug Use.* Binghamton, New York. Hayworth Medical Press, 1993. Chapters on marijuana, hallucinogens, nicotine, solvents and sports all provide a good source of data on a variety of addictive substances.

Chapter 7: Recovery and Thinking

Martin, Faher Joseph C. *No Laughing Matter; Chalk Talks on Alcohol.* San Francisco, California. Harper & Row, 1982. This book, based on a well-known training film used in most treatment centers in the United States, is well worth reading. If you have the opportunity, see the film!

DuPont, Robert L., M.D. *Getting Tough on Gateway Drugs: A Guide for the Family.* Washington D.C. American Psychiatric Press, 1984. This book is written by a psychiatrist who formerly directed the National Institute on Drug Abuse. It is recommended because it provides understandable discussions on the effect of alcohol and marijuana on the brain and behavior.

Chapter 8: Recovery and the Body

Edwards, et al. *Alcohol Related Disabilities.* Geneva, Switzerland. World Health Organization, 1977. A reference report on alcohol and physical disability.

Rubin, Emanuel, editor. *Alcohol and the Cell.* New York, New York. New York Academy of Sciences, 1987. A collection of scientific papers concerning how alcohol effects types of cells throughout the body.

Chapter 9: Recovery and Sex

The Dilemma of the Alcoholic Marriage. Revised, expanded edition. New York, New York. Alanon Family Group Headquarters, 1984. This book has been expanded from it's first edition printed in 1971. It deals frankly with problems in family relationships that occur in the first years of recovery. The chapter **Sex in the Alcoholic Marriage** gives real-life accounts of how couples solved situations in which past feelings had spoiled sex after recovery. If this is not available at your local bookstore or library, obtain it through a local Al-Anon Family Group meeting.

McFarland, Barbara, Ed.D. *Sexuality and Recovery.* Center City, Minnesota. Hazelden, 1984. Baudhuin, John. *Now About Sex.* Center City, Minnesota. Hazelden, 1985. Weiss, Karen. *Women's Experience on Sexuality and Recovery.* Center City, Minnesota. Hazelden, 1992. These three pamphlets are part of a series intended for use by patients in treatment centers. Dealing with basic issues, they are intended to initiate a dialogue about sexuality in recovery.

Chapter 10: Finding Recovery

Hart, Stan. *REHAB: A Comprehensive Guide to Recommended Drug-Alcohol Treatment Centers in the United States.* New York, New York. Harper & Row, 1988. Although facilities and situations change, this is the best guide available for locating the best inpatient rehabilitation programs in the United States.

Chapter 11: Following the Twelve-Step Path

Brown, Stephanie Ph.D. *Treating the Alcoholic: A Developmental Model of Recovery.* New York, New York, 1985. This is an excellent guide for professionals. Written by an experienced psychologist, it utilizes a wide range of psychological theory to explain to the professional how the twelve steps of recovery not only work but are well grounded in scientific theory.

Robertson, Nan. *Getting Better: Inside Alcoholics Anonymous.* New York, New York. William Morrow, 1988. This critically acclaimed book by a veteran reporter for the New York Times is equally informative reading for people in recovery from addiction as well as those wishing to help them. It is a factual and accurate guide as to what to expect, and what not to expect from recovery programs.

Twelve Steps and Twelve Traditions. New York, New York: Alcoholics Anonymous World Services, 1952. Referred to as the **12 and 12** this pocket sized book offers thought provoking ideas on the importance of working each step. It is frequently used at A.A. "Step Meetings" to provide a starting point for discussion about how to utilize the steps of recovery.

Chapter 12: Other Paths to Recovery

Lowison, J.H., Ruiz, P.R. and Millman, R.B., editors. *Substance Abuse: A Comprehensive Textbook.* Second edition. Baltimore, Maryland. Williams and Wilkins, 1992. This is a multi-authored textbook for alcoholism counselors. "Part V. Treatment Approaches" offers a mixture of treatment approaches written by the proponents of each of those approaches, some theoreticians others from experience. Additional data, including critical and historical data on other treatment approaches can be found in the earlier first edition.

Chapter 13: Avoiding Relapse

Living Sober. New York, New York: Alcoholics Anonymous World Services, 1975. a simple and straight-forward guide making the modest claim "Some methods A.A. members have used for not drinking," I recommend it highly to everyone in early sobriety as well as to those who help them. The simple and practical wisdom found in this short text works. It is available through the A.A. General Services Office (see Appendix D), at local A.A. meetings or through local A.A. groups if it is not available at your local bookstore or library. It is short on theory and long on practical suggestions for maintaining continuous sobriety.

Moody, Al J., M.D., Eisenberg, A. and Eisenberg H. *The Recovery Book.* New York, New York. Workman Publishing, 1994. This book, by the director of a respected treatment center in Georgia offers practical advice for the newly recovering addict on leading a sober life.

Miller, M., Gorski, T.T. and Miller, D.K. *Learning to Live Again: A Guide to Recovery from Chemical Dependency.* Updated and Revised Edition. Herald House-Independence Press. Independence, Missouri, 1992. A popular guide, suggested by many counselors who follow Gorski's model of relapse prevention.

Chapter 14: Prevention is Possible

American Society of Addiction Medicine. *Public Policy Statement on National Drug Policy. Journal of Addictive Diseases.* 1994;13(4):231–8. This gives the current recommendations regarding a national drug policy from a society comprised of physicians specializing in the treatment of addictive disorders.

INDEX

205

About the Author

Irv Cohen, M.D., M.P.H., is a physician who lives in Kansas with his wife Lauren (a psychologist) and two youngest sons. He currently treats patients suffering from addiction at the Colmery–O'Neill V.A. Medical Center in Topeka. He holds faculty appointments at the University of Kansas School of Medicine, Department of Preventive Medicine, as well as the Karl Menninger School of Psychiatry and Mental Health Sciences.

In the past Dr. Cohen has served as Deputy Director of the New York State Research Institute on Addiction (Buffalo, NY), held faculty appointments at the State University of New York at Buffalo, School of Medicine, in the Departments of Medicine as well as Social and Preventive Medicine. He has been in private practice, specializing in addiction treatment and has started and directed addiction treatment programs. In Baltimore, Maryland, he served as Chief Resident in Preventive Medicine at the Johns Hopkins University, School of Hygiene and Public Health.

Dr. Cohen is Board-Certified in Preventive Medicine and Public Health by the American Board of Preventive Medicine and is also Certified in Addiction Medicine by the American Society of Addiction Medicine. He was the first physician in the United States to simultaneously hold this combination of credentials.

Dr. Cohen wrote this book because he believes that too many people have suffered needlessly on the roller coaster of addiction. He knows that addiction is a powerful trap and hopes that people will recognize that addicts are neither weak nor bad people. They are just people who underestimated the danger they were facing!